A VIEW FROM ROME

D0030218

A VIEW FROM ROME

On the Eve of the Modernist Crisis

Daᴠɪᴅ G. Sᴄʜᴜʟᴛᴇɴᴏᴠᴇʀ, S.J.

Fordham University Press
New York
1993

Copyright © 1993 by Fordham University Press
All rights reserved
LC 92–23892
ISBN 0–8232–1358–7 (clothbound)
ISBN 0–8232–1359–5 (paperback)

Library of Congress Cataloging-in-Publication Data

Schultenover, David G., 1938–
A view from Rome : on the eve of the modernist crisis / David G.
Schultenover.
p.   cm.
Includes bibliographical references and index.
ISBN 0-8232-1358-7 : $30.00. — ISBN 0-8232-1359-5 (pbk.) : $19.95
1. Modernism—Catholic Church—History. 2. Catholic Church—
Doctrines—History—19th century. 3. Catholic Church—Doctrines—
History—20th century. I. Title.
BX1396.S38   1993
282'.09'034—dc20   92-23892
CIP

Printed in the United States of America

During my many months of research and writing, certain fellow Jesuits graciously welcomed me and smoothed my path in so many ways—Bob Hagan, John Navone, Joseph Pittau, and Philip Rosato in Rome; Benny Goodman in England; Ina Echarte in Spain; and, at home, Don Doll, Dick Hauser, John Holbrook, John Laurance, Eddie Mathie, and Bert Thelen. To these Jesuits, who have made my life richer as well as easier, I dedicate this book.

CONTENTS

ACKNOWLEDGMENTS

My gratitude goes out to so many who have helped me along the way. A grant from the National Endowment for the Humanities enabled me to carry on extended research in Europe. While in the Jesuit archives in Rome I had the good fortune to meet Ignacio Echarte, a young Basque Jesuit historian, who informed me of the existence of General Luis Martín's memoirs at Loyola and facilitated my access to them. But for him this book would have not been written. Various Jesuit archivists were also most generous with their time and suggestions: Edmond Lamalle (now deceased), Georges Bottereau, József Fejér, Joseph de Cock, and Wiktor Gramatowski in Rome; Filippo Iapelli in England. The librarians of Creighton University always met my requests with good cheer and competence: Jo Browning, Chris Le Beau, Gerry Chase, Sinora Garrett, Ray Means, Mary Nash, Mike Poma, Lynn Schneiderman, Julia Trojanowski, and Russell Warzyn. My departmental colleague Bruce Malina supplied me with just the right bibliography on Mediterranean anthropology. He and his wife, Diane, also an expert in the field, both read my typescript and offered helpful suggestions, as did Gary Lease, professor in the history of consciousness, University of California at Santa Cruz, and fellow Jesuit William J. Kelly, Marquette University. My colleagues in the Roman Catholic Modernism Working Group of the American Academy of Religion read and critiqued preliminary drafts of materials used for Parts I and II. Ron Burke, George Gilmore, Bob Krieg, Mary Lou Kuhlman, Paul Misner, Frank Nichols, Rosemary O'Neil, and Nick Pope, s.j., assisted in proofreading. Don Doll, s.j., designed the cover. To all these generous people I am deeply grateful. I hope they will be pleased with how I used their counsel.

ABBREVIATIONS

AAW	Archives of the Archdiocese of Westminster, London
AEPSJ	Archives of the English Province of the Society of Jesus, London
AL	Maude D. Petre, *Autobiography and Life of George Tyrrell*, 2 vols. London: Arnold, 1912
ANGL	Papers in the Archives of the Society of Jesus in Rome pertaining to the English Province. Many of these papers are letters to the Jesuit superior general from members of the English Province.
APF	Archives of the Congregation Propagande de Fide, Rome
ARSJ	Archivum Romanum Societatis Jesu (Archives of the Society of Jesus), Rome
ASS	*Acta Sanctae Sedis*
BL	British Library, London
LN	*Letters and Notices of the English Province of the Society of Jesus*, an in-house quarterly for Jesuits of the English Province
PP	Maude Dominica Petre Papers, British Library, London
Reg. Epp. Angl.	Registrum Epistolarum ad Provinciam Angliae, a register of letters in ARSJ from the Jesuit superior general to members of the English Province
VP	Cardinal Herbert Alfred Vaughan Papers, Westminster, London

INTRODUCTION

"WOE TO YOU LAWYERS! You have taken away the key of knowledge; you did not enter yourselves, and you hindered those who were entering" (Luke 11:52). Jesus aimed this reproach at the Pharisees. George Tyrrell, the Anglo-Irish Catholic "modernist" who was dismissed from his religious order in 1906 and excommunicated a year later, enjoyed hurling it at ecclesiastical officials, who he thought were claiming far too much authority for themselves and far too little for everyone else. Tyrrell saw, as few others did, that the fundamental issue of the crisis facing the Western religious world at the turn of the century was access to truth—truth in general and religious truth in particular. The issue was about the nature of the access, about who controlled it, and about who defined the particular perceptions of truth once access had been gained or acknowledged. In other words, the crisis was largely about perception and lack of perception, awareness and lack of awareness, questioned and unquestioned presuppositions about human knowledge and expression of truth.

With his encyclical *Pascendi dominici gregis* (1907) defining and condemning "modernism" in the Catholic Church, Pope Pius X left little doubt about where he stood on this issue. Any lingering doubt was dispelled by two practical implementations of the condemnation: (1) the establishment of secret vigilance committees in every diocese worldwide to delate suspected modernists to Rome and (2) the enforcement among clerics and professors of philosophy and theology of an oath against modernism (1910) as a condition for ordination, employment, and advancement. The rigorous implementation of these two measures swept the church clean of most of its independent thinkers who were trying to bridge the growing gap between the church and the post-Enlightenment world.

The outside observer might well be astonished and wonder at the ferocity of the pope's response to the modernist effort, but when one analyzes the encyclical and attendant documents with their emotion-laden description and denunciation of modernism as the "compendium of all heresies," one must conclude that the counter-measures prescribed were little compared to the arsenal of the *perceived* enemy. Certainly that was the conclusion of the so-called "integralists" who took the papal condemnations as license indiscriminately to bash modernists, real or imaginary. And certainly that was the conclusion of the vast majority of the bishops who loyally enforced the prescriptions. The effect was devastating and deadening to the immediate and subsequent generations of Catholics, but it only postponed by sixty years the *aggiornamento* of Vatican II that modernists had struggled for and predicted would happen by historical necessity.

It has frequently been observed that Vatican II is a watershed marking the Catholic Church's departure from a classicist to an historical world view. If one grants the truth of this observation, then one must also conclude that the effort to prevent such a departure—seen in the integralist campaign against modernism—is one of the most significant antithetical movements in modern religious history.

Safeguarding belief is a perennial charge for the church's magisterium. Why at this particular juncture in history the shrillest alarm should be sounded and a pogrom announced against the perceived enemy is one of the more pressing questions surrounding the modernist crisis and the one the present study seeks to address. An analysis of the anti-modernist campaign, a search for causes, a sifting out of the forces leading up to it, a probing and defining of energies that fueled the reaction, all to disclose the fear of that alleged hydra of heresies, modernism, can go a long way toward developing more creative and constructive strategies to meet perceived dangers in the future.

Historiographical Pitfalls

Such an explanatory study, however, is rife with historiographical handicaps and dangers, and the honest historian must enter on such a project keenly aware of them. These handicaps and dangers arise out of numerous limitations, of which surely the most pervasive, far-reaching in its effects, and difficult of resolution is the limitation of human perception. Immanuel Kant has taught us—though not all accept it—that for various reasons, some natural, some perverse, there is not a one-for-one correspondence between reality (or truth) and perception of reality (or truth) or between perception and the expression of perception. Relative to the modernist crisis, sociologist Lester Kurtz has pointed out that there was not a close correlation between the number of the enemy as perceived by the anti-modernists and the few singled out for condemnation.[1] The enemy *as perceived* was far more numerous and quite other than the enemy *as defined* in official documents of condemnation. For church authorities saw far more at stake than the doctrinal issues they addressed—indeed, doctrine was not the main issue—and the modernists were merely set up to serve notice that a line had been drawn between the Catholic Church and the "modern world." In other words, the modernists were scapegoats, symbols of the hidden enemy within allied to the more formidable and less accessible enemy without.

Stated as a corollary to Kurtz's compelling characterization, the controlling historiographical thesis of the present study is that modernism in Roman Catholicism was perceived by church officials to exist within the context of that much larger and far more dangerous root-modernism known as liberalism, and that the latter rather than the former was the real target of the anti-modernist campaign.

The operative word for the present study, as the reader must have already guessed, is *perception.* The intent of the following pages is to try to enter into the perceptions of the principal ecclesiastical figures who defined modernism and so to begin to expose the motivation for the sequence of condemnations of various "isms" throughout the nineteenth and early twentieth centuries. For it is the perceivers themselves who hold the key to the lessons that the history of modernism can teach us today.

But this goal raises another historiographical difficulty: How does one accurately perceive the perceivers, especially when all we have left of their perceptions is their writings? This is the hermeneutical problem that every interpreter of a text faces. It is not in place here to try to "solve" the hermeneutical problem, but it is in place to alert the reader to the present investigator's awareness of the problem, as well as to his self-conscious wrestle with it. Briefly to state the outcome of the match, I am aware of having applied the following hermeneutical steps: (1) On the basis of all available sources, I first formed in my own mind *a guiding idea* of an author's true mind; (2) I then determined the disclosure value of texts by judging how true they were to the guiding idea previously formed; (3) I drew tentative conclusions on the basis of the disclosure value attributed to the texts; (4) I regularly returned to step one to re-evaluate and revise my guiding idea as new sources were brought into dialogue with old; and (5) I revised my earlier conclusions accordingly.

It goes without saying that the mind behind a text is not completely transparent in the text, especially in texts meant for other eyes. Documents intended for public scrutiny will reveal, at least on the surface, only as much as their authors want their publics to know, so that the historian must read such documents "between the lines," always aware of the risk of eisegesis, but running that risk to get at the fuller truth that usually lies not in the public documents themselves but behind them in the lives of all who collaborated in the production of those documents, wittingly or unwittingly.

The honest historian, therefore, begins a research project and carries it through with humility—humility marked by (1) daring because of the risk of misreading perceptions; (2) a keen awareness of limitations, those stemming from personal bias and ideology as well as those stemming from the nature of the sources themselves; and (3) gratitude for whatever archival digging and investigation yield. Such an historian presents interpretations and conclusions as more or less tentative and subject to revision, the degree of tentativeness depending largely on the nature of the sources.

SOURCES FOR THIS STUDY

In the present case, what marks my awareness is rather more gratitude and less tentativeness than I am accustomed to, due primarily to two factors: the fortuitous discovery of a massive and exceptionally revealing document that serves as the core of this study, and the private and self-disclosing nature of the other sources related to this document.

The core document in question is the unfinished memoirs of the Spanish Jesuit Luis Martín Garcia (1846–1906), the superior general of the Society of Jesus at the time of the modernist crisis. When Martín died in 1906—two months after having dismissed Tyrrell from the order—he left behind a manuscript of 2,712 quarto folios front and back (5,424 quarto pages!), and that took him only up to 1901.[2]

These memoirs are extraordinary on several counts. First of all, their sheer size—which might lead one to expect verbosity. But, surprisingly, they are usually terse, always careful, and, best of all, replete with names, scenarios, and commentaries rarely found in Vatican and curial archives. Second, as far as is known, this is the only autobiography of any of the principal anti-modernist figures, and so it occupies a place of pride among all the archival sources for modernist studies. Third, it is the only autobiography of a Jesuit superior general since Ignatius of Loyola left his small account to satisfy the appeals of his companions.

But whereas Ignatius was clear about his intentions in writing his autobiography, Martín was not. It is difficult to imagine that he had ever intended his *Memorias* for public scrutiny, especially the part about his early life. One might draw this conclusion from two remarkable anomalies: (1) the fact that he wrote his memoirs in six languages (Spanish, English, French, Italian, Portugese, and Latin), sometimes passing from language to language in mid-sentence—as an exercise, he said, to sharpen his skills in those languages; and (2) his unusual candor about his upbringing, schooling, and private struggles. But the fact that he was so candid—sometimes brutally so—instills confidence in the judgment that he left a reliable account of his most private thoughts, for which subsequent unintended (?) readers may be duly grateful.

Why Martín decided to enter on such a startling and colossal departure from tradition by writing his memoirs requires more of an explanation than the following brief ascetical reason he supplied as a preface:

In the name of Our Lord Jesus Christ, today (15 May 1895) I begin to write in French and in English these recollections of my life, in order to exercise myself in these languages and to acquire the habit of speaking them less incorrectly. And I wish to choose this argument or subject in preference to some others because in it I find the opportunity to make a general examination of conscience of my entire life, in order to confess many miseries, and to praise God who has shown me such abundant indulgence and infinite mercy.[3]

Though I could accept this explanation with some reservation for the years up to 1892 when Martín became superior general, I find it less easy to accept for the succeeding years. The historical detail of the later years of the *Memorias* demands some other explanation, such as Martín's keen personal interest in providing a full scientific account of Jesuit history. The general congregation of 1892 which elected him general mandated the writing of histories of each Jesuit assistancy, as well as a general history of the whole Society, and Martín energetically devoted himself to the task.[4] He assembled competent archivists and writers, personally instructed them at great length on the most rigorous modern historical methods, and, to facilitate the project, moved the Jesuit archives to Exaeten in Holland where they would be more open and accessible to historians and less subject to confiscation by hostile governments.[5]

Amazingly, Martín wrote his *Memorias* in almost absolute secrecy—amazing because of the project's enormous size, the time commitment, the documents required, and the constraints of space in the curia.[6] None of his general assistants knew about it. Only one man knew—Father Eduardo Gallo, the secretary for Martín's Spanish assistant. When he found out is not known. But it was he whom Martín, on his deathbed, charged with the mission to smuggle the *Memorias* back to his home province of Castille. Under no circumstances were his *Memorias* to be left in Rome. So Gallo consigned them at the last minute with the luggage of the Castillian provincial, Ignacio María Ibero, on his way home after participating in the election of Martín's successor. Ibero did not know the contents of the box.[7]

Whatever his motives, Martín began writing his memoirs in 1895—two and a half years after his election, and four and a half months after he moved his curia from Fiesole to Rome—and continued probably until sometime in 1902 when illness forced him to stop. From 1902 until late November 1904 when his fatal illness first appeared, he probably worked at his memoirs only sparingly, if at all.[8] Given his open and confessionary stance, it is most regrettable from the historian's viewpoint that Martín did not live long enough to retrospect the crucial years of the modernist crisis. But what we do get is a privileged perspective on the all-important *background* to the modernist crisis, as well as to several other not-unconnected ecclesiastico-political crises—the Spanish-American War, for example—seen through the eyes of one of the key figures of fin-de-siècle European and ecclesiastical history.

THE PLAN OF THIS STUDY

The year 1892 when Martín assumed office was a fateful year. It brought together a constellation of the three main protagonists of the events played out on the eve of the modernist crisis. In that year Leo XIII, on the heels of his two boldest encyclicals, *Rerum novarum* and *Au milieu des sollicitudes*, made perhaps the most dramatic and symbolically significant gesture of his papacy—the transfer of the remains of Pope Innocent III from Perugia to the Lateran Basilica.[9] Less dramatically, but in the long run of greater consequence for the modernist crisis, Leo appointed Monsignor Rafael Merry del Val his chamberlain, thus poising him for decisive influence in the years ahead. Finally, with Martín having been mandated by the 1892 general congregation to move the Jesuit curia back to Rome, it was he—with his great intellectual and moral resources and special relationship to the papacy—whom Leo would call on more than anyone else to devise and/or execute strategies to meet the impending crisis.[10]

Although the time-frame of the present study coincides with the last years of Leo XIII's reign, we begin in Part 1 with the perception of Leo's successor, Pope Pius X, as disclosed in *Pas-*

cendi dominici gregis, probably the most historically significant
document of his papacy. An exegesis of that document will
provide a general background and historical context for the
chapters to follow, even though the subsequent chapters arise
out of chronologically antecedent documents. Such a procedure may seem anomalous, if not methodologically backwards,
but it provides a retrospective of the entire papal tradition of
anti-liberalism of the nineteenth century on which Pius X and
the framers of the anti-modernist campaign self-consciously
built. Popes, after all, do not idly choose their names. When
Giuseppe Sarto was elected pope on 4 August 1903, he announced that he would bear the name Pius in honor of the pontiffs "who in the last century battled with such courage against
proliferating sects and errors."[11] With this name he claimed his
lineage and specified the direction for his pontificate.[12] The intention of Part I, then, is to evoke a sense of the ecclesiastico-
political atmosphere on the eve of the modernist crisis as a context for the narrative constructed in Part II from Luis Martín's
Memorias and related documents from various Jesuit and ecclesiastical archives in Rome, England, and Spain.[13]

Part III is an historiographical essay which attempts to interpret Parts I and II from a perspective that is new to many historians. It is a perspective that strives to read and interpret documents from within the social, cultural, and psychological
framework of the authors of those documents, insofar as this
framework can be determined. Such a procedure may seem obvious, but the obvious is so only after it occurs to one. The fact
is that, although this effort had been called for since the
Enlightenment's invention of modern history, cultural contexts
were not systematically attended to in historical circles until
just a few years ago, except for scriptural and to some degree
medieval studies. Geoffrey Barraclough in 1978 called historians to a greater honesty and integrity of purpose by pointing
out the utter necessity of taking into account social contexts of
historical events: one cannot understand an event without understanding its context.[14] But to understand historical contexts,
historians have to broaden their field of investigation to include
such other related disciplines as social, cultural, and psychological anthropology. The era of the isolated scholar working

alone in his or her private study is ended. Today historically significant work requires the collaboration of numerous scholars from numerous disciplines.

Part III, then, attempts to show the historical necessity of the modernist crisis from the perspectives of those who defined it. It tries to enter into those perspectives from the viewpoint of the anthropology of the Mediterranean world, since the subjects of this study—Luis Martín, Popes Leo XIII and Pius X, and Rafael Merry del Val—are from that world.[15] In so doing I accept the findings and descriptions of respected Mediterranean anthropologists and simply apply their findings to my subjects.

The application of anthropology to historiography is relatively new to history in general and to the history of modernism in particular. This is my first effort at such a hermeneutic. It has turned on lights for me. I hope it does the same for my readers.

NOTES

1. Lester R. Kurtz, *The Politics of Heresy: The Modernist Crisis in Roman Catholicism* (Berkeley: University of California Press, 1986), esp. pp. 139–87.

2. Alerted to the existence of this source by Ignacio Echarte, a Basque Jesuit I met in 1984 in the Jesuit archives in Rome, I traveled to Loyola castle, the ancestral home of St. Ignatius, the founder of the Jesuits, at Azpeitia in the Basque province of Guipuzcoa, and there discovered this exceptionally rich resource for turn-of-the-century European history in general and for modernist studies in particular. Since my first encounter with Martín's *Memorias*, a large portion has been rendered entirely in Spanish and published, in two large volumes of more than a thousand pages each, under the title *Memorias del P. Luis Martín, General de la Compañía de Jesús*, Vol. 1 (1846–1891), Vol. 2 (1892–1906) (Rome: Historical Institute of the Society of Jesus; Madrid: Pontifical University of Comillas; Bilbao: University of Deusto and Ediciones Mensajero, 1988); edited by three Jesuits, Manuel Revuelta González and Rafael Maria Sanz de Diego, professors at the University of Comillas (Madrid), and José Ramón Eguillar, archivist of the Loyola Province. About the end date of Vol. 2 (1906), it should be noted that the *Memorias* themselves go only up to the end of 1901.

Illness between 1902 and 1904 forced Martín to suspend work on them almost entirely. On 9 April 1905, Martín's right arm was amputated to try to prevent the spread of cancer. Twenty-one days later he began writing with his left hand, in an amazingly clear and well-proportioned script, an account of his last infirmity, *Cuadernos de la última enfermedad*. The editors included this work of 32 pages (21 × 16 cm.) as the final chapter of the *Memorias*, but it does not, strictly speaking, belong to it. In fact, the *Cuadernos* are kept in the Roman archives of the Society of Jesus (hereafter, ARSJ), not at Loyola with the *Memorias*.

3. Martín quickly reverted to writing in Spanish and added other languages as he went along.

4. On 1 June 1894 Martín disseminated a decree to the whole Society of Jesus on his intention to promote the writing of a complete history of the Society according to proposition 21 of the twenty-fourth general congregation (1892) (copy of the *Decreta XXIV Congregationis* in the archives of the English Province of the Society of Jesus [hereafter AEPSJ], BT[1]). Martín's decree is entirely objective in tone. It says nothing about the need to refute enemies. Indeed, as far as the English Province is concerned, there is some evidence that Martín did not want the history of the Society in England to proceed at all, in order to avoid controversy and harmful repercussions against the Society. See p. 120 n. 44.

5. When Bismarck expelled the Jesuits from Germany in 1872, they established a retreat house and novitiate at Exaeten in Holland. In 1885 the novitiate was moved, and a philosophate with spacious libraries was added to the existing buildings at Exaeten. The German Jesuit periodicals *Stimmen aus Maria-Laach* and *Die katholischen Missionen* were located here, along with most of the German Jesuit writers. See Count Paul von Hönsbröch, *Fourteen Years a Jesuit: A Record of Personal Experience and a Criticism*, trans. Alice Zimmern, 2 vols. (London: Cassell, 1911), 2:369–98; Michael J. King, S.J., "The German Fathers at Ditton and Portico," *Letters and Notices* (hereafter, LN) 28 (July 1905) 190–93 (LN is an in-house quarterly of the English Province, published by their own Manresa Press, Roehampton). Martín went beyond the mandate and instigated the production of critical editions of documents on Jesuit origins and history. To date, this enterprise has resulted in the publication of 131 weighty volumes of *Monumenta Historica Societatis Jesu*. See Peter J. Chandlery, S.J., "The Very Rev. Father General Luis Martín, S.J.: A Biographical Sketch," LN 29 (April 1908) 367. Chandlery, secretary to Martín's assistant for the English-speaking provinces and for twelve years almost daily companion to the gen-

eral on his walks, knew him probably as well as or better than anyone else on the curial staff. After Martín's death Chandlery became editor of LN and serialized in it an important biography of Martín of some 180 pages: LN 28 (July, October 1906) 433–50, 510–17; LN 29 (January, April, July, October 1907; January, April, July, October 1908) 1–13, 73–84, 145–57, 217–30, 296–307, 361–75, 442–57, 535–47; LN 30 (January, April, July, October 1909; January 1910) 21–36, 119–30, 191–98, 256–63, 291–97.

6. The Jesuit curia at that time was housed in temporary quarters on the upper floor of the Collegium Germanicum–Hungaricum in the Via S. Nicolo da Tolentino. See below, n. 10.

7. See Revuelta, Introduction to *Memorias*, 1:xxvii–xlvii, esp. xxviii–xxix.

8. The onset of Martín's fatal illness was marked by an attack of influenza on 28 November 1904 and a fever that stayed with him off and on to the end. The first sarcoma appeared on his right forearm on 14 or 15 January 1905 and was surgically removed on 20 January. On 14 February a second sarcoma erupted higher up the arm and was removed on 17 February. In both surgeries Martín refused anesthesia. Only when his arm had finally to be removed, on 9 April 1906, did he consent to anesthesia. Chandlery chronicled the course of Martín's battle against cancer and sent the following reports to LN: "Father General's Illness," LN 28 (April 1905) 73–82; "Father General's Recent Illness," LN 28 (July 1905) 169–70; "Father General's Convalescence," LN 28 (October 1905) 217–19; "Fatal Termination to Very Rev. Father General's Long Illness," LN 28 (April 1906) 361–69.

9. See below, pp. 20–22.

10. The move occurred in January 1895. Pieter Johann Beckx, general from 1853 to 1887, had moved the curia to the ancient monastery of San Girolamo in Fiesole outside Florence in 1873 after Piedmontese troups entered Rome, seized the Jesuit colleges, museums, libraries, and observatories, and ordered the expulsion of the Jesuits. See William V. Bangert, s.j., *A History of the Society of Jesus* (St. Louis: Institute of Jesuit Sources, 1972), pp. 438–39. The special relationship of the Jesuits to the pope stems from the so-called "fourth vow." The Formula of the Institute of the Jesuit order, par. 4, states the relationship briefly: "In addition to that ordinary bond of the three vows, we are to be obliged by a special vow to carry out whatever the present and future Roman pontiffs may order which pertains to the progress of souls and the propagation of the faith; and to go without subterfuge or excuse, as far as in us lies, to whatsoever provinces they may choose to send us." Ignatius of Loyola, *The Constitutions of the Society*

of Jesus, trans. George E. Ganss, S.J. (St. Louis: Institute of Jesuit Sources, 1970), p. 68. Leo XIII's regard for, and reliance on, the Jesuits was, according to Peter Chandlery, so extreme as to be embarrassing to Martín, and Pius X's relationship was in some respects even closer. See below, pp. 164–67.

11. See Roger Aubert, *The Church in a Secularised Society,* trans. Janet Sondheimer, vol. 5 of *The Christian Centuries* (New York and Ramsey, NJ: Paulist, 1978), pp. 16–17.

12. According to Cardinal James Gibbons of Baltimore, the resemblance of Pius X to Pius IX was even physical. During a visit to the Jesuit curia in Rome on 11 August, just after Sarto's election, Gibbons remarked to Luis Martín: " 'Pius X. is a worthy successor to Leo XIII. I was struck with Cardinal Sarto's appearance immediately he entered the Conclave. He reminded me strangely of Pius IX., his simple, dignified bearing giving him a truly Apostolic exterior.' " Quoted in Chandlery, "Biographical Sketch," LN 30 (January 1909) 30.

13. It should be noted that most of the Jesuit letters to and from Martín were written in Latin. The translations are mine. Although Martín wrote his *Memorias* in six languages, the published version translates all the letters into Spanish. Thus, when I refer to the published version, I supply the translation from the Spanish. When I refer simply to folio numbers, I am working from the languages in which Martín wrote.

14. Geoffrey Barraclough, *Main Trends in History* (New York: Holmes & Meier, 1978).

15. Of the four figures mentioned here, only Merry del Val's Mediterranean status might be in dispute, for indeed he was born and spent his first twelve and two later years in England. But the identification and association of his family with Spain was long-standing and intimate. His father, Rafael senior, was a Spanish marquis and spent his entire adult life in the Spanish diplomatic service, first as secretary to the Spanish legation in London, then as ambassador until 1877, when he became Spanish minister in Belgium; in 1885 he became ambassador to the Austro-Hungarian empire; and from 1898 to 1903 ambassador to the Vatican where his son was serving in various capacities. He spent his youth in the palace of Queen Isabella II, where his mother served as a lady-in-waiting. During those days he became friends with Eugenia María de Montijo de Guzmán, daughter of the Count de Teba and later empress of France (1853–1879) as consort of Napoleon III (Sister M. Bernetta Quinn, O.S.F., *Give Me Souls: A Life of Raphael Cardinal Merry del Val* [Westminster, MD: Newman, 1958], p. 4). That friendship helped his diplomatic career. When Napoleon was

captured by the Prussians in 1870 during the Franco-Prussian War, Eugenia fled to England, retiring after the death of her only child to Farnborough on the Bournemouth–London route. That route was well traveled by the Merry del Vals. They had a home in London but sometimes lived in Bournemouth, especially during the years of the Spanish Revolution (1866–1874), with Rafael senior's father-in-law, Pedro José de Zulueta, second Count de Torre Diaz, who had fled Spain in 1823 and established a banking firm in England (Marie Cecilia Buehrle, *Rafael Cardinal Merry del Val* [Milwaukee: Bruce, 1957], pp. 6–9).

Merry del Val's mother, Josefina de Zulueta, was of Scottish-Dutch descent on her mother's side and was born in England, but her father, although a British subject, was pure Spanish, or, rather, Basque, by blood. When Queen Isabella was deposed in 1868 during the Spanish Revolution, she fled to Paris, where Rafael senior, then Spanish ambassador in London, met her and accepted her jewels for safekeeping in England. He then journeyed to the Pyrenees to muster forces to fight for the restoration of the monarchy. Isabella's young son, King Alfonso XII, stayed with the Merry del Vals in London when he was not in school at Sandhurst near Farnborough, and Rafael senior accompanied him back to Spain when he acceded to the throne in 1874. The Merry del Vals kept a summer home near San Sebastian, where the Spanish court repaired during the summer months. Rafael senior died there in 1917.

As to Rafael junior, his English-speaking biographers tend to emphasize the English influence on him. They make much of his early schooling in England and especially his two years of seminary at Ushaw College in Durham. But Jerome Dal-Gal, in his *The Spiritual Life of Cardinal Merry del Val*, trans. Joseph A. McMullin (New York: Benziger, 1959) and Merry del Val's official biographer, Pio Cenci, archivist of the Secret Vatican Archives, in his *Il Cardinale Raffaele Merry del Val* (Rome and Turin: Berruti, 1933), emphasize his Spanish heritage and nationality. Cenci remarks that, although his father's line descended from the O'Hoolichans of Hy-Main, County Connaught, Ireland, they emigrated to Seville in the second half of the eighteenth century and "became in all respects completely Spanish" ("fu sotto tutti i riguardi interamente spagnuola" [p. 4]).

Thus I would argue that the Mediterranean influence clearly dominated Merry del Val's outlook and that his preferred cultural ties were with his father and Spain. After early schooling in England and Belgium, he spent his major seminary years in Rome and never left except for nearly annual visits to England. He passed most of his vacation time either in Spain or with Spanish nobility at the Hapsburg court in Vienna where his father was ambassador. During at least one of his vacations in Spain, he said Mass every morning in the private chapel of the Palacio de Ayete, temporary summer home of the Queen Regent Maria Christina, the young King Alfonso XIII, and other members of the royal family prior to the construction of the Royal Palace of Casa de Campo of Miramar. He prepared the king for his first communion and taught catechism to the royal infantas. See Buehrle, *Merry del Val*, p. 48, and Charles Petrie, *King Alfonso XIII and His Age* (London: Chapman & Hall, 1963), p. 49.

Merry del Val, although born in London, was Spanish by nationality. Pius X testified that this was one reason why he chose him as secretary of state (Cenci, *Merry del Val*, p. 138). His older brother Alfonso continued in his father's footsteps as Spanish ambassador in London and in Copenhagen (Quinn, *Give Me Souls*, pp. viii–ix).

Certainly the Spanish regarded Merry del Val as one of their own. It was at the request of the Spanish hierarchy that Merry del Val's cause for canonization was opened by Pope Pius XII on 26 February 1953 (Charles Ledré, "Rafael Merry del Val," *New Catholic Encyclopedia*).

I

PAPAL PERCEPTIONS

1

Rome's General Synoptic of Antecedent "Isms"

"*Instaurare omnia in Christo*," the first and last words of Pope Pius X,[1] announced his goal to restore all things in Christ. "Restoration" implies a return to a prior condition. What condition Pius had in mind we shall presently see, but his inaugural letter, *E supremi apostolatus* of 4 October 1903, stated his rationale: "We were terrified beyond all else by the disastrous state of human society today . . . suffering more than in any past age from a terrible and radical malady which, while developing every day and gnawing into its very being, is dragging it to destruction. . . . This disease is apostasy from God." That apostasy Pius characterized generally as "the substitution of man for God," which meant—in Counter-Reformation logic—rationalism, individualism, Protestantism. His prescribed remedy was to include, first, renewal of priestly holiness among the ordained, and, second, the "greatest diligence" in "the right government and ordering" of seminaries "so that they may flourish both in sound doctrine and upright morals"; but, third and most important, it summoned bishops and other ordinaries to be "co-operators" with Christ's vicar against "that sacrilegious war which is now almost universally being stirred up and fomented against God." They were to "exercise the greatest diligence in preventing members of the clergy from being drawn into the snares of a certain new and fallacious science, which . . . with masked and cunning arguments strives to open the door to the errors of rationalism and semi-rationalism."[2]

To spearhead the campaign against this "new and fallacious science," Pius X selected Archbishop Rafael Merry del Val as his secretary of state.[3] The campaign culminated in the 1907 encyclical *Pascendi dominici gregis*, which defined and condemned modernism and mandated the establishment of secret vigilance committees in every diocese worldwide to ferret out suspected offenders. The condemnation was reinforced in 1910 by the promulgation of an oath against modernism to be taken annually by all teachers of philosophy and theology in Catholic colleges, universities, and seminaries and by all clerics as a condition for ordination and advancement to higher offices in the church. To the outsider, the ensuing campaign would seem often to violate the principles of Christian morality, as unsuspecting preachers and professors were summarily removed from posts without explanation or opportunity of defense. However, when one enters into the perception of the framers of the condemnation of modernism, one realizes that their response was proportional and appropriate to the danger perceived and, as will be seen, quite within the framework of Mediterranean morality.

The logic of the condemnation seemed to go like this: Modern society, at least from the onset of the French Revolution, was in a disastrous state—especially for Catholicism because of its alignment with the embattled *ancien régime*. But if Catholicism especially was threatened, then so was society itself, because, in the ascendant Vatican ecclesiology, the Catholic religion alone constituted the secure foundation of society.[4] To safeguard society, therefore, one had to safeguard Catholicism. But to safeguard Catholicism, one had to address those responsible for the ills besetting it—namely, the theologians. Pius X's condemnation, therefore, took aim at specific, if unnamed, theologians because, he argued, it was their Protestant-inspired religious philosophy of vital immanence that necessarily followed a trajectory through agnosticism to atheism and thence to the destruction first of religion, then of society.[5] At stake was civilization itself.

What was that "modern world," and what was Catholicism's relation to it? To the Vatican party, the modern world was the religio-political complex held in bondage to the ideology previously known as liberalism with its straight-line ancestry through Enlightenment rationalism to Protestantism. But liberalism was now renamed modernism, because—in the ultramontane perception—it had penetrated the ageless and ahistorical Catholic Church and with insidious design had adapted to the environment of its new host. It was now the enemy within.

. . . THROUGH THE EYES OF POPE LEO XIII

The key to the identification of the enemy and his lineage, and so also the key to methods of counter-assault, is to be found more in Leo XIII than in Pius X, because Pius merely succeeded Leo in the conviction that all power, including all civil power of whatever executive form, is derived from God and that therefore the social foundation and support of government are religious. Leo drew a circle on a venerable lineage of ultramontane argument that government and social order depend on religion,[6] and this dependency gave the papacy a claim of moral primacy in world affairs.

Leo was convinced, therefore, that his only effective tactic for the renewal of society was the renewal of religion, where there was no challenge to his claim of primacy. But he was also convinced that for the pope to exercise primacy, even in religion, he had to have a free base of operation. This meant temporal sovereignty, that is, a free papal state. But this in turn meant resolving the Roman Question, which Leo was never able to do, and it remained for him the single most vexing preoccupation of his papacy. This preoccupation is the background against which all other issues were played out.

The answer to the question why the Roman Question was such a consuming preoccupation for Leo is linked to his perception of the role of the papacy within history, particularly as it intersected with world affairs. Oskar Köhler's observation that Leo XIII had a "very pronounced awareness of the history of the papacy" is pertinent. In Leo's writings "quotations from Innocent III abound, and the latter along with Leo the Great, Alexander III, and Pius V appear as models of his pontificate."[7]

Why did Leo focus precisely on Innocent III? There were reasons of personal history as well as of principle. As to the latter, it is safe to assume with Köhler that Leo was well aware of Innocent's great goal of raising the papacy " 'in the realm of *christianitas* to a sacerdotal–royal position'," with himself " 'as head of the super-national *populus christianus*, which would be his direct responsibility'."[8] But while royal–temporal primacy— even in some kind of throne-and-altar coalition—was long since out of the question, there was still the sacerdotal–moral primacy that Leo believed was the sacred patrimonial mission of the papacy to the world. But to exercise that mission the papacy required two attributes: (1) the papacy must have a recognizable and recognized supra-national prominence—that is, the papacy could not be identified with any given state or nationality, otherwise its moral primacy would be vitiated by a lack of catholicity; and (2) the papacy must exercise freedom (which exercise in turn implies temporal sovereignty) if the papacy was to be an effective symbol of freedom to the world—first, freedom of religion, then freedom of the working classes from oppression either by the ruling classes or by socialist ideologies. A papacy that could be held hostage by a civil government would be unable to exercise its sacred mission. Therefore, to Leo, temporal sovereignty was the God-given *conditio sine qua non* of the papacy.[9] It was not a question of whether but of how much temporal sovereignty. Three popes later that question was resolved.

Leo's personal reasons for evoking Innocent III involved the providential, historical links in birth, life, and—as Leo would arrange it—death. Both were born in Anagni. During his papacy Innocent was a powerful crusader against lawlessness, rebellion, and disorder. On his way to preach the Fourth Crusade at the close of the Fourth Lateran Council, he died suddenly in Perugia. His unguarded body was plundered by thieves,[10] then interred in the cathedral with the remains of two other prelates in a tomb bearing a small, unobtrusive marker. This shameful treatment was an outrage and a sacrilege that seven centuries later Bishop Vincenzo Gioacchino Pecci of Perugia—the later Pope Leo XIII—determined to redress in due course.

Leo was nothing if not a master of symbolic action. In 1882

he mandated a wholesale restoration of the Lateran Basilica, the cathedral of Rome, the pope's church, built on land donated by Constantine—the church where Innocent III had realized his last and greatest triumph, the Fourth Lateran Council. Ten years later, upon completion of the project, while under the heel of an occupying government, Leo brazenly if quietly transferred Innocent's remains from Perugia to the Lateran Basilica, thereby sending to the Italian government and perhaps to all governments a forceful message about his own intentions. Leo then ordained that his own tomb be erected on the right side of the basilica directly facing that of Innocent.

Clues to Leo's intentions in his identification with Innocent III are given in his address to the cardinals on 1 March 1892— the anniversary of his coronation (1878)—shortly after the transfer of Innocent's remains. He justified the transfer by declaring that ever since his episcopate in Perugia, he had wanted to honor the memory of this pope. Transferring Innocent's remains to the Lateran would, he declared, allow Innocent's voice to echo from the "symbol of Christian unity." Then, as if to underscore his own agenda, Leo recounted the great goals of Innocent's pontificate: the "conquest of the Holy Land and the independence of the Church." Under the "freedom of the papacy," he said, the Christian faith, "like our blood, revitalized the social and political organism" and tied the "peoples" to the authority of the church, the "moral center of the world." Is not "a strong faith, embodied [inviscerata] in the conscience of the peoples, rather than the restoration of medieval institutions," the way to achieve "final victory"?[11]

None of Innocent's triumphs figured more prominently in Leo's imagination than the securing of papal sovereignty over Rome. Innocent ordered Roman civil officials to acknowledge him rather than the emperor as their sovereign and substituted his own appointees for the imperial judges. They obeyed him, and he got away with it.[12] It would not be stretching the point too far to suggest that Leo wanted to find for his own day a formula such as Innocent had found to raise the papacy to a power to be reckoned with in every arena of world affairs—not by returning to medieval polity but by serving "a strong faith, embodied in the conscience of the peoples" and *thereby* achieving "final victory."

That was a fateful year, 1892.[13] The transfer of Innocent's remains occurred in the wake of Leo's boldest encyclicals: *Rerum novarum* (15 May 1891), against the social injustices of the industrial age, and *Au milieu des sollicitudes* (16 February 1892), the encyclical of the *ralliement*. Leo's argument for his papacy was circular. On the one hand, he sought a cure for the social and political disruptions of the modern world in order to safeguard freedom of religion. On the other, he sought a cure for the ills of religion so that it could in turn stabilize society. He saw little hope for a return to the medieval polity of *christianitas*—his every effort to regain temporal power through political channels and alliances had so far failed. What was still open to him was a spiritual and moral sovereignty that would lift Catholics caught in a pluralistic maelstrom of menacing cultures, governments, and ideas into a transcendent *populus christianus*.[14] This goal he figured to prosecute by sidestepping refractory heads of states and appealing directly to the people. It was a forced option.

Thus, in that same year Leo addressed *Au milieu des sollicitudes* directly to the French people and, in a significant gesture, used the French language. He appealed not to Catholics alone but to "all upright and intelligent Frenchmen" to rally behind their legitimate government for the sake of peace. Contrary to certain calumnies, he declared, the church does not seek political domination over the state. Nor does it seek any particular form of government; "Catholics, like all other citizens, are free to prefer one form of government to another." The church seeks only freedom of religion within whatever form of government the political powers of a nation assume, and citizens are bound to accept that government and refrain from all attempts to overthrow it or change its form. The basis of this conformity to various forms of legitimate government, Leo asserted, is religion, because "religion, and religion only, can create the social bond; . . . it alone maintains the peace of a nation on a solid foundation."[15]

In Leo's thinking, the more fundamental and significant need that the papacy could especially serve was the moral perfecting of the human person. It was as if the irretrievable loss of temporal power forced the papacy self-consciously to claim the realm of moral influence still left to it. In so doing, Leo XIII set the agenda of the modern papacy down to John Paul II.

Charles Stanton Devas, an English political economist, remarking on Leo XIII's lasting influence, perceptively observed that, whereas in former epochs the church had been called "the Church of the catacombs," or "the Church of the Fathers," or "the Church of the Middle Ages," the church of Leo's period could best be called "the Church of the people."[16] Indeed, in Leo's direct appeal to the people, he began to move beyond national politics to transnational politics. In *Graves de communi* (18 January 1901), one of his last encyclicals, Leo returned to a theme of *Rerum novarum* and protested that the social problem was not purely economic. "In point of fact," he argued, "*it is above all a moral and religious matter*, and for that reason must be settled by the principles of morality and according to the dictates of religion."[17] Again, therefore, Leo underscored the priority of the religious issue and thus claimed a more significant papal primacy than could be realized through any union of throne and altar.

To accomplish this defined mandate, however, nothing was more necessary to Leo than independence from the state. That meant answering the Roman Question in favor of papal temporal sovereignty.

Pascendi—THE FINALE TO THE ANTI-LIBERAL PROGRAM

The perceptions of Pius X and the framers of *Pascendi* were filtered through the antecedent perceptions of Leo XIII. Pius and his writers knew that the program announced in *Pascendi* was not a new departure. In fact, they took pains at every point to demonstrate its lineage. Pius X perceived his mandate to be an effectual continuation, if not decisive conclusion, of the consistent efforts of his predecessors of the nineteenth century—Leo XIII, Pius IX, and Gregory XVI—to combat the errors of the modern world.[18]

In the logic of *Pascendi*, the progenitor of modernism was Luther. Modernists "feel no especial horror in treading in the foot-steps of Luther. . . . The error of Protestantism made the first step on this path; that of Modernism makes the second; athe-ism makes the next."[19] The working out of the error took its philosophical form in Kantianism, its theological form in liber-alism, and its world-political form in the French Revolution (al-though, as will be seen shortly, that revolution was intimately connected with the American Revolution and the "heresy" of Americanism defined by Leo XIII's encyclical *Testem benevolen-tiae* of 1899).

That the authors of *Pascendi* saw modernism as continuous with and nothing but a further expression of nineteenth-cen-tury liberalism can be demonstrated from the traditional au-thorities they cited against modernism. The authors began their description and analysis of modernism by exposing the alleged root of the malady—agnostic depreciation of the intel-lect—and by arraying against it the canons of Vatican I on faith and revelation which had been explicitly aimed at Protestant rationalism and liberalism, and which pronounced anathemas against whoever teaches that God "cannot be known with cer-tainty by the natural light of human reason," "that divine rev-elation cannot be made credible by external signs, and that therefore men should be drawn to faith only by their personal internal experience or by private inspiration."[20]

It is telling that the first papal authority cited in *Pascendi* was Gregory XVI and his encyclical *Singulari nos* (1834) condemning Lamennais' anarchic jeremiad, *Paroles d'un croyant* (1834). E. E. Y. Hales observed that "the *affaire Lamennais* . . . has always occupied a prominent place in the modern history of the Church because the attitude which Gregory XVI took up to-wards the tenets of [Lamennais' journal] *L'Avenir* became a precedent of great importance. On such matters as the relations of Church and State, toleration, or liberty of the press, it went far to mark out the line taken later by Pius IX when he issued his Syllabus of Errors."[21] A digression here on the elements of the *affaire Lamennais* pertinent to the present study is appropri-ate because that *affaire* decisively formed Vatican policy against liberalism from Gregory XVI through Pius X and beyond.

THE *Affaire Lamennais*

Of the despotisms of the French Revolution, none more outraged loyal Catholics than Napoleon's imprisonment of Pope Pius VII from 1809 to 1814. That atrocity confirmed the royalist conviction that the Revolution and the Roman Catholic Church were simply incompatible. Count Joseph Marie de Maistre's *Du Pape* gave classic expression to this conviction. The thought of popular sovereignty horrified him. The greatest crime of the Revolution, he maintained, was that it sought to make the people "free." Both the king and the pope, he declared, were ordained by God with absolute authority, albeit with the pope above the king. And Viscount Louis Gabriel Ambroise de Bonald (1754–1840) virtually absolutized the value of a monarchic social order with his contention that the king could not be deposed under any circumstances. For him Roman Catholicism under a Catholic monarch meant order; and Protestantism, disorder.

There were, to be sure, outstanding Catholics who believed that their faith and political democracy were not mutually exclusive—among them, Félicité Robert de Lamennais (1782–1854), Lacordaire, and Montalembert. Early on, however, Lamennais had supported the basic spirit of de Maistre and de Bonald. He acquired fame with the first volume of his *Essai sur l'indifférence en matière de religion* (1817), in which he argued that the right of private judgment passes through indifference (or toleration) to atheism and the collapse of society, and that religion alone could restore a ruined society—precisely the later contention of Leo XIII and Pius X. Lamennais' next three volumes (1820–1823), however, stirred up heated controversy because of their odd mixture of ideas from his eclectic reading of the *philosophes.* On the one hand, he argued that Catholicism alone could shore up society, and that Europe could be regenerated only by accepting ecclesiastical authority.[22] On the other, he argued that the foundation for certitude was the *raison générale* or *sens commun,* a view strongly redolent of Rousseau.

Lamennais wanted a political system that would allow Christianity both to penetrate and to undergird the fabric of society. He thought at first that a legitimist union of throne and altar would be the answer. But he was quickly disillusioned by the ultraroyalist policies of the Bourbon restoration that subsidized and controlled the church and used religion to domesticate the people, just as the Empire had done. His hope dashed for a moderate church–state alliance, he swung to radical ultramontanism. He contended that, although certitude rested on the *sens commun*, the pope was God's anointed expression of that *sens* and so was the trustee of the entire human race. Necessary consequences were that the pope must be endowed with the most absolute power, including infallibility and the right to intervene in world affairs, in order to effect the principles of the Gospel. The pope alone, he argued, could safeguard the freedom of God's children against state interference.

Lamennais was now advocating a theocratic democracy, in which the church would be free from all civil domination and beholden to the pope alone. To advance his views he founded the periodical *L'Avenir* and attracted some of France's greatest writers, including Victor Hugo and Lamartine, but mostly free-thinking intellectuals and social revolutionaries. Lamennais' targeted opponents were now no longer doctrinaire atheists but Catholic lackeys of secular government, Gallicans bent on scattering the people from Rome's protective mantle. The Gallicans reacted vigorously and quickly embroiled Lamennais in controversy with powerful church authorities, among them even many non-Gallicans put off by his extravagant claims to truth and his immoderate invective against the episcopacy.

In 1831 Lamennais went to Rome to submit his quarrel to Pope Gregory XVI. But the pope, however much he valued aspects of Lamennais' program, mistrusted him and his theology. Nor was he about to let Lamennais dictate papal policy, especially regarding the episcopacy. After lengthy examination, Gregory issued the encyclical *Mirari vos* (15 August 1832) condemning the main theses of *L'Avenir*.

Disillusioned, Lamennais retired from public life but two years later reappeared a non-Catholic. His *Paroles d'un croyant*, the greatest work of this period, described the world as divided into two opposing camps: on one side, the people, the living embodiment of the City of God; on the other, the city of Satan with his executioners and oppressors, kings and priests. Gregory XVI responded with *Singulari nos* (25 June 1834), summarily condemning in particular Lamennais' view that the evolution of truth was part of the progressive evolution of the people—a view later labeled immanentism and condemned by Pius X's *Pascendi*.[23]

Pascendi CONTINUED: EFFECTS OF MODERNISM/LIBERALISM

Pascendi in fact connected Lamennaisian liberalism with modernism by invoking *Singulari nos* against the modernists as philosophers: "They are seen to be under the sway of a blind and unchecked passion for novelty, thinking not at all of finding some solid foundation of truth, but, despising the holy and apostolic traditions, they embrace other and vain, futile, uncertain doctrines, unapproved by the Church, on which, in the height of their vanity, they think they can base and maintain truth itself."[24]

The encyclical goes on to address the modernist as believer and purports to show how the modernist, by separating reason from belief, arrives at the liberal demand for separation of church and state. It argues that, because modernists give no legitimate place in belief to reason, they have no foundation for belief but must necessarily fall into sentimentalism and base belief on some vague religious sense, or feeling, or experience. The experience is then expressed in formulas, which, they say, belong entirely to the realm of phenomena and so fall under the control of science. That works out fine for them, since they regard formulas of faith as mere symbols of the divine. Thus modernists separate faith and science, and subject the former to the latter. They apply this same argument to church and state to separate them and subject the former to the latter— although they do not yet openly admit this subjection. The result is what many liberal Protestants advocate: individual religion devoid of social embodiment and manifestation. The implications for the church's disciplinary authority are obvious. It is bankrupt.

More pernicious still, *Pascendi* asserted, is modernism's view of *doctrinal* or *dogmatic* authority. Here the modernist premise is that religious society becomes unified to the extent that there is a shared common mind. The magisterium's function is then relegated to finding and giving expression to that common mind or conscience, while not hindering individual consciences from urging dogma forward in its evolutionary path. It follows that the magisterium is dependent on the individual consciences and must bow to popular ideas. But to entertain such a view is to introduce "that most pernicious doctrine which would make of the laity the factor of progress in the Church."[25]

Against all these pernicious views, *Pascendi* invoked Pius IX's first encyclical, *Qui pluribus* (9 November 1846), which, correctly read, debunks the common view that Pius IX was initially a liberal and puts him squarely in continuity with the program of his predecessor, Gregory XVI:[26] " 'These enemies of divine revelation extol human progress to the skies, and with rash and sacrilegious daring would have it introduced into the Catholic religion as if this religion were not the work of God but of man, or some kind of philosophical discovery susceptible of perfection by human efforts.' " *Pascendi* then adds significantly, "On the subject of revelation and dogma in particular, the doctrine of the Modernists *offers nothing new*. We find it condemned in the Syllabus of Pius IX., where it is enunciated in these terms: 'Divine revelation is imperfect, and therefore subject to continual and indefinite progress, corresponding with the progress of human reason.' "[27]

The Vatican Council, *Pascendi* continued, reiterated this condemnation:

The doctrine of the faith which God has revealed has not been proposed to human intelligences to be perfected by them as if it were a philosophical system, but as a divine deposit entrusted to the Spouse of Christ to be faithfully guarded and infallibly interpreted. Hence also that sense of the sacred dogmas is to be perpetually retained which our Holy Mother the Church has once declared, nor is this sense ever to be abandoned on plea or pretext of a more profound comprehension of the truth.[28]

More telling still for the perceived continuity betwen modernism and liberalism are the authoritative citations in the brief second and third parts of the encyclical on the causes and remedies of modernism.[29] Modernist scholars remark the recurrence of the word "novelty" and its cognates in the anti-liberal/modernist literature. *Pascendi* offers a rationale for this preoccupation in the assertion that the remote causes of modernism "may be reduced to two: curiosity and pride. Such is the opinion of Our Predecessor, Gregory XVI, who wrote: 'A lamentable spectacle is that presented by the aberrations of human reason when it yields to the spirit of novelty, when against the warning of the Apostle it seeks to know beyond what it is meant to know, and when relying too much on itself it thinks it can find the truth outside the Catholic Church wherein truth is found without the slightest shadow of error.' "[30] There we have it again: The basis of liberalism is rationalism—by which the framers of *Pascendi* meant *prideful* curiosity that accords the intellect unbridled power for truth—that is, unbridled from the reins of the magisterium. Such an affirmation of reason's power, the encyclical contended, is the foundation of intellectual democracy, which spills over to social democracy and thence to anarchy.

The surest sign of inflamed passion for novelty and therefore modernism, *Pascendi* declared, is the aversion to scholasticism. Indeed, " 'certain it is that the passion for novelty is always united in them [the modernists] with hatred of scholasticism,' " but they must remember that Pius IX condemned their proposition that " 'the method and principles which have served the ancient doctors of scholasticism when treating of theology no longer correspond with the exigencies of our time or the progress of science.' "[31] Thus again *Pascendi* joined modernism with liberalism.

Jean-Baptiste Lemius, whose brother Joseph was the principal drafter of *Pascendi*,[32] viewed the modernist passion for novelty in terms of a "war" against authentic tradition and authority. In his *A Catechism of Modernism*—approved on 14 December 1907 by Cardinal Merry del Val for "the less cultured"—Lemius turned *Pascendi*'s propositions into questions that bear his own editorial stamp. Paragraph 42, for example, typifies his tactics:

Q. In the war against scholastic philosophy and Tradition, what is the third obstacle which the Modernists feel obliged to remove?

A. They propose to remove the ecclesiastical magisterium itself. . . .
Q. In their war against the "magisterium of the Church," may we not apply to the Modernists the earlier condemnations?

Here Lemius quotes in reply the encyclical's own invocation of Leo XIII's motu proprio, *Ut mysticam* (14 March 1891): " 'To bring contempt and odium on the mystic Spouse of Christ, who is the true light, the children of darkness have been wont to cast in her face before the world a stupid calumny, and perverting the meaning and force of things and words, to depict her as the friend of darkness and ignorance, and the enemy of light, science, and progress.' "[33]

It is not always possible to say with certainty what specific cases or events the framers of *Pascendi* had in mind when they made general accusations of the modernist lust for novelty. Most commentators have pointed to the immediate cases of Loisy, Tyrrell, von Hügel, and Houtin, among others. But the Vatican memory is long, and it is perhaps not too far-fetched to suggest—as we shall see in some detail below—that certain celebrated cases connected with Americanism and liberalism are equally well described by *Pascendi*'s exposé of modernist artifices:

[Modernists] seize upon professorships in the seminaries and universities, and gradually make of them chairs of pestilence. In sermons from the pulpit they disseminate their doctrines, although possibly in utterances which are veiled. In congresses they express their teachings more openly. In their social gatherings they introduce them and commend them to others. Under their own names and under pseudonyms they publish numbers of books, newspapers, reviews, and sometimes one and the same writer adopts a variety of pseudonyms to trap the incautious reader into believing in a multitude of Modernist writers. . . . They are possessed by the empty desire of having their names upon the lips of the public, and they know they would never succeed in this were they to say only what has always been said by all men.[34]

Pascendi: REMEDIES FOR MODERNISM

In the section on the remedies for modernism, *Pascendi*'s course of choice was to make scholastic philosophy "the basis of the

sacred sciences."[35] The first citation of papal tradition in support of that course came from the papal champion of Thomism,
Leo XIII:

Against this host of grave errors, and its secret and open advance,
Our Predecessor, Leo XIII, of happy memory, worked strenuously,
both in his words and acts, especially as regards the study of the
Bible. But . . . the Modernists are not easily deterred by such weap-
ons. With an affectation of great submission and respect, they pro-
ceeded to twist the words of the Pontiff to their own sense, while they
described his action as directed against others than themselves.[36]

Pius X was referring, of course, to Leo's prescription of Thomism with his encyclical *Aeterni Patris* (4 August 1879) and the
ensuing flap among various rival schools of scholasticism, on
the one hand, and the rejection of scholasticism by the modernists, on the other.

The principal cause of the grave errors referred to was the
same as that which Leo XIII had indicated in his allocution of 7
March 1880 — namely, the pursuit of positive theology and natural sciences to the proportionate neglect of scholastic theology. The result, asserted *Pascendi*, is that the former splendor
of theology is dimmed and "disfigured by perverse doctrines
and monstrous errors."[37]

At the heart of that principal cause was the "love of novelty."
It was to be counteracted "without compunction" by excluding
from positions in universities and seminaries anyone openly or
secretly "tainted with Modernism" as evident in their "carping
at scholasticism, and the Fathers, and the magisterium," their
"love of novelty in history, archaeology, biblical exegesis," or
finally their preference for secular sciences to the neglect of the
sacred.[38] Great vigilance was to be exercised over publications,
especially over "the writings of some Catholics, who . . . are ill-
instructed in theological studies and imbued with modern philosophy, and strive to make this harmonise with the faith, and,
as they say, to turn it to the profit of the faith. The name and
reputation of these authors cause them to be read without suspicion, and they are, therefore, all the more dangerous in gradually preparing the way of Modernism."[39]

Then, in a move that would darken the church's atmosphere

even to the present day, the encyclical appealed several times to Leo XIII's apostolic constitution *Officiorum ac munerum* (22 January 1897) as precedent for extending to all ordinaries the power of proscription invested in the Sacred Congregation of the Index. Such an extension of power was needed, the pope argued, because the number of modernist writings had exceeded the Congregation's means to censure them all. He admonished bishops and religious superiors not to be fooled by the wiles of these writers. The *imprimatur*, for example, may be bogus or "granted through carelessness or too much indulgence or excessive trust placed in the author, which last has perhaps sometimes happened in the religious orders."[40]

To enforce the prescriptions against modernism, *Pascendi* appealed for precedent to an earlier action of Leo XIII, who in 1849, as archbishop of Perugia, led the Congress of the Bishops of Umbria to establish a vigilance committee in each of their dioceses to take note of " 'the existence of errors and the devices by which new ones are introduced and propagated, and to inform the Bishop of the whole, so that he may take counsel with them as to the best means for suppressing the evil at the outset and preventing it spreading for the ruin of souls or, worse still, gaining strength and growth.' "[41] This appeal anchored *Pascendi* firmly in the anti-liberal tradition, as the act it appealed to was taken in the midst of the Italian revolution and became the model for the subsequent "Syllabus of Errors."[42]

Pius X's injunctions to the new worldwide vigilance committees also found inspiration in Leo XIII. In their combat against "novelties of words," the committees were to enforce Leo's instruction of 27 January 1902 to the Sacred Congregation of Extraordinary Ecclesiastical Affairs: " 'It is impossible to approve in Catholic publications a style inspired by unsound novelty which seems to deride the piety of the faithful and dwells on the introduction of a new order of Christian life, on new directions of the Church, on new aspirations of the modern soul, on a new social vocation of the clergy, on a new Christian civilisation, and many other things of the same kind.' "[43]

Pius X's final injunction to the committees was "the duty of overlooking [read "overseeing"] assiduously and diligently social institutions as well as writings on social questions so that they may harbour no trace of Modernism."[44] This last, but certainly not least, injunction suggests that his overriding concern, like Leo XIII's, was the tranquillity of order; for, the encyclical charges, the implications of modernism are profound, far-reaching, and devastating for religion and the churches as well as for the state whose social bond depends on them. This concern rested on the argument that modernism, because it originates from individual sentiment and internal authority, necessarily denies external authority and therefore must end, on the one hand, in atheism and the destruction of all religion and, on the other, in anarchism and the destruction of all society.

MODERNISM AND AMERICANISM

We have reflected above on the continuity between the anti-modernist perceptions of Pius X and the framers of *Pascendi* and the anti-liberal perceptions of Pius' nineteenth-century predecessors. It is time now to trace in some detail the continuity between the campaign against modernism and the campaign against Americanism because the latter campaign was at its climax in the precise time-frame of the present study. In the process it will become apparent that (*a*) the very errors cited by *Pascendi* were those repeatedly denounced in the years leading up to the condemnation of Americanism in the encyclical *Testem benevolentiae* (1899); and thus (*b*) the preoccupations of Vatican officials in the time-frame of this study were the same as those that precipitated three resounding condemnations: first, of Americanism; last, of modernism; but, sandwiched in between, liberalism—condemned by the bishops of England with their joint pastoral of 29 December 1900. The same motivations as impelled the forceful rhetoric and measures of Pius X and *Pascendi* were operative in Leo XIII and *Testem benevolentiae* and in the principal figures of the present study: the Jesuit superior general Luis Martín, Bishop Merry del Val, and Cardinal Herbert Vaughan of London, all of whom, as we shall see, collaborated in the production of the joint pastoral. The contention here will be that their preoccupations, while self-consciously defined as religious and theological, were surrounded and sustained by socio-political concerns.

NOTES

1. See Vincent A. Yzermans, ed., *All Things in Christ: Encyclicals and Selected Documents of Saint Pius X* (Westminster, MD: Newman, 1954), p. xiii.

2. Pius X, *E supremi apostolatus*, par. 2, 4, 9, 12. Paragraph numbers are those given in the official English translation in *The Papal Encyclicals*, vol. 3, *1903–1939*, ed. Claudia Carlen (Wilmington, NC: McGrath, 1981).

3. After eight years as Leo XIII's chamberlain, Monsignor Merry del Val was appointed in October 1899 president of the Accademia dei Nobili Ecclesiastici, which trained promising clerics for diplomatic service in the Vatican. The following year he was consecrated titular archbishop of Nicaea. A few days before Leo XIII died (20 July 1903), Monsignor Alessandro Volpini, secretary of the Consistorial Congregation, a close personal friend of Merry del Val's and collaborator on the Anglican Orders question and the Canadian education crisis, died suddenly. As secretary of the college of cardinals, Volpini would have been secretary of the coming conclave to elect Leo's successor. Cardinal Oreglia de Santo Stefano, dean of the college of cardinals, secured Merry del Val's unanimous election as Volpini's replacement. It was in that capacity that Merry del Val gained the new pope's confidence and nomination as his secretary of state. See Cenci, *Merry del Val*, pp. 117–46; Quinn, *Give Me Souls*, pp. 75–88, 59–62; Del-Gal, *Spiritual Life of Merry del Val*, pp. 19–23. All the biographies of Merry del Val that I have seen depend on Cenci's. Often they simply paraphrase or translate Cenci's words.

4. This was the ultramontane argument influenced especially by Count Joseph de Maistre (1753–1821). His dominating work, *Du Pape* (1819), was the textbook of such prominent disciples as Félicité Robert de Lamennais (1782–1854) and Juan Donoso Cortés (1809–1853). See, e.g., Donoso's widely influential *Ensayo sobre el catolicismo, el liberalismo y el socialismo* (1851); translation: *Essay on Catholicism, Liberalism, and Socialism*, trans. Madeleine Vinton Goddard (Philadelphia: Lippincott, 1862). See also the fine studies of John Thomas Graham, *Donoso Cortés, Utopian Romanticist and Political Realist* (Columbia: University of Missouri Press, 1974) and Stanley G. Payne, *Spanish Catholicism:*

An Historical Overview (Madison: University of Wisconsin Press, 1984), esp. pp. 71–148.

5. *Pascendi*, par. 39. The official text of *Pascendi* in *Acta Sanctae Sedis* (hereafter ASS) 40:593–650 contains no paragraph numbering. The numbers used here are those assigned in the official English translation, *Tablet* 110 (28 September 1907) 501–15; in *The Papal Encyclicals*, vol. 3, *1903–1939*, ed. Claudia Carlen (Wilmington, NC: McGrath, 1981), pp. 71–97.

For excellent analyses of these issues, see Pierre Colin, "Le Kantisme dans la crise moderniste," and Dominique Dubarle, "Modernisme et expérience religieuse: Réflexions sur un cas de traitement théologique," in *Le Modernisme*, Institut Catholique de Paris Philosophie Series 5 (Paris: Beauchesne, 1980), pp. 9–81 and 181–244, respectively.

6. See Leo XIII's encyclical to the church in France, *Au milieu des sollicitudes* (16 February 1892), *Acta Leonis* 12:21–34; in *The Papal Encyclicals*, vol. 2, *1878–1903*, ed. Claudia Carlen (Wilmington, NC: McGrath, 1981), pp. 277–81.

7. Oskar Köhler, "The World Plan of Leo XIII: Goals and Methods," in *The Church in the Industrial Age*, trans. Margit Resch, vol. 9 of *History of the Church*, ed. Hubert Jedin and John Dolan (New York: Crossroad, 1981), pp. 18–19. The urgency of the Roman Question can be inferred from the important study by Halvor Moxnes, "Patron–Client Relations and the New Community in Luke-Acts," in *The Social World of Luke-Acts: Models for Interpretation*, ed. Jerome H. Neyrey (Peabody, MA: Hendrickson, 1991), pp. 241–68. In the patronage system of Mediterranean society central control plays the critical and dominant role. Without it, the entire system collapses.

8. F. Kempf, *Lexikon für Theologie und Kirche*, 2nd ed., 5:688; quoted in Köhler, "World Plan," p. 19.

9. See Köhler, "World Plan," p. 21.

10. M. David Knowles, "The Thirteenth Century," in *The Middle Ages*, vol. 2 of *The Christian Centuries: A New History of the Catholic Church*, ed. M. David Knowles and Dimitri Obolensky (New York: McGraw-Hill, 1968), p. 291.

11. Leo XIII, "Onorare le ceneri" (1 March 1892), *Acta Leonis* 12:383–85, here p. 385. See Köhler, "World Plan," pp. 18–19.

12. See Kenneth Scott Latourette, *A History of Christianity* (New York: Harper & Row, 1953), p. 485.

13. In this year, in addition to the events about to be described, the Spanish Jesuit Luis Martín was elected superior general of the Society

of Jesus, and Monsignor Merry del Val was appointed papal chamberlain.

14. For an authoritative background study of the issue of pluralism and its impact on the nineteenth-century church, see Gerald A. McCool, S.J., *Nineteenth-Century Scholasticism: The Search for a Unitary Method* (New York: Fordham University Press, 1989)—repr. of *Catholic Theology in the Nineteenth Century: The Quest for a Unitary Method* (New York: Seabury, 1977)—esp. the epilogue, "The Reemergence of Pluralism," pp. 241–67.

15. Leo XIII, *Au milieu des solicitudes*, *Acta Leonis* 12:19–31; *Papal Encyclicals*, pp. 277–83.

16. See René Fülöp-Miller, *Leo XIII and Our Times: Might of the Church-Power in the World*, trans. Conrad M. R. Bonacina (London: Longmans, Green, 1937), p. 137. Charles Stanton Devas (1848–1906) was a convert to Roman Catholicism. In the Introduction to his *The Key to the World's Progress, Being Some Account of the Historical Significance of the Catholic Church* (London: Longmans, Green, 1906), pp. v–vi, he acknowledges his discipleship to Newman and his indebtedness to the works of George Tyrrell and Wilfrid Ward. He drew on several ideas from Tyrrell's *Hard Sayings* and *Lex Orandi*.

17. Leo XIII, *Graves de communi* (18 January 1901), *Acta Leonis* 21:8–10; in *The Papal Encyclicals*, vol. 2, *1878–1903*, ed. Claudia Carlen (Wilmington, NC: McGrath, 1981), pp. 481–82. Emphasis added.

18. See *Pascendi*, par. 40ff.

19. Ibid., par. 18, 30.

20. Vatican I, *De revelatione*, can. 1, 2, 3 and *De fide*, can. 3, cited in ibid., par. 6. See Colin, "Le Kantisme," and Dubarle, "Modernisme et expérience religieuse."

21. E. E. Y. [Edward Elton Young] Hales, *The Catholic Church in the Modern World: A Survey from the French Revolution to the Present* (Garden City, NY: Doubleday Image, 1960), p. 94.

22. This was the ultramontane argument, influenced especially by de Maistre. See above, n. 4.

23. See Hales, *Catholic Church in the Modern World*, p. 94, and Henri Daniel-Rops, *The Church in an Age of Revolution (1789–1870)*, trans. John Warrington, vol. 8 of *History of the Church of Christ* (New York: Dutton, 1965), pp. 162–71, 199–213.

24. *Pascendi*, par. 13.

25. Ibid., par. 27.

26. See Daniel-Rops, *Church in an Age of Revolution*, pp. 240–42. It is curious that Hales does not even mention *Qui pluribus* either in his *Pio Nono: A Study in European Politics and Religion in the Nineteenth Cen-*

tury (New York: Kenedy, 1954) or in his *Catholic Church in the Modern World*.

27. *Pascendi*, par. 28, emphasis added; Syllabus of Errors (December 1864), prop. 5.

28. *Pascendi*, par. 28; Vatican I, Constitution *Dei filius*, chap. 4. Given this declaration, it would seem inconsistent that *Pascendi* should legislate a philosophical system as the *basis* for a revealed religion. See below, n. 35.

29. *Pascendi*, par. 40–56.

30. Ibid., par. 40, quoting *Singulari nos* (25 June 1834), which condemned Lamennais.

31. *Pascendi*, par. 42, quoting Syllabus, prop. 13.

32. Adolf Schönmetzer, in his 1963 edition of Denzinger, noted: "De theologis, qui hanc epistolam composuerunt, nihil quidem certi constat; opinio favet praesertim cardinali Ludovico Billot S.I. et Iohanni B. Lemius O.M.I." (DS 3475), but Gabriel Daly, o.s.a., *Transcendence and Immanence: A Study in Catholic Modernism and Integralism* (Oxford: Clarendon, 1980), pp. 232–34, certainly identified *Joseph* Lemius as the principal drafter of *Pascendi*, not his brother, Jean-Baptiste. Whether or not Billot or anyone else had a hand in its preparation is still an open question.

33. Jean-Baptiste Lemius, o.m.i., *A Catechism of Modernism* (New York: Society for the Propagation of the Faith, Archdiocese of New York, 1908; repr. Rockford, IL: TAN, 1981), pp. 127–28. The *motu proprio* was issued on the occasion of the restoration and expansion of the Vatican observatory.

34. *Pascendi*, par. 43. Émile Poulat, *Histoire, dogme, et critique dans la crise moderniste* (Paris: Casterman, 1962), pp. 621–77, provides a helpful treatment of pseudonymous and anonymous publications during the modernist period. Thomas Michael Loome, *Liberal Catholicism, Reform Catholicism, Modernism: A Contribution to a New Orientation in Modernist Research*, Tübinger theologische Studien 14 (Mainz: Grünewald, 1979), pp. 269–71, provides a list of pseudonyms used in Germany during the crisis; and elsewhere in his extensive bibliographies Loome lists and identifies many other pseudonyms and anonymous works in other European countries.

35. There seems to be an internal contradiction here in *Pascendi*'s recommendation that a rational system of philosophy be the basis of a revealed religion.

36. *Pascendi*, par. 44.

37. Ibid., par. 47. It should be noted that Leo's allocution followed

on the heels of *Aeterni Patris* (4 August 1879) with its advocacy of scholastic philosophy.

38. *Pascendi*, par. 48.

39. Ibid., par. 50. Certainly Tyrrell would fit here. So would Newman, although Pius X would be loath to say so openly.

40. Ibid., par. 51; see also par. 50–53. Certainly it happened in the case of George Tyrrell and his *Lex Orandi*. Religious orders, especially the "exempt" orders like the Jesuits, had their own censorship process. See David G. Schultenover, S.J., *George Tyrrell: In Search of Catholicism* (Shepherdstown, WV: Patmos Press, 1981), pp. 241–42. See Leo XIII's detailed apostolic constitution on the prohibition and censorship of books, *Officiorum ac munerum*, in ASS 30:39–53, with extensive commentary, pp. 55–81.

41. Acts of the Congress of the Bishops of Umbria, November 1849, tit. 2, art. 6, quoted in *Pascendi*, par. 55. See Giacomo Martina, S.J., *Pio IX (1846–1850)*, Vol. 1, Miscellanea Historiae Pontificiae 38 (Rome: Gregorian University Press, 1974), p. 524.

42. To deal with the problems of the modern world, Pecci and his bishops urged the pope to define the Immaculate Conception and papal infallibility, issue a point-by-point condemnation of errors, and call an ecumenical council. See Raymond Corrigan, *The Church and the Nineteenth Century* (Milwaukee: Bruce, 1938) p. 177, and Raymond H. Schmandt, "The Life and Work of Leo XIII," in *Leo XIII and the Modern World*, ed. Edward T. Gargan (New York: Sheed & Ward, 1961), p. 19.

43. Quoted in *Pascendi*, par. 55.

44. Ibid., par. 55.

2

Rome's More Particular and Immediate Synoptic: Americanism/Modernism

WAS AMERICANISM ALSO THE TARGET OF *Pascendi*? Certainly the common anti-modernist hermeneutic regarded Americanism as the practical precursor of modernism. The connection was first made in print by the French Jesuit Maurice de la Taille in September 1907, prior to the publication of *Pascendi*.[1] Pius X and *Pascendi* officially endorsed the connection. "With regard to morals," the encyclical asserted, the modernists "adopt the principle of the Americanists, that the active virtues are more important than the passive, and are to be more encouraged in practice."[2] Granted this authoritative connection, subsequent commentators can be expected to take it as fact. And indeed they do—notably, the influential Bishop Anton Gisler and Jean Rivière.[3] A strong case can be made that the integralist mentality of European Catholicism cut first Americanism, then modernism out of the same cloth.[4]

THE SCIENTIFIC CONGRESS: TOWARD A BAN ON CONTROVERSY

Avowed Americanists and "modernists" were well known to each other. Denis O'Connell, John Keane, and John Zahm, along with Charles Grannan and Edward Pace, professors at Catholic University, chose the International Catholic Scientific Congress at Fribourg in August 1897 as the setting to articulate the Americanist platform. Zahm delivered a paper on evolu-

tion, and O'Connell read a paper on the meaning of Americanism entitled "A New Idea in the Life of Father Hecker." Important papers by Marie-Joseph Lagrange on the authorship of the
Pentateuch and by Baron Friedrich von Hügel on historical criticism and the Hexateuch were also presented. Some three thousand scholars attended that congress—almost every European
Catholic scholar of note—including subsequently identified
"modernists" and "modernist" sympathizers Blondel, Se-
meria, Minocchi, Mignot, Rose, Ward, Laberthonnière, and
Klein. Loisy was absent from the congress, but, as we shall see,
he later commented sharply on its proceedings.[5]

The rabid anti-Americanist/anti-modernist bishop of Nancy,
Charles-François Turinaz (1838–1918), also attended the congress and, according to Felix Klein, provoked a major row. Turinaz had come to the congress specifically to hear and refute
O'Connell's paper on Americanism, but he missed the paper
because O'Connell had been unexpectedly shifted from third
to first speaker in the morning session on "Judicial, Economic,
and Social Sciences." When Turinaz arrived, undaunted by his
ignorance of the proceedings, he launched into a lengthy "re-
buttal" that bore little on O'Connell's thesis but broadsided
Isaac Hecker, charging him with fomenting individualism and
a Protestant doctrine of the direct inspiration and guidance of
the Holy Spirit in each soul. That criticism, Klein wrote,

was the first of a series of inconsistent, illogical diatribes against
everyone associated with Americanism. Repeatedly we had to face
adversaries who attributed to us ideas that we never entertained, who
tried to fasten upon us opinions forged from bits extracted here and
there out of our writings and speeches, who condemned us for parts
of sentences taken out of context or for expressions interpreted in a
sense that no ordinary reader would ever dream of.

If we should say that God acts in each soul by His inspirations but
that, in order to know whether or not an inspiration comes from Him,
we need the aid of the Church, they would seize upon the first part
of the sentence and suppress the conclusion; then they would charge
us with teaching that today the Holy Spirit suffices for the direction
of souls and there is no need for external authority.[6]

La Semaine religieuse, the diocesan paper of Soissons, reported
a further encounter between Turinaz and Professor Gaspard

Decurtins of the Catholic University of Fribourg, a particularly significant altercation for pointing up not only Turinaz' imbalance but also, and more importantly, the intimate connection drawn by his ideology between theology and political systems. Immediately after Professor Giuseppe Toniolo of the University of Pisa had spoken on the ancient political system of Florence, Turinaz began to discourse on the Middle Ages and Christian democracy. Decurtins' reply to Turinaz indicated that he and the bishop held two different views of Leo XIII's idea of Christian democracy. This discrepancy is revealing, particularly in light of the fact that Decurtins enjoyed high favor in Rome and was thought to have collaborated in preparing *Rerum novarum*.[7] Moreover, according to Émile Poulat, Decurtins, at least in 1906, was the acknowledged leader of the conservative majority at the University of Fribourg—the "German party"—over against the minority but active "French party: Dominicans (Fr. Mandonnet, Fr. Rose, etc.), Marianists (self-proclaimed neo-Kantians), and laymen (Jean Brunhes, J. Zeiller, Gustave Michaut, P. M. Masson, V. Giraud, etc.). For this second tendency," Poulat noted, ". . . Fribourg had several times been denounced as a 'modernist lair.' "[8]

Whatever the subtleties of disagreement were between Decurtins and Turinaz, Leo XIII's understanding of Christian democracy was anything but the understanding prevalent among Americanists. Leo's early view, from which he never significantly departed, is given in his encyclical *Diuturnum illud* (29 June 1881), in which he deplored the *cupiditates populares* that emanate from a distorted doctrine of popular sovereignty and affirmed that patriarchal monarchy is unquestionably the ideal, although not the only legitimate, form of government.[9]

Twenty years later, in *Graves de communi* (18 January 1901), a letter occasioned by the tensions of the Italian Opera dei Congressi,[10] Leo distinguished between the terms "Christian Socialism" and "Christian Democracy" and asserted that the latter, rather than the former, "was regarded as offensive among many good persons" due to an "inherent ambiguity and danger." It could be taken to mean that Christianity somehow advocates a people's state in preference to other forms of government. Leo then clearly rejected the distortion of the term

"Christian Democracy" into a political term. "Democracy" in connection with "Christian," he declared, could only mean "a benevolent and Christian movement in behalf of the people,"[11] not *by* the people.

The Jesuit Joseph Brucker, who covered the Scientific Congress for *Études*, wrote forebodingly of the future of such congresses. Referring specifically to the section "Juridical, Economic, and Social Sciences," he served notice of the existence of a commanding body of opinion that in such congresses " 'disputes on the most burning issues of the day were entirely out of order,' " as they do nothing but foment conflict. They may be attractive to the younger delegates, he observed, " 'but it would be unfortunate if these disputes should cause more peaceful undertakings to be forgotten or neglected.' "[12]

LOISY'S REJOINDER

It should be noted, however, that the section of the congress on "The Science of Exegesis," at which the papers of Lagrange and von Hügel were read, also entertained vigorous controversy. But, inexplicably, the press completely ignored von Hügel's paper and the stir it created. To correct this oversight, the mischievous Loisy began a series of articles under the pseudonym Isidore Desprès. Truth to tell, he had a few other objectives in mind for that series: to advance his own congruent thesis of the documentary nature and multiple authorship of the Pentateuch, to expose "the true purpose" of Lagrange's paper, but especially to refute the Jesuit Lucien Méchineau's wrongheaded defense of "tradition" against Lagrange's implications.[13]

Loisy's first salvo, "Opinions catholiques sur l'origine du Pentateuque," was brash enough for taking Lagrange beyond his exquisitely restrained conclusions. "Let us not be deceived," Desprès wrote; "from critical analysis to refutation is but a step; and what we have here is, in fact, a refutation of the traditional thesis" (about Mosaic authorship).[14] But Loisy's June 1900 article, "La Lettre de Léon XIII au Clergé de France et les études d'Écriture Sainte," was positively inflammatory. Here he abandoned the air of innocence of his earlier article and "coldly pushed home some cruel truths."[15] His main point was that Leo XIII's recent letter, *Depuis le jour* (8 September 1899),[16] to the French clergy on ecclesiastical studies clearly betrayed what the pope had intended in *Providentissimus Deus* (1893)— namely, "to condemn all criticism without exception." The reason for the condemnation, Loisy alleged, was that until now biblical exegesis had been subsumed in the scholastic system as "merely an auxiliary science or, more accurately, a branch of theology" whose sole function was to support dogmatic theses or furnish arguments against heresies. That it could now "enjoy a relatively independent existence, like every other branch of human knowledge, with its own object and method, both purely historical' " was " *'an idea absolutely new and almost revolutionary for Catholic theology. . . .* This is why Leo XIII condemns the new criticism.' " The arguments recently advanced by Catholic exegetes on the origin of the Pentateuch, Desprès explained, seem to the pope to destroy the entire structure of Christian apologetics, as they compromise the authority both of the Old Testament and of our Lord who appealed to it and to Moses, not to mention the entire ecclesiastical tradition.[17]

Loisy seems to have accurately interpreted Leo XIII's mind in *Providentissimus Deus*, for Leo wrote in *Depuis le jour* that in *Providentissimus Deus* he had already laid down instructions to "guard against the disturbing tendencies" that "some Catholic writers" were trying to insinuate into biblical interpretation under the "specious pretext" of refuting adversaries, whereas their real motivation was to turn an ostensible apologetic goal to private purpose. Thus "they have worked to make a breach with their own hands in the walls of the city they were charged to defend." Leo then called attention to his stern letter of 25 November 1898 to the minister general of the Friars Minor, warning against "this rash, dangerous policy."[18]

Post hoc if not *propter hoc*, the exegetical section of the International Scientific Congress for Catholic Scholars meeting in Munich the summer of 1900 was canceled. That cancellation spelled the beginning of the end for all such congresses. Indeed, that was the last congress.[19]

ANOTHER KIND OF CONGRESS, ANOTHER BAN

Another interesting connection needs to be pointed out here between the now ended scientific congresses and another kind of congress that drew—in the Roman view—oblique lines from Americanism to modernism. That congress was the Parliament of Religions held 11–28 September 1893 in Chicago in conjunction with the World's Columbian Exposition. Just prior to the parliament, the Catholic Congress of laity had met. Patterned after the 1889 Plenary Council of Baltimore, its purpose was to offer Catholic laity opportunity to speak on Catholic aspects of the problems of the day. The congress was planned by such prominent lay Catholics as Henry Brownson and William J. Onahan, but it was well supported by the more progressive bishops, notably Archbishop John Ireland of St. Paul.

Shortly before this congress, Rome had appointed Archbishop Francesco Satolli its first permanent apostolic delegate to the United States. Satolli knew little English at the time and appeared to be in the tow of Ireland and the progressives who knew him from their Roman days and who could interpret for him. Indeed, the speech that Satolli delivered at the Catholic Congress—with Ireland translating—advanced ideas much like Ireland's on the great benefits to religion of the democratic form of government and on the separation of church and state. Satolli concluded his peroration with the Americanist-sounding exhortation, "Go forward, in one hand bearing the book of Christian truth and in the other the Constitution of the United States."[20] The progressive prelates were elated, but their enthusiasm was quickly dampened by Satolli's unfavorable reaction to the Parliament of Religions—a gathering, he reported to Cardinal Ledóchowski of the Vatican Sacred Congregation de Propaganda Fide, where Catholics consorted with Protestants and where all religious errors were voiced, but which could only propagate religious indifferentism.[21] Cardinal Gibbons, well aware that the Vatican might not understand this particular expression of American religious liberty, submitted an apologia to Leo XIII's secretary of state, Cardinal Rampolla, arguing that the parliament was "a solemn affirmation of religious principles against the great evils [sic] of our days, materialism, agnosticism, atheism" and that to have refused to participate would have harmed the Catholic cause. Rampolla's reply was unenthusiastic. He said he had shown the report to the pope who *recognized the good intention*—a Roman euphemism for *disapproved*—of those who has participated.[22]

If Satolli, Rampolla, and the pope were unenthusiastic, conservative Americans were resoundingly reactionary. A campaign of criticism ensued both in the press and in the correspondence of certain bishops. The anti-parliamentary campaign climaxed with papal prohibition of Catholic participation in any such future parliaments.

When Leo XIII finally issued the prohibition, the Jesuit-run *La Civiltà Cattolica*—regularly called upon to support and explain papal directives—used its annual "chronicle of events" to editorialize on the meaning of the papal action. The anonymous author (Salvatore Brandi?) asserted that Satolli's vigorous action on two fronts checked the evil tendency in the United States toward Pelagianism or neo-Pelagianism.[23] Action on the first front secured the condemnation of secret societies—the Odd Fellows, the Knights of Pythias, and the Sons of Temperance—all of which were in some way Masonic and sowers of religious indifference if not intolerance. Action on the second front secured the prohibition against future participation in parliaments of religions. The latter prohibition, the author crowed, came none too soon, since a similar parliament had already taken place in Toronto, and certain French clerics were agitating for a sensational affair at the World's Exposition in Paris in 1900.

A third alarming front, the author pointed out, was emerging in America out of a false interpretation of American political traditions into a kind of Gallicanism that shows little sympathy for the pope's efforts to regain temporal power. A fourth front was a "sectionalism" that divides Catholics into national or racial groupings and then accuses them of anti-Americanism if, for example, they support parochial schools over public schools. The same charge had also been levied against some religious orders.[24] Indicative of this fourth tendency, the author asserted, is the growth of the "malignant" American Protective Association, which deserves unqualified condemnation.[25]

THE POLITICAL BASIS OF ANTI-AMERICANISM

Behind all the charges of "separatism"—which, in the Vatican mind, was spawned by Protestantism—lay a growing fear among established European powers that the United States, as an increasingly assertive and resourceful giant, would at least realign, if not replace, the old world powers. What Klein said about Turinaz' specious style of criticism[26] would hold *a fortiori* for Charles Maignen's intemperate conflation *Le Père Hecker est-il un Saint?* as well as for the average European royalist/ecclesiastical view of America's world designs.[27] But, while Klein's complaint may be entirely justified in his own regard, the correspondence of the principal Americanist figures suggests that the fabrications of Maignen and other anti-Americanists were not spun entirely out of thin air.

Ever since James Monroe on 2 December 1823 proclaimed the United States' opposition to European interference in the Americas—specifically a projected attempt by the Holy Alliance to return newly independent Latin American countries to colonial status—European states suspected U. S. intentions.[28] Matters went considerably beyond suspicion on the eve of the Spanish-American War, when American officials regularly appealed to the Monroe Doctrine (in a now expanded version) to justify a projected intervention by the United States in Cuba's struggle for independence. Spain could not let the vulgar challenge go unanswered. In the heat of August 1896, Foreign Minister Carlos O'Donnell y Abreau attempted to galvanize European sentiment against the United States by drafting a memorandum to be circulated through all European Spanish embassies, calling for a united and forceful European response to any actual or threatened U. S. intervention. But to what could O'Donnell appeal to convince European powers to lay aside their own nationalistic interests and cooperate in such a venture? His tactic was to raise the specter of a death-threat represented by the United States to the monarchical principle and to alarm European heads of state with a domino theory:

If America intervened, Cuba would be lost. If Cuba were lost, the monarchy would fall. If the monarchy fell, then what of Czar Nicholas, Kaiser Wilhelm, Emperor Franz-Joseph, Queen Victoria, and the other crowned heads? Would their own thrones remain secure? Or would the republican elements in their kingdoms seize on the first opportunity to follow the Spanish example? And what of their colonies? Did not even republican France have cause to fear for her possessions in Guiana and the West Indies if the Americans continued to broaden the interpretation of their Monroe Doctrine?[29]

At the beginning of 1898 anti-American feelings in Europe were running as high as anti-Spanish feelings in the United States. For months the U. S. Congress had debated and filibustered with sometimes unflattering speeches about Spaniards and things Spanish. Reports of these debates, laced with ethnic slurs, reached Spain and ignited riots and demonstrations throughout the country. In the face of this reaction, O'Donnell's point to Europe's rulers was this: the European sky is falling, and disaster can be averted only by a united front against U. S. expansionism. European diplomats and heads of state applauded O'Donnell's design, but they all held back from practical commitment, each one waiting for the other to initiate action. In the end, they all simply let matters run their course between the young and wealthy United States and the old, depleted Spain.[30] Why throw resources at what they privately regarded as ultimately a losing proposition?

AMERICANISM REVEALED

For some years now, the Americanist clergy had sensed the reins of power passing from the Old World to the New. Some had indeed, as Maignen complained, made this passage into a racial issue by speaking of a transfer of power from the politically and morally bankrupt Latin races to the Anglo-Saxon races. This notion received considerable propagation in the American church as early as 1855 from Isaac Hecker's essay *Questions of the Soul,* where the closing pages considered the specifically American manifestations of human nature and their providential, messianic significance for world culture or for—in Hecker's term—the "age."[31] Hecker's later *Exposition of the Church in View of the Recent Difficulties and Controversies, and the Present Needs of the Age*—which followed his disillusionment at Vatican I's definition of papal infallibility—focused his general notion of the agency of converted America as Europe's sole hope for regeneration.[32] The work received wide circulation in Europe through simultaneous French and German translations.

In the last years of the century, the arch-monarchist Maignen, under the psuedonym M. Martel, fanned this Americanist/racial issue to flames with a series of daily articles in *La Vérité Française*, beginning 3 March 1898. These articles were immediately collected and expanded into the infamous *Études sur l'Américanisme: Le Père Hecker est-il un saint?* published under his own name.[33] Refused imprimatur by the archbishop of Paris, Maignen went to the Master of the Sacred Palace in Rome, the Dominican Father Albert Lepidi, and obtained it with the pope's personal consent.[34] Archbishop John J. Keane (1839–1918), himself one of Maignen's targets—having recently been removed from the rectorship of Catholic University, and "elevated" to archiepiscopal rank and labor in Vatican congregations—protested forcefully, suggesting that Lepidi as a Dominican had been swayed by his master general's bitter opposition to the United States in the Spanish-American War.[35]

Most outside observers recognized Maignen's blatant tendentiousness, not least of all in his conflation of Hecker's views with a recent and widely circulated book by the French economist Edmond Demolins, *A quoi tient la supériorité des Anglo-Saxons?* It was an exceptionally devious association, because Demolins' book had recently been acclaimed by the highly suspect *"néo-chrétien"* movement, thus throwing Hecker into the same category as that movement.[36] In fact, in one of his essays, Maignen related how Americanists in Rome were attempting to influence Vatican opinion and thereby use the church to further the cause of the United States during the Spanish-American War. To support his point, Maignen reported that Keane and O'Connell regularly entertained cardinals, Roman aristocracy, and diplomats. At one such dinner in O'Connell's apartment, Ferdinand Brunetière, editor of the *Revue des Deux Mondes* and a principal figure of the Neo-Christian Movement, was said to have proposed a toast to the United States, to which Keane replied that the American Revolution had produced happier results than the French Revolution, because it was founded on truer and wiser ideas. Maignen went on to call attention to the account of this banquet in the *Washington Herald*, which suggested that Keane would soon be made a cardinal. The upshot of all of this pro-American campaign, Maignen alleged, was to establish an American Rome. But to subvert such a scheme, Maignen simply mentioned Archbishop Ireland's diplomatic failure to prevent the Spanish-American War, after Pope Leo had asked him to intercede with his friend President McKinley. Maignen then quoted a letter of a Frenchman in the United States who expressed fear that Ireland was about to go into schism and create an American church.[37]

Whatever Ireland's chances had been for a red hat, they were certainly done in by Maignen's book. The Jesuit Salvatore Brandi, meddling editor of *La Civiltà Cattolica*, in a letter of 11 July 1898 to the anti-Americanist Archbishop Michael A. Corrigan of New York, made it clear that Maignen's view had deeply influenced most of the Roman prelates. How could it not have, given the pope's personal approval and the subsequent outpouring of support spearheaded by Jesuit writers and possibly even by a Jesuit–Dominican alliance?[38]

That there was substance to anti-Americanist concerns is indicated in the views expressed in correspondence between Archbishop Ireland in St. Paul and Denis O'Connell in Rome.[39] A particularly revealing exchange occurred in early May 1898 on the *mixtum gatherum* of issues involved in Americanism and the war with Spain. On the previous 15 February, the sinking of the American battleship *Maine* exploded into a virtually irresistible clamor for armed U. S. intervention in Cuba. On 25 March, Merry del Val's father, Rafael, now the Spanish ambassador to the Vatican, requested papal intervention. Cardinal Rampolla, papal secretary of state, channeled an urgent request to Ireland to use his considerable personal influence with President McKinley to avert war. Ireland tried, but matters had gone too far too fast, and he failed. He told O'Connell that, had he been asked two months earlier, he might have succeeded. But once the United States declared war, he stood patriotically united with liberals and conservatives alike. Given the war, both Ireland and O'Connell saw it as a crisis of supreme advan-

tage for America and Americanism. " 'Evidently,' " Ireland observed prophetically to O'Connell on 2 May 1898,

"you wish America to be in a situation to frighten Europe. Well, she
is in that situation. And henceforward she will be more so. The result
of this war will be to strengthen & enlarge our navy—& reach out for
new territory. If the Pope in the future is to have any world-wide
prestige, he must deal as never before with America. Tell all this in
Rome. And even if we do not hold Cuba & the Philippines—the
church there will be organized on the lines of Americanism."[40]

A few days later, having learned of Rome's indignation over his
diplomatic failure, Ireland complained to O'Connell, " 'What
those people want is success, & when success does not come
they make no allowance.' "[41]

O'Connell replied on 24 May with an important letter of remarkable messianic hubris and chauvinism that characterizes
the worst aspects of Americanism and writes large what anti-
Americanists feared:

"It seems to me that you have now reached the providential period of
your life;—it seems to me the culminating point—where all your
dreams are to be realized and all your poetic visions are to be turned
into prophecies. Now is a moment in which it will be utterly impossible for you to expand your power or your personality too much: 'for
this were you born for this you came into the world' [sic][42] to realize
the dreams of your youth for America and to be the instrument in the
hands of Providence for spreading the benefits of a new civilization
over the world. To this point has really tended, even without your
knowing it, everything you have hitherto done in all the period of
your activity, and now from this point you are to radiate your influence as far and as intensely as you can all the world over. You have
now the whole field free and you are a citizen in America, and a
Bishop in the Church without a rival. All the former little questions
of local content in the Church in America are now for you as nothing,
and henceforth you are to consider yourself as a figure in history with
no Corrigan beside you. Your dreams were for the Church but you
were born for the country and it will be through your direct labors for
the country that you will later prepare greater benefits for the church.
At the Vatican of course they did not reap all they hoped from your
intervention. . . . The fault is their own. . . . From the beginning I
trembled for you and I thank God that you have escaped a terrible
danger with universal triumph. . . . You have put John Ireland to the

front in America & Europe as no other American Bishop was ever put before. You have compelled the Vatican to publicly and solemnly recognize him and the cause he represents. And instead of hurting yourself in the eyes of the public in working for the odious cause of Spain you have only increased & confirmed & sanctified the confidence reposed in you by your fellow citizens. I congratulate you and thank God for you. And now only one word more: all doubts & hesitation to the wind and on with the banner of Americanism which is the banner of God & humanity. Now realize all the dreams you ever dreamed, and force upon the Curia by the great triumph of Americanism that recognition of English speaking peoples that you know is needed.

For me this is not simply a question of Cuba. If it were, it were no question or a poor question. Then let the "greasers" eat one another up and save the lives of our dear boys. But for me it is a question of much more moment:—it is the question of two civilizations. It is the question of all that is old & vile & mean & rotten & cruel & false in Europe against all this [sic] is free & noble & open & true & human in America. When Spain is swept of [sic] the seas much of the meanness & narrowness of old Europe goes with it to be replaced by the freedom and openness of America. This is God's way of developing the world. And all continental Europe feels the war is against itself, and that is why they are all against us, and Rome more than all because when the prestige of Spain & Italy will have passed away, and when the pivot of the world's political action will no longer be confined within the limits of the continent; then the nonsense of trying to govern the universal church from a purely European standpoint—and according to exclusively Spanish and Italian methods, will be glaringly evident even to a child. 'Now the axe is laid to the root of the tree.' Let the wealth of Convents & Communities in Cuba & the Philippines go; it did nothing for the advancement of religion. No more patching of new pieces on old garments; it serves neither one nor the other. And the foundation of religion need be laid anew 'in spirit and in truth.' Begin there anew with the Gospel and with such accessories & canon law as the Gospel requires without making paramount the interests of comfortable-living personages or communities.

After having reflected on this matter a long time and after long interviews with European diplomats, especially with attachés of the English Embassy I am convinced that the material progress of America lies likewise on the lines I have indicated above."[43]

Then, in a passage that throws full light on the intermingling of theology and politics, O'Connell argued that, for religious

Americanism to succeed, American had to succeed politically and economically as a world power. Europe was prepared " 'to save themselves from the invasion of American influences' " by erecting a Chinese wall against trade. America must counter by building a naval power second to none so that " 'no continent will be strong enough to conspire against her.' " The time of America's childhood was past, when she could live in a state of domestic isolation. Her power and potential were now forcing her to take into account her " 'relations to the rest of the world whose financial, commercial & industrial harmony [she] is continually and almost unconsciously disturbing.' " America must compete for and take possession of her own markets—" 'the more, it seems to me, the better.' "[44]

O'Connell then articulated his version of America's "manifest destiny." Such economic expansionism, he observed, was all part of the " 'constant action of a tender divine Providence' " that was using America to help all nations,

"moving them on along the path of civilization to better, higher, happier modes of existences . . . towards that common & destined end; to more brotherhood, to more kindness, to more mutual respect for every man, to more practical and living recognition of the rule of God. At one time one nation in the world now another, took the lead, but now it seems to me that the old governments of Europe will lead no more and that neither Italy, nor Spain will ever furnish the principles of the civilization of the future. Now God passes the banner to the hands of America, to bear it:—in the cause of humanity and it is your office to make its destiny known to America and become its grand chaplain."

America had a God-given duty beyond its individual states and nation to humanity itself. " 'Go to America,' " he exhorted Ireland, " 'and say, thus saith the Lord! Then you will live in history as God's Apostle in modern times to Church & to Society. Hence I am a partisan of the Anglo-American alliance, together they are invincible and they will impose a new civilization. Now is your opportunity—and at the end of the war as the Vatican always goes after a strong man you will likewise become her intermediary.' "

Even the War was part of the plan:

War is often God's way of moving things onward. . . . The "horrors of war" often a sentimental phrase is often better "the glories of war" the triumph of Providence, see the war of secession & negro emancipation.[45] The whole history of Providence is the history of war; survival of the fittest. There is not room in this little world for anything else and bad as the world is today how much worse it certainly would be if by war & struggle the worse [sic] elements had not to go to the wall.

Then build navies & give your men employment, enroll an army picking up for it as England does fellows fit for nothing else. Take the place God has destined for America and leave John Ireland's name imperishable among those achievements. You are the only man in America lay or cleric who can properly take in and give the right initiative to this design.[46]

The confrontation was indeed, as the Americanists observed, between two civilizations. The fall of the *ancien régime* in the French Revolution and the ensuing struggle throughout Europe to replace monarchy with democracy made that observation commonplace. On the one hand, there was Abbé de Salinis, a disciple of Lamennais', arguing in *L'Ère nouvelle* that " 'democracy is the movement imposed on the world by the Gospel. . . . Earth accepts Heaven's programme.' "[47] On the other, there was Charles Maignen arguing that "the sovereignty of the people is a heresy"—a view not far from that of Leo XIII.[48]

What gave the confrontation new poignancy and energy in the era of the Spanish-American War was the spectacle of a democratic and largely Protestant republic, grown rich while still young and vibrant, unmistakably in control of its own destiny and poised to unseat the old Catholic monarchies and to take its seemingly predestined place at the head of world powers. Thus for many European liberals who struggled toward the same goal, America became a symbol and rallying cry of "the new age." Politics and theology were one. The ecclesiastical powers, who for centuries had been identified with the monarchies and so with them were finding their political power rapidly fading, now turned their energies to the only other sphere where they could still exercise power, the sphere of internal ecclesiastical discipline, where they sought to contain theology within a narrowly defined system of scholasticism by condemning liberalism within.

The following chapters describe the Roman view of this effort as seen through the eyes of Luis Martín, the Jesuit superior general and principal executor of Vatican designs on the eve of the modernist crisis.

NOTES

1. Maurice de la Taille, s.j., "Ami du clergé," *Études* 29 (26 September 1907) 872 and Alfred Firmin Loisy, *Mémoires pour servir a l'histoire religieuse de notre temps*, 3 vols. (Paris: Nourry, 1930–1931), 1:478–81).

2. *Pascendi*, par. 38.

3. See Jean Rivière, *Le Modernisme dans l'Église: Étude d'histoire religieuse contemporaine* (Paris: Letouzey, 1929), pp. 27–30, and the extensive treatment by Anton Gisler, *Der Modernismus dargestellt und gewürdigt*, 2nd ed. (Einsiedeln, Waldshut, Cologne: Benziger, 1912), pp. 27–222. Contrariwise, Thomas T. McAvoy, c.s.c., *The Great Crisis in American Catholic History, 1895–1900* (Chicago: Regnery, 1957), pp. 346–48, 361–63, 369, vigorously argues that Americanism cannot be construed as modernism, even if contemporary historians and religious commentators saw them as directly linked. On this issue see R. Scott Appleby's superb study *"Church and Age Unite!" The Modernist Impulse in American Catholicism* (Notre Dame and London: University of Notre Dame Press, 1992) and Margaret M. Reher, "The Church and the Kingdom of God in America: The Ecclesiology of the Americanists," diss., Fordham University, 1972, esp. pp. 175–238.

4. See Gerald P. Fogarty, s.j., *The Vatican and the American Hierarchy from 1870 to 1965* (Wilmington, DE: Glazier, 1985), pp. 188–90. I wish to emphasize that it is not I who am attempting to reduce Americanism and modernism to liberalism. I argue that this reduction was in the minds, and sometimes the very words, of anti-modernists and the framers of *Pascendi*. Liberalism is far too complex a phenomenon for any related "ism" simply to be reduced to it. It embraces both Protestants and Catholics, "liberals" and "conservatives" (e.g., Lamennais), theological and political views. I would argue, however, that Americanism is allied primarily with the political wing of liberalism. Of course, Isaac Hecker's theology is replete with liberal theological ideas, but the later Americanists like John Ireland, John Keane, and Denis O'Connell were rather much more involved with the political implications of Hecker's programs for making Catholicism more har-

monious with American socio-political and religious realities. I see modernism, on the other hand, as much more allied with liberalism's theological wing stemming from Kantian epistemology and Schleiermacher, who emphasized subjectivity as the source and norm of religious truth, without discounting the necessity and validity of dogma. Modernists emphasized subjective religious experience to counter-balance the excesses of counter-Reformation Catholic externalism. Unlike some Protestant liberals, however, most modernists did not dismiss the importance of dogma, authentic tradition, and authority. Of course, a few modernists went—or were driven—too far, as the majority of the modernists themselves recognized. But modernists cannot be lumped together, as *Pascendi* tried to do, and be praised or blamed for holding this or that position. There were no modernist "dogmas" to which all alike subscribed. As support for my contention that modernism is not essentially different from theological liberalism, see Daly, *Transcendence and Immanence*, esp. pp. 1–6. The one characteristic of modernism not much found in liberalism at the century's turn is a trenchant criticism of Neo-Scholasticism. Protestant liberals, with the exception of Ernst Troeltsch, largely ignored it, although early in the nineteenth century they pilloried the scholasticism of orthodox Protestants.

5. Marie-Joseph Lagrange, O.P., *Père Lagrange: Personal Reflections and Memoirs*, trans. Henry Wansbrough (New York and Mahwah, NJ: Paulist, 1985), pp. 55–56.

6. Félix Klein, *Americanism: A Phantom Heresy* (Atchison, KS: Aquin Book Shop, 1951), pp. 68–69. Klein also noted (pp. 70–71) that "O'Connell's address was heard by the largest audience assembled for any single paper during the congress, and that the speaker was repeatedly interrupted by the applause of intellectuals from every country of Europe." Klein (pp. 71–75) reproduced O'Connell's address from the *Freeman's Journal* because of its unavailability. Klein's criticism of Turinaz' mentality was precisely the criticism Loisy lodged against Auguste Sabatier and Adolf von Harnack in his second "Firmin" article, "La Théorie individualiste de la religion," *Revue du clergé français* 17 (1 January 1899) 202–14.

7. Klein, *Americanism*, pp. 68 and 76–77 n. 4. Paul Misner, whose peerless work *Social Catholicism in Europe: From the Onset of Industrialization to the First World War* (New York: Crossroad, 1991) thoroughly nuances Leo XIII's understanding of "Christian democracy," observes that what set Toniolo apart from intransigents like Turinaz and Louis Billot, S.J., was that, even though he was a neo-Thomist, he

"was used to thinking in historical terms, of contemplating the evolution of social institutions" (p. 243).

8. Poulat, *La Crise moderniste*, p. 275 n. 19.

9. "From that heresy [Protestantism] there arose in the last century a so-called philosophy [*falsi nominis philosophia*], and what they called a *new* right, along with popular sovereignty and unrestrained license, which many regard as the only true liberty. From these have come the ultimate horrors, namely *Communism, Socialism*, and *Nihilism*, hideous threats to civil society and its virtual ruin." Leo went on to assert that "religion . . . is in every society the best guardian of security." For that reason, the popes "are to be regarded as having served the common good, for they have endeavored to break the prideful and disturbing spirits of *Innovators* and have repeatedly warned of their danger to civil society." He then offered monarchies the continued "protection of religion, . . . than which no protection is stronger," in return for the church's liberty. For "it is God," Leo concluded, quoting Ps. 144:10, "who gives salvation to kings.'" Leo XIII, *Diuturnum illud*, in *Acta Leonis* 2:269–87; here, pp. 283–87 (my translation). Leo regularly attributed the distorted doctrine of popular sovereignty, like most other modern evils, to the Reformation. See Oskar Köhler, "The Relationship to the State and the Parties," in *The Church in the Industrial Age*, trans. Margit Resch, vol. 9 of *History of the Church*, ed. Hubert Jedin and John Dolan (New York: Crossroad, 1981), pp. 233–45.

10. The Opera dei Congressi e dei Comitati Cattolici in Italia originated in 1875 as a lay Catholic organization loyal to the pope and dedicated to combating the secularization of Italy and keeping the Roman Question before the Catholic eye. The movement was religiously and politically intransigent but split into factions largely over the question of direct political action. Romolo Murri (1870–1944) and his youthful coterie advocated autonomous action in the spirit of a "Christian democracy" over against the policy of Toniolo's older party. See Sandro Fontana and Francesco Traniello, "Aspetti Politico-Sociali," in *Romolo Murri nel storia politica e religiosa del suo tempo*, ed. Sandro Fontana, Maurilio Guasco, and Francesco Traniello (Rome: Cinque Lune, 1977), pp. 15–68; Mario Bendiscioli, "Italian Catholics Between the Vatican and the Quirinal: The *Non expedit* at the Time of Leo XIII," in *The Church in the Industrial Age*, trans. Margit Resch, vol. 9 of *History of the Church*, ed. Hubert Jedin and John Dolan (New York: Crossroad: 1981), pp. 84–96.

11. Leo XIII, *Graves de communi*, in *Acta Leonis* 21:3–20, here, p. 5 (my translation); in *Papal Encyclicals*, p. 480. A note of caution: Pub-

lished translations of papal documents seem to be biased either for or against papal positions. One simple case in point among very many that I came across: In this quotation, *bonos* was translated in one case (for Leo's position) as "many excellent men." In another case (hostile to Leo's position), it was translated "many right-minded people."

12. Joseph Brucker, "Un congrès et un centenaire à Fribourg en Suisse," *Études* 72 (1898) 788–93; quoted in Klein, *Americanism*, p. 77.

13. Loisy, *My Duel with the Vatican: The Autobiography of a Catholic Modernist*, trans. Richard Wilson Boynton (London: Dutton, 1924; repr. New York: Greenwood, 1968), pp. 201–202. See also Loisy, *Mémoires*, 1:478–81; *Choses passées* (Paris: Nourry, 1913), pp. 210–11; Lawrence F. Barmann, *Baron Friedrich von Hügel and the Modernist Crisis in England* (Cambridge: Cambridge University Press, 1972), pp. 68–71; McAvoy, *Great Crisis*, pp. 173–77; Klein, *Americanism*, pp. 63–68; Fogarty, *Vatican*, p. 153; Schultenover, *George Tyrrell*, pp. 80, 376–77, nn. 100–101.

14. Isidore Desprès, "Opinions catholiques sur l'origine du Pentateuque," *Revue du clergé français* 17 (15 February 1899) 526–57, quoted in Loisy, *Duel*, p. 201.

15. Loisy, *Duel*, p. 202.

16. Leo XIII, *Depuis le jour* (8 September 1899), *Acta Leonis* 19:157–90; ASS 32:193–213; in *The Papal Encyclicals*, vol. 2, *1878–1903*, ed. Claudia Carlen (Wilmington, NC: McGrath, 1981), pp. 455–64.

17. [Isidore Desprès], "La Lettre de Léon XIII au clergé de France et les études d'Écriture Sainte," *Revue du clergé français* 22 (1 June 1900) 5–17, quoted in Loisy, *Duel*, p. 203. Indeed, *Providentissimus Deus*, par. 15, provides some basis for Loisy's argument: "The sense of Holy Scripture can nowhere be found incorrupt outside the Church and cannot be expected to be found in writers who, being without the true faith, only gnaw the bark of Sacred Scripture and never attain its pith." P. Leclair, s.j. (pseud.), "Leo XIII et le modernisme biblique," *Le Revue apologétique* (Brussels) 9 (16 January 1908) 631–44, also asserted, albeit from an animus opposite Loisy's, that *Providentissimus Deus* "condemns rather than sanctions the new exegesis."

18. Leo XIII, *Depuis le jour*, in *Acta Leonis* 19:171–72; in *Papal Encyclicals*, p. 459. See Loisy, *Duel*, p. 340. The document Leo referred to was a very forceful apostolic letter, *Nostra erga Fratres Minores*, in ASS 31:264–67. He especially called attention to the words, "genus interpretandi audax atque immodice liberum" ("an audacious and intemperately liberal kind of interpretation," p. 265). An interesting question poses itself: Might it have been this apostolic letter that converted the Franciscan David Fleming from a liberal to a conservative—if not

reactionary—theologian? See below, n. 39. Five months after the Desprès article, Loisy, under the pseudonym "A. Firmin," published the first installment of his infamous article, "La Religion d'Israël," which provoked his first formal denunciation from Rome.

19. Loisy and others believed that the exegetical section was canceled to avoid the kinds of doctrinal discussions that had occurred at the previous congress. See Loisy, *Mémoires* 1:481; Pierre Benoit, O.P., in Lagrange, *Père Lagrange*, p. 56, n. "g" (Benoit supplied most of the footnotes); Edgar Hocedez, S.J., *Le Règne de Léon XIII, 1878–1903,* vol. 3 of *Histoire de la théologie au XIXe siècle* (Brussels: Universelle; Paris: Desclée de Brouwer, 1947), pp. 95–96; Oskar Köhler, "The Position of Catholicism in the Culture at the Turn of the Century," in *The Church in the Industrial Age,* trans. Margit Resch, vol. 9 of *History of the Church,* ed. Hubert Jedin and John Dolan (New York: Crossroad, 1981), pp. 245–56.

20. Francesco Satolli, *Loyalty to Church and State,* ed. John R. Slattery (Baltimore: Murphy, 1895), p. 150.

21. Letter of Satolli to Cardinal Mieczyslaw Ledóchowski, Prefect of the Sacred Congregation Propaganda de Fide, 6 October 1893, reported in Fogarty, *Vatican,* p. 131.

22. See Fogarty, *Vatican,* p. 131.

23. McAvoy, *Great Crisis,* p. 116, suggests that this remark was a nod to the contentious Fr. David Phelan, editor of the St. Louis *Western Watchman,* who claims to have invented the term "neo-Pelagianism." That term was, of course, a salvo at Hecker's teaching on the active *vs.* the passive virtues. Phelan's paper was regularly sent to the Jesuit curia, among other Roman addresses. On Salvatore Brandi see below, pp. 115–16, n. 13.

24. Certainly the charge had been made against the Jesuits.

25. "Cronaca contemporanea," *La Civiltà Cattolica* 5, ser. 16 (28 December 1895) 118–24.

26. See quotation above, p. 40.

27. On Maignen and the production of this volume, see above, pp. 48–49 and below, p. 59 n. 33.

28. See Frederick Merk, *The Monroe Doctrine and American Expansionism* (New York: Knopf, 1966), and William Penn Cresson, *The Holy Alliance: The European Background of the Monroe Doctrine* (New York: Oxford University Press, 1922).

29. A paraphrase of O'Donnell's memorandum, from George J. A. O'Toole, *The Spanish War: An American Epic—1898* (New York and London: Norton, 1984), p. 71.

30. When Práxedes Mateo Sagasta assumed office, Spain had al-

ready committed over a quarter of a million military personnel to overseas duty—225,000 in Cuba and 28,000 in the Philippines—and was six months in arrears on military salaries. On 8 August 1897, Miguel Angiolillo, an Italian anarchist, assassinated Spain's prime minister Antonio Cánovas del Castillo to avenge the torture and deaths of Spanish anarchists in the horrific Montjuich prison. (Internal anarchism was a persistent preoccupation for the ruling parties primarily of Spain and Italy, as well as for Leo XIII). See O'Toole, ibid., p. 88.

31. Isaac Thomas Hecker, *Questions of the Soul* (New York: Appleton, 1855).

32. Isaac Thomas Hecker, *Exposition of the Church in View of the Recent Difficulties and Controversies, and the Present Needs of the Age* (London: Montagu, 1875); also in *Catholic World* 21 (April 1875) 117–38. See William L. Portier, "Isaac Hecker and *Testem Benevolentiae*: A Study in Theological Pluralism," in John Farina, ed., *Hecker Studies: Essays on the Thought of Isaac Hecker* (New York and Ramsey, NJ: Paulist, 1983), pp. 11–48.

33. Abbé Charles Maignen, *Études sur l'Américanisme: Le Père Hecker est-il un Saint?* (Paris: Retaux, 1898; Rome: Desclée, Lefébvre, 1898); translated and adapted under the title *Studies in Americanism—Father Hecker, Is He a Saint?* (London: Burns & Oates, 1898). This volume began as a series of articles from 3 March to 19 April 1898 in *La Vérité* entitled "L'Américanisme Mystique" and signed "Martel." To these articles were added several new ones, and the entire set was published in book form. McAvoy, *Great Crisis*, p. 189, claims that, on the later articles, Maignen apparently received the collaboration of Abbé George Périès, who had vowed revenge against liberal critics of his reactionary views for getting him dismissed from the faculty of the Catholic University of America.

34. See McAvoy, *Great Crisis*, pp. 210–11, and Klein, *Americanism*, pp. 135–51.

35. The Dominican General was the Frenchman Père Berthier. Thomas M. Schwertner, O.P., "The Genius of Père Berthier," *Catholic World* 122 (January 1926) 452–58, says that Berthier "was literally an arm fellow of Pope Leo XIII., with whom he walked in the Vatican Gardens three or four times each week" (p. 453). See also McAvoy, *Great Crisis*, pp. 220–21.

36. Edmond Demolins, *À quoi tient la supériorité des Anglo-Saxons?* (Paris: Firmin-Didot, 1897). The book went through at least ten printings within a year—the first American edition, *Anglo-Saxon Superiority: To What It Is Due* (New York: Fenno, 1898) was translated from the

tenth printing. Rivière, *Le Modernisme*, p. 110, names this work and the impetus it gave to the Neo-Christian movement as one of the *incidents précurseurs* of modernism. See also Klein, *Americanism*, pp. 19, 126.

37. Maignen, *Études sur l'Américanisme*, pp. 274–76. See Fogarty, *Vatican*, p. 165, and McAvoy, *Great Crisis*, pp. 211–17.

38. See McAvoy, *Great Crisis*, pp. 221–60; Fogarty, *Vatican*, p. 175.

39. Although this correspondence was private, the attitudes and views of Ireland and O'Connell were generally known, both from their speeches and publications and from the usual channels of ecclesiastical gossip. O'Connell's apartment in Rome was dubbed "Liberty Hall" or O'Connell's "Club" or "Lodge," a sobriquet mocking the Vatican fear of secret societies. And, although it was a gathering place for liberal sympathizers, screening was not perfect. An early member of the "Club" was Father David Fleming, O.F.M., an English consultor to the Holy Office and friend of Merry del Val's. Ireland expressed an unflattering view of Fleming pseudonymously but publicly in the May 1900 *North American Review*. After cataloging the principal French *réfractaires*, he pilloried the Jesuits of *La Civiltá Cattolica* and Cardinals Mazzella (see p. 115, n. 13) and Satolli. To these figures he then added Fleming—"the friend and co-laborer of Dr. St. George Mivart. He was formerly highly respected at Rome as an exemplar of large-mindedness. Recently, however, in obedience to the edict of his Order, he has become the exponent of English reactionary views, and he is rapidly atoning by his zeal in his new cause for his theological escapades of former years." J. St. Clair Etheridge (pseud.), "The Genesis of 'Americanism,' " *North American Review* 170 (May 1900) 679–93; reprinted in Klein, *Americanism*, pp. 299–312, here p. 308. See Fogarty, *Vatican*, pp. 140–60, passim.

40. Ireland to O'Connell, St. Paul, 2 May 1898, Archives of the Diocese of Richmond, quoted in Fogarty, *Vatican*, p. 162.

41. Ireland to O'Connell, 11 May 1898, St. Paul, Archives of the Diocese of Richmond. Ireland's report to Rome is contained in the Secret Vatican Archives, papers of the Apostolic Delegation of the United States, "Stati Uniti," doss. 25; quoted in Fogarty, *Vatican*, p. 162. Ireland had long sought the red hat. His diplomatic failure here probably precluded his ever gaining it.

42. A rather blasphemous application of Jesus' self-testimony to Pilate in John 18:37, especially in view of the fact that O'Connell goes on to suggest that God was using Ireland without his awareness or consent based on that awareness.

43. O'Connell to Ireland, 24 May 1898, Archives of the Archdiocese of St. Paul; printed in full in McAvoy, *Great Crisis*, pp. 206–10.

44. Ibid.

45. This awkward sentence and punctuation are O'Connell's.

46. Ibid.

47. Quoted in Daniel-Rops, *Church in an Age of Revolution*, p. 247. Abbé Antoine Louis de Salinis (1798–1861) later became professor of theology at Bordeaux, then bishop of Amiens, and finally archbishop of Auch. See Alec R. Vidler, *Prophecy and Papacy: A Study of Lamennais, the Church, and the Revolution* (London: SCM, 1954), pp. 141f.

48. Charles Maignen, *La Souveraineté du peuple est une hérésie* (Paris: Roger & Chernoviz, 1892).

II

PERCEPTIONS
OF THE
JESUIT GENERAL

3

Martín and the English Jesuits: Behind the Joint Pastoral Condemnation of Liberalism

ON 29 DECEMBER 1900, Cardinal Herbert Vaughan and the bishops of the province of Westminster issued a joint pastoral letter roundly condemning liberalism in the Catholic Church.[1] The influence of that pastoral on the impending modernist crisis is pointed up in Wilfrid Ward's contention that the pastoral " 'had almost a determining influence in driving Father Tyrrell to the extreme left.' "[2] Though one might wish to nuance that judgment, one can hardly overstate the case that the pastoral set a standard for the anti-modernist campaign that culminated with Pius X's *Pascendi dominici gregis* of 1907 and the celebrated anti-modernist oath of 1910.[3] The following account, based on the Jesuit General Luis Martín's *Memorias* and related documents, will support this judgment.

In 1902, when the English Jesuit James Hayes was sent as representative of the English Province of the Society of Jesus to a congregation in Rome, his provincial superior Reginald Colley had ordered him to secure a private interview with Fr. General Martín in order to get some straightforward answers to straightforward questions. The English Province at this juncture was feeling particularly aggrieved by persistent criticisms and queries from Martín regarding numerous suspected infractions of religious discipline, not the least of which was their lax attitude toward some of their writers.[4] Representation by Hayes was advantageous for the English Province in that he was a friend of Martín's from seminary days at Poyanne in southern France, where Spanish Jesuits, exiled in 1868, had established a house of study.[5] Thus Hayes was fluent in Spanish.

In a letter of 5 October 1902 to Colley from Rome, Hayes reported the results of two lengthy interviews with Martín. After they had dealt with several comparatively objective issues and were "chatting in a most friendly way in Spanish," Hayes asked "if I might state with full frankness the feeling of the Eng. Province with regard to H. P. [His Paternity] & his way of ruling us." Permission granted, Hayes put the first sharp question: "We in England think that Y. P. [Your Paternity] & the English Assist[ant] have no love for the English Province & are prejudiced against us." "This is absolutely untrue," Martín replied. "I love & esteem much, very much, the Prov. of England, & have always regretted deeply the difficulties & unpleasantnesses that have arisen between us. I am longing for mature & thorough understanding between us."[6]

Several observations need to be made here. First, Martín shows himself in these remarks, as well as in his *Memorias* and voluminous correspondence, to be extraordinarily circumspect and politically adept. However, though he was able here to profess his *love* for the English Jesuits, he was not able to deal with the more deeply seated issue of prejudice. In a subsequent question from Hayes dealing with delations to Rome about excessive consumption of alcoholic beverages in the English Province, Hayes told Martín, among other things, "We felt under a cloud & not trusted, simply because a few sensational pessimists had been too easily & willingly listened to by H. P. [His Paternity], & that excellent & virtuous FF [Fathers] had suffered irreparably in their reputation by heed being given to irresponsible defamers."[7] This question, Hayes noted, made Martín "very uneasy as I was speaking, but [he] listened patiently," then admitted that gross exaggerations had been sent to him.[8]

Second, on the issue of the general's distrust of the English Province, it would be difficult for the English Jesuits to come to any other conclusion, after Martín had three years earlier removed from office their well-liked and respected provincial John Gerard, largely for resisting what Gerard regarded as ill-advised orders from Martín dealing mostly with George Tyrrell, the staff of the *Month*, and censorship.[9] Moreover, Martín seems by personality to have been cautious and distrustful—qualities that are quite accountable to several formational factors: (1) Luis Martín was the only one of seven children in his family to have survived beyond adolescence; (2) from age twelve he lived in various seminary settings away from his parents and had to deal alone with several personal insecurities; and (3) because of constant ecclesiastico-political turmoil in Spain, he grew up in a socially insecure environment.[10] In addition to these personal factors is the larger cultural factor—considered at some length in the concluding chapter—that contributed to Martín's distrustful nature.

Third, on the ability of superiors in Rome to understand the English, Hayes reported in his first letter to Colley of 25 September 1902 that his initial impression of Rudolf Meyer, Martín's assistant for the English-speaking provinces, had led him to "a confirmed conviction that we have no friend in him," and so he had little hope for his mission.[11] After his two long interviews with Martín and several with Meyer, Hayes made the following telling observation: "As to Fr. Assist[ant], he seems to me to take his views & colour from Fr. Gen. I don't think him a man of strong independent character. *He does, however, wish that Fr. General could understand better the character of us awkward Britons.*"[12] Thus the difficulties that arose between Martín and the English Province seem to have been due less to ill will than to ill understanding, and where ill will might have entered in, it can be said to have been at least aggravated by cultural bias and suspicions generated by many years of European socio-political destabilization, including most recently the Spanish-American War.[13] What follows will substantiate this assertion.

BACKGROUND ISSUES

Martín's Program

The context for General Martín's dealings, first, with the English Province on the issue of liberalism, then, with modernism is patently set by his first letter to the whole Society of Jesus. Probably nothing he ever wrote commanded as much attention and preparation, and therefore it requires a rather full exposition here.

Significantly, the letter bears the title "On Some Dangers of Our Times" and is dated 4 October 1896, just prior to the time-frame of the present study. It is an especially reliable barometer of Martín's mind because he deliberated over it for some four years. It is, as he intended it to be, programmatic. Jesuits around the world placed this letter among the greatest letters of their fathers general from Ignatius of Loyola to the present. It was included in at least two anthologies;[14] and, more impor-tant, it was included in a volume called *Renovation Reading*, which consists of devotional and legislative documents to be read at table in Jesuit houses twice a year during the custom-ary, semi-annual three-day retreats prior to the renewal of relig-ious vows.[15] Thus it was a letter used for decades to form the views of Jesuits around the world.

Exposition of Martín's First Letter to the Society of Jesus

At the time that Martín had completed his first letter to the whole Society of Jesus, he had been in Rome nearly two years. During that time, as a frequent consultant to and confidant of Pope Leo XIII, he learned the challenges facing the Catholic Church as well as the Society of Jesus from the intimate per-spective of the papal and Jesuit curias. It is safe to assume that, as he composed "On Some Dangers of Our Times," Leo XIII's agenda as well as his own was at the forefront of his mind, and he was prepared to carry them out.

The opening paragraphs explain the four-year delay of this first letter and also disclose Martín's caste of mind. Note the immediate recourse to wartime rhetoric: "Prudence . . . de-manded that before addressing the whole Society, I should first gain a thorough knowledge of its present condition, ascertain what works were being carried on for the glory of God, what obstacles thwarted the success of its labors and what dangers in these our evil times were threatening us." Martín then asked all Jesuits to join him in thanking God, who "in these latter days 'hath showed might in His arm' by shielding [the Society] with His divine power against the furious onslaught of her en-emies and increasing and extending her in the teeth of many difficulties." God had been pleased not only "to raise the Society from the grave,"[16] but also to bring her "to such a marvellous condition as not only to strike our adversaries and fiercest enemies with astonishment but to fill our own souls with wonder."[17]

Then briefly and without analysis Martín made his first point: the root evil of the modern world was liberalism. It masquerades as "a specious love of that noble liberty" which it misunderstands and so, "impatient of the bridle of authority, seeks to throw off all restraint." The church, he noted sadly, had been "despoiled of all her wealth by her own rebellious children"—that is, the liberals—and so the Society had lost generous support from well-disposed prelates. As to secular rulers, some had offered assistance, while others had viciously turned against the Society. "For many of them, tainted and captivated with those principles which are absurdly called 'liberal,' . . . have more than once waged an open and deadly war against her, carried on a pitiless persecution, besmirched her good name, robbed her of her property, driven her forth from their cities as if she were a deadly plague; in a word, have left nothing undone to wipe out her name from the memory of men."[18]

Martín's second point constitutes the bulk of the letter: an analysis of liberalism's infiltration of the Society of Jesus and a scheme of counter-strategies. Liberalism's entrance was facilitated, the general asserted, by "a natural levity of mind and character" which develops in due course into a "habit" leading to a constant "craving for fresh excitement, ever bent upon seeing and reading something new," so that "in place of God and the laws of our Institute" one takes "the natural impulse of the senses as his rule of action."[19]

But the modern world with its heedlessness in child-bearing and -rearing has exploited this natural levity of mind and opened the door to "the foul enemy of the human race":

This levity of mind is fostered and encouraged from early days by that delicacy of body which, in the opinion of men of experience, growing apace and bearing a punier offspring, renders the nervous system more and more excitable. And thus it comes to pass that our youth are becoming indolent, hare-brained and unfit for the battle of life; and far from seeking vigorous mental exertion they shrink from all serious effort of body and mind and are ever looking for relaxation and comfort. Small wonder that this evil propensity of nature brings forth in our day the most lamentable results, since the home-training, which is of paramount influence for good as well as for evil, seeing that it is for the most part soft, inconsistent, mainly bent on satisfying and pleasing the child's whims and flattering his passions that grow apace with the body's growth, only develops levity of mind while debilitating and enervating the will.

The subsequent college discipline and literary education are altogether incapable of remedying the many faults committed in this effeminate domestic training.[20]

Then the wretched system of education that is almost everywhere prescribed, in which the student gets a smattering of everything and nothing of substance, merely excites curiosity and produces only conceited ignorance, out of which the student "is emboldened to pronounce rash judgment on matters of which he understands nothing."[21] It is precisely that kind of education—the methods and programs of the public schools—that liberals argue is superior and ought to replace the Society's venerable *Ratio studiorum* for our scholastics.[22]

Martín went on to describe the more obvious dangers to religious life that come from the failure to observe strictly all the rules of the Institute: namely, that one is easily led from intellectual levity to moral levity. But there were also the more subtle, and so more pernicious, snares of the enemy, who induces many to set aside their total dedication to God by amusing themselves with "foolish trifles" and "frittering away the time that belongs to God, in reading periodicals, newspapers and novels." These practices were not in themselves violations of the rule, but they became dangerous under changed circumstances: "the flood of newspapers and periodicals that are being poured into town and country alike, so that they can scarcely be kept from invading even the cloister be it ever so closely guarded; the danger is greater than ever before, lest we too, yielding to the spirit of the age, choose a life of ease rather than a life of toil."[23]

Martín was referring not merely to "bad newspapers or periodicals" but to newspapers and periodicals of whatever stripe, even Catholic papers, because reading them, he argued, takes Jesuits away from "all serious application to those studies which are for us a necessity, and, in a special sense, peculiarly our own."[24] The problem, he asserted, was twofold. On the personal level, such reading opens the door to vain and ridiculous notions that are "utterly foreign to and inconsistent with our religious life," such that "the soul will grow weak, and the imagination, aroused and agitated by so many phantasms, will often obtrude upon the mind" and "violently" withdraw one from heavenly things. Then "all that is spiritual and divine will no longer possess any relish" or "afford solace and help, but will become irksome and produce only disgust and torment. From these beginnings will flow all those consequences which have been already described at length."[25]

Besides the personal problems occasioned by such reading, community problems also arise—"partisan strife and fierce rage"—through the airing of political and religious controversies.

For our Society especially, what ruin should we not fear from such a pest? What would become of the rule by which we are all commanded to think, to speak, as far as possible, the same thing, according to the Apostle, so that not only are different doctrines not to be admitted either by word, in public discourse, or by written books, but even diversity of views on matters of business is, as far as can be, to be avoided? What would become of fraternal charity and union, which cannot exist where there is difference of opinion, opposition of will and sentiment, disagreement as to the lines on which we are to carry out our work? What would become of religious simplicity; of gentlemanly manners, of easy intercourse and common life, of united efforts, of mutual confidence, if, in order not to hurt the feelings or opinions of others we had to practise continual dissimulation to conceal our own sentiments, and in word, sign and look stand carefully on our guard in all points on which we are at variance?[26]

Rather, Jesuits are to model themselves after their founder and master, Ignatius, who was "*a man of few truths*, which did not ebb and flow with the tide of passion" but "went as a torch before all his actions" to "preserve him from deviating even a hair's breadth from the path which led straight to God." Those truths are "the glory of God as the aim of all our actions" and "the perfect imitation of Christ, as the means of fully attaining that sublime end." These truths were the measure of all his transactions, and from them "followed also the contempt with which he regarded what was novel, vain, or trivial."[27]

But striving after the noblest ideals is equally fraught with danger, "for the enemy of our souls" takes advantage of our lofty sentiments to hurl us upon "another dangerous rock: I mean the spirit of license, private judgment and pride." The cause of this spirit Martín laid to the French Revolution:

This ungovernable plague of license which has seized upon all hearts and which we too, even though unwillingly, breathe with the very air, threatens to shake and shatter the very foundations of the religious life. For a century and more, not only throughout Europe but in all other countries likewise, the nations have been proclaiming a lawless liberty; they praise it with extravagant eulogy; they imperiously demand it as a sacred birthright for the individual as well as for cities, countries and nations.

Hence war is declared against all authority and any attempt to put a check or limit upon liberty is fiercely resisted. Books and pamphlets filled with these pernicious teachings are daily published and whole nations are being tainted and corrupted by them; popular assemblies, meetings of men and women re-echo with the boisterous assertion of these false doctrines. Nay, the teachings of the corrupters of the people are every day translated into lawless actions by the populace who have become convinced of their inalienable right to throw off the yoke of all laws, to criticise and amend whatsoever has been enacted by legitimate authority, to seat or unseat, by inherent right, kings and rulers; in a word, to proclaim as a right the crime of rebellion.[28]

Out of this confusion of ideas, Martín lamented, the true idea of authority is dismantled. "Rights and duties . . . are no longer deduced from the divine law and the natural order, but are forced upon the rest of the people by the overbearing will of the majority, acting in accordance with that atrocious maxim of modern politics: 'Might makes right.' "[29]

As matters now stand, Martín continued, the plague of liberalism has "contaminated and subverted the whole fabric of civil and political life" and now only waits for the chance to enter the cloister, where, once inside, "it will overturn and utterly ruin religious life." And how easy it is for liberalism to gain entrance! It is in the very air we breathe, and "in breathing this pestilential atmosphere we receive the germs of the deadly poison into our blood and taint our religious life at the very core." Moreover, it permeates society as a whole, and so it enters the Society of Jesus with her young candidates.

For it is a lamentable fact that so irrational is not seldom the early home training of children that infatuated parents proudly call their little boy clever and winning when in truth he is forward and impudent. The result is that when such boys reach the years of adolescence they will brook no rule but their own judgment, chafe under authority, carp at, criticise and condemn the words and actions of their teachers and superiors. Now those who wish to enter the Society, must of course come to us out of the world just described.[30]

Allowing entrance to the virus of liberalism is all the more to be dreaded, Martín continued, because it leads to a false notion of authority that can destroy religious life from within. For "the spirit of liberty which to-day they dignify with the pretentious name of *independence*, but ought rather to call license" advances the error that orders from superiors ought to pass "the bar of our private judgment as human injunctions." For liberalism regards the superior "merely as a man more or less prudent and experienced, and not as God's minister and the herald of His will, whose orders we need not reverence as God's commands," but may regard as merely human injunctions to be obeyed or not according to whim. But Ignatius' desire was that the virtue of perfect obedience, requiring the "entire submission of the intellect," be the distinguishing mark of the Society, such that "they who did what they were bid while disagreeing in judgment, stood with only one foot in the Society." Indeed, Martín concluded, "what I dread most are not the enemies and perils from without: persecutions, spoliations, exiles, and whatever foes there are that plot our destruction," but the loosening of the bond of union between superiors and subjects through the exaltation of private judgment. This dissolution would be sufficient in itself, "without the intervention of persecutions and violent attacks from without, to undermine and overthrow" the Society. That is "why the enemy of the human race, to-day more fiercely than ever before, applies his engines to the blasting of the rock of humility and obedience."[31]

Thus we have in outline the content of Martín's long and carefully considered first address to the Society of Jesus. What requires illumination are the motives of such a letter. Motives stemming from a superior's duty to warn his subjects against the real dangers of the modern world are obvious enough. But there are perhaps underlying motives that add an exceptional impetus to his language and a peculiar twist to his message, motives that arise out of perceptions so skewed by cultural background as to lead to judgments that persons from other cultures could not endorse. But the illumination of this letter from the viewpoint of Martín's cultural characteristics will be postponed to Chapter 5. Here we need to pass on to one of liberalism's many eruptions—namely, Americanism—to see how it impinged on Martín's relations with the English Province.

Americanism and the Dreyfus Affair

Americanism, Martín noted in his *Memorias*, was the issue that initiated doctrinal difficulties with the English Province, and it caught him by surprise. He had had differences with the English Province on matters of the Jesuit Institute and religious discipline ever since the twenty-fourth general congregation that elected him superior general in 1892. But since he regarded the English as "little given to purely intellectual speculation and eminently practical in everything," he did not think that he would ever have to straighten out their ideas on doctrine.[32] But that was not to be so.

In retrospect, Martín observed, liberalism was the rank heresy behind the English involvement with Americanism as well as with every other doctrinal aberration entertained on the English scene. According to Martín, the English Jesuits' flirtation with liberalism/Americanism first showed itself with Herbert Lucas' articles on Hecker and Heckerism in the *Tablet*. These, he said, were "nothing more than a particular manifestation of a rather liberal spirit which was insinuating itself into various Fathers without their knowing it."[33] In fact, in a letter of 16 May 1899 to the English provincial superior, John Gerard, Martín quoted an unnamed American newspaper that linked the Lucas articles, Americanism, and liberalism. Referring to the articles, the author wrote: "It seems that the London Tablet, too, has opened its columns of late to the defence of Liberalism, and seeks to discredit Dr. Maignen." The latter charge doubly disturbed Martín because Lucas had publicly attacked Charles Maignen's *Le Père Hecker: est-il un Saint?* which had been approved by the Vatican (and was immediately translated for the American church).[34] For Martín, such an attack was tantamount to attacking the pope himself. "Without a doubt," he continued, "Fr. Maignen's book has been approved by the Supreme Pontiff, and indeed after strict censorship, and therefore it ought not to be refuted publicly by a Father of the Society, especially since that book will do good by dragging out before the eyes of the Holy See the insidious and dangerous errors of 'Americanism.' " Then to drive his point home, Martín related Bishop Turinaz' account of his recent audience with Leo XIII. The bishop had presented Fr. Leclerc, the Vincentian superior general, to the pope. After the latter two had exchanged brief comments, Leclerc interjected proudly, "I am the superior of Fr. Maignen." To which Leo replied, "Was my letter on Americanism agreeable to him?" "Most agreeable, Holy Father," Leclerc responded, "and he was most grateful for it, as were we all." To which Leo added energetically, "But one must be vigilant!" "Which," Martín explained, "must be taken as directed also to us."[35] Martín then recalled how he had repeatedly, but to little effect, complained to the English provincial that their journal, the *Month*, was bland and ineffectual, because its writers "had no stomach for battling the protestants and liberals."[36] It was "the English spirit" that accounted for this languor, habituated as it was to tolerating Protestant errors.[37] On numerous occasions, particularly during the foreshortened tenure of the provincialate of John Gerard (1897–1900),[38] Martín wrote sternly to and about English Jesuits, so that they could only wonder whether a man with such a negative perception of the English scene could sincerely *trust* his English confreres as he claimed to do. In fact, at a meeting of 11 June 1897 of Gerard and his consultors, the following minutes of proceedings on a letter from Martín were recorded:

The CC. [Consultors] feel that such a remark shows that His Paternity is not in touch with the mind of the Province, and they think the time has come for trying to make him understand our position better. Perhaps the best way would be to ask him if he would like to have the thoughts of some of our leading men about the present position of the Catholic Church in England and the demands upon our Province for help in the conversion of the country. They are beginning to feel that His Paternity does not care for the opinions of those who understand the state of things in England and they cannot help thinking that those who have been living and working in England in contact with English Protestants and with full knowledge of the movement in the midst of which they are deserve to be listened to. We are in a great crisis and a false move will ruin our Province and make it ineffectual for good to the Church in this country at the time of the greatest promise and also of the greatest need.[39]

Concurrent with the altercation over the Lucas articles another more explosive issue arose: the involvement—or, from the English Jesuits' viewpoint, an equally censurable *non*-involvement—of French Jesuits in the Dreyfus affair.[40] On 18 December 1898 Gerard complained to Martín that the debacle in France was having serious repercussions in England and chided him for not taking their complaints seriously. To justify his concern, Gerard quoted a letter from Professor Conybeare of Oxford, an alumnus of a Jesuit college, who was still kindly disposed toward English Jesuits, although he took a dim view of Jesuits elsewhere:

I have gathered the impression that there are two categories inside the order: one of quietists, students who keep the books and religious offices, the other of administrators and men of affairs. The latter class in foreign countries, notably the Latin countries, harbours many intriguers, intolerant spirits, who would like to put back the [clock] by several centuries. I may be wrong, but the moral obliquity so observable in France seems to me due to the predominance exercised by the Jesuits.

These charges, Gerard continued, although exaggerated, could not be summarily dismissed. Indeed they could be substantially credited from French Catholic newspapers and private conversations with French Jesuits—of which Gerard had been apprised by Sydney Smith, editor of the *Month*, whom he had sent to France specifically to investigate Jesuit involvement in the Dreyfus case. Gerard recounted for Martín some of Smith's findings: "A certain one [French Jesuit] said, for example, that it does not matter whether or not Dreyfus is innocent. It must be insisted that, given the situation, the greatest possible condemnation must be brought against the Jews." Now, if such sentiments become public, Gerard warned, they will stir up such hatred against the Society that the stigma would not be removed for many long years.[41]

Martín dismissed Gerard's alarm by reading the French Jesuit's remark as nothing more than the " 'boutade' of some imprudent young man who was deeply impressed by the publications of Drumont, but who did not express the sentiments of our Fathers."[42] On the other hand, he read in Gerard "the tendency of the English to presuppose the innocence both of Dreyfus and of the Jews in general of the many charges brought against them. And of course there was in this the fear of attacks against the Society and religion by Protestants and the impious, whom they [the writers of the *Month*] did not want to provoke" by confronting them. To Martín, Protestantism was endemically pernicious, and the age called for duels, not dialogue. Those who had no stomach for duels were to be replaced by those who did, for, indeed, toleration was but a platform of liberalism, which in turn was of a piece with English nationalism. The Lucas articles, Martín charged, used Hecker merely as an excuse to introduce the Saxon-*vs.*-Latin issue, and were but one more example of how liberalism and nationalism suffused every contingent of English culture, including the English Jesuits. "English nationalism," Martín observed, "has been a real and dangerous tendency for our English Fathers, inasmuch as they are disposed to believe many historically false charges against the pope" and against the principal defenders of Catholicism, solely because what the pope and his supporters stood for was not in the Saxon interest.[43]

Martín brought forward two other cases to support his contention. Nationalism, he claimed, was the operative force several years earlier when Gerard and others insisted that Father John Hungerford Pollen (1858–1925) write the history of the Jesuits in England, but Pollen had rightly demurred that there were too many points about which the truth would only arouse English nationalism and Anglican fanaticism. The nationalist tendency was also at work in an incident under the previous provincial, Francis Scoles (1840–1909), when anxieties were raised over Edmund Purcell's intention to include anti-Jesuit materials in his *Life of Cardinal Manning* (1895), particularly Manning's contention that—in Martín's words—"the Saxon race could not tolerate the Society's way of proceeding and its Constitution (approved by so many popes) as the work of a Spaniard (S. Ignatius), so it deserves to be forever suppressed." In that case, Martín lamented, even though the English fathers abominated such ideas, their nationalism prevented their defending themselves against them, since they were ideas of Catholics and bishops who were held up as eminent representatives of modern civilization and the glory of the English race.[44]

Frustrated with the English fathers over the issue of the Lucas articles and Americanism, Martín concluded that the English Jesuits were simply not open to criticism. Gerard retorted that, after reviewing the articles again, he "found nothing abhorrent to sacred doctrine or offensive to pious ears," that there were no Americanists in the province, and that everyone was glad about the condemnation of Americanism.[45] And in a final word of 9 May, he reiterated that he could not understand why Lucas' articles were found censurable; nor could several other fathers of good judgment who had reviewed them. He reminded Martín that the Society in England was beleaguered by critics just waiting to pounce at a Jesuit miscue, so that the only reasonable tactic to take in refuting errors and teaching the truth was "a conciliatory rather than a severe manner, which tends to alienate and create enemies—a tactic which seems plainly to agree with the tenor of the apostolic letter on Heckerism." Gerard then seized the opportunity to return some criticism of his own: "If I may take this occasion to note . . . how very displeased many were that the *Civiltà Cattolica* for January had so harshly treated the illustrious Bishop of Newport (R. D. [*sic*] Hedley) for his article in the *Dublin Review*. He is learned, very pious, and orthodox, and it seems very harmful that our writers deal with a prelate in this way."[46] With that volley, Martín realized that the English were not going to capitulate to his criticisms, so he ended the exchange by merely ordering Gerard roundly to reprimand Lucas for his great imprudence and to see that his future writings would be subjected to the strictest censorship, but no penalty was to be imposed since his intentions had been good.[47]

But matters worsened for Martín. Directly on the heels of the Lucas issue came the distressing news that the Jesuits of London's Farm Street church—to which was attached the curia of the English Province—had scheduled a conference for 26 June by the reputedly liberal American Archbishop John Ireland, of whom Martín had an exceedingly low opinion. This sponsorship of Ireland only sharpened Martín's suspicions that the English Province was rife with liberalism. He wrote at once to Alexander Charnley, rector of the Farm Street community and vice provincial for Gerard who was visiting a mission in British Guyana, and demanded a full explanation.[48] Charnley replied that in the first place no one knew at the time of the hall's reservation—two or three months in advance—that Ireland would be the speaker. Second, the sponsoring organization was the Catholic Union, a respectable society of prominent laymen, who had for years been renting the hall several times a year, so permission was rather automatic. Third, Cardinal Vaughan had given permission for Ireland to speak in his diocese and had informed the Jesuits that he himself would ensure that Ireland would not offend pious ears. (In fact, Vaughan did not attend.) Fourth, because the meeting was held under the auspices of the Duke of Norfolk, secretary of the Catholic Union, and because Archbishop Ireland was a personal friend of the Duke's, permission to use the hall could hardly have been withdrawn without causing grave scandal.[49]

Later Martín retorted to Gerard that he might at least have forbidden Jesuits to attend Ireland's conference, for, despite the Cardinal's precaution, "it cannot be foreseen what that man will say; and if by chance he might have said something offensive, our Fathers could have been seen by their presence to have given at least implicit approval." Besides, there were the other provinces to think of, which had had problems with Ireland, to say nothing of the damage to the Society's reputation and the troubles that such sponsorship would undoubt-edly stir up in Rome. But what was done was done, and Martín could do nothing more than instruct Gerald to admonish all who had attended the conference that they would have done better to have imitated Cardinal Vaughan's prudence by staying away.[50]

Several other issues complicated Martín's comportment toward the English Province. Although they cannot be pursued here, they deserve at least a notice to indicate how utterly sty-mied Martín felt and why he would resort to removing a pro-vincial from office. It could certainly not have improved his dis-position, for example, to hear from Gerard that one of his recently ordained fathers, who had earlier been dismissed from an American province and readmitted in England, had recently become "infected with this pernicious Americanism," was now completely disillusioned with the Jesuits, and had requested dismissal from the Society, after having secretly requested in-cardination in Archbishop Ireland's diocese.[51] To compound the affront, Ireland acceded to the man's request, pending the outcome of his dimissorial process.[52]

Two other nettlesome issues were the revision of the plan of higher studies for Jesuit seminarians—central to which was the question of establishing a house of studies at the University of Oxford—and the enforcement of the Vatican's rule of cloister at the rural parishes and grammar schools. Bad feelings between English Jesuits and Rome were raised once again, particularly around the latter issue, because Jesuits on the scene were find-ing Rome's position of strict enforcement impractical and un-duly burdensome. It would have meant firing the women, who were needed to care for the smaller children, and hiring men, who would have required wages too high for the poor par-ishes.[53]

The argument over Archbishop Ireland lasted to the end of August 1899. Then the Dreyfus issue rekindled. Alexander Charnley arrived in Rome as representative of the English Prov-ince to an international congregation of Jesuits. He was charged by his provincial and the writers of the *Month* to renew com-plaints about the repercussions in England of the bad press Jesuits were receiving in France "as fanners of the flames of hatred against Dreyfus as merely racial hatred for Jews." Martín's considered response was that, although he regretted the situation, he could not prudently support the English Jesuits in such aggravating circumstances without a fuller investigation. But at the same time, he deplored, on the one hand, the English Jesuits' reluctance to speak out publicly "because of what liberal Catholics, Protestants, and the impious might say," and, on the other, their readiness to think badly of their French confreres and other Catholics just because they "were inclined to believe that Dreyfus was guilty and that the Jews were stockpiling gold."[54]

The disturbance in France intensified as the year wore on, and apprehensions in England grew apace. On 12 December Gerard wrote Meyer that he had received

an earnest appeal from the Lord Chief Justice, Lord Russell of Killowen, who is, as you know, a Katholic [sic], begging me to use what influence I can abroad to incline our FF. [Fathers] to set their face against the anti-jewish [sic] crusade so far at least as concerns the charge of ritual murder so constantly repeated in some quarters, but as it seems without any evidence, and in opposition to the pronouncements of various Popes. Cardinal Waughan [sic] is likewise earn[es]t in the same side. They say that in this country at least the Jews are our only allies in the battle of religious education and alone besides ourselves will make no termes [sic] with the advancing tide of secularism.[55]

Martín was not impressed with Lord Russell's appeal, as it "proved nothing on the question of ritual crimes." He wanted hard evidence. On 19 December Gerard wrote again to Meyer on the question of ritual murder. He complained about an article in the latest *Civiltà*, in which the writer, while professing absolute impartiality,

uses this profession as a mere literary device under cover of which to insinuate the general charge [of ritual murder] for which he brings no evidence and I believe none can be brought. It is hard for them not on the spot to realize the immense harm that is done by this kind of thing, not only by deepening Protestant prejudice against us but by distressing and even grievously shocking catholics [sic]. As I told [Father General,] Card. Vaughan is extremely indignant against writers who take this line, (He had not seen the Civilta when we last met) and speaks of their action as a scandal.[56]

Martín was not pleased by Gerard's admonition, especially because at the same time the English Jesuits, and in particular Herbert Thurston, one of the *Month*'s staff-writers, were supporting Cardinal Vaughan's line by publishing articles in the *Tablet* and the *Month* which argued a papal tradition of pro-Jewish sentiment and sought to demonstrate insufficient evidence for the charge of ritual murder. Nor was Martín pleased by a concurrent letter of Thurston's to Meyer urging the latter to press Martín to forbid the *Civiltà* to publish in a contrary sense.[57] Martín replied that if Thurston had arguments to demonstrate his position, he should send them to him. Thurston then sent two articles, which Martín found impressive but unconvincing, as they "failed to prove the general thesis or establish anything relative to the lack of testimony about ritual murder."[58]

Martín tried to get to the bottom of the question, but his search for qualified Jesuits in Rome who could speak to the issue with authority proved fruitless. Chandlery then pointed out to Martín that a certain Englishman in Rome had written to the *Tablet*, persisting in the accusations against the Jews; that a rabbi had protested and challenged the Englishman to supply evidence; and that the latter sought help from Brandi, who sent him to several old Bollandist articles in *La Civiltà*. These articles, Chandlery suggested, might help the general to formulate some idea of his own about the controversy. Upon reading them, Martín found his earlier understanding confirmed. Thus he formulated for Meyer the following position:

The accusations against the Jews, especially with regard to ritual murder, were to be considered exaggerated and anachronistic: at that time the effort of Fr. Thurston and others to clear the Jews of such a ritual crime and other serious accusations down the ages was also exaggerated and undemonstrable, since it did not contend with the ritual texts brought forth in the old Civiltà articles and the explicit and published confessions of some Jewish converts: it seemed better and more prudent not to commit the exaggerations which the Civiltà and others had [recently] committed . . . by crediting fables; but at the same time not to jump to the defense of a cause which, although it can be defended well in some particular points restricted to certain ages and countries, cannot be defended in general, as with the ritual crimes.[59]

By the beginning of 1900, interest in the Dreyfus case was dying in the press, and the Jewish question in England was coming to a close. Martín's assessment of the whole affair was, again, decidedly unfavorable to the English Jesuits. He saw them as acting "under the guise of impartiality and yielding to the liberal inspiration of the English press, of Lord Russell, and of C[ardinal]. Waughan [sic]," and as "more inclined to what was convenient with regard to the liberal Catholic party" than to what was a matter of principle.[60]

TYRRELL'S WRITINGS: "A MORE SERIOUS MATTER"

Given all the aforementioned points of contention with the English Province, Luis Martín had to have been in a testy mood when, at the beginning of January 1900, a deeply disturbed Rudolf Meyer laid before him Salvatore Brandi's annotated copy of the 16 December 1899 number of the *Weekly Register* containing George Tyrrell's inflammatory article "A Perverted Devotion" impugning the extravagances of popular preaching on hell.[61] Martín immediately attempted a reading, but found his comprehension balked by "Tyrrell's complex manner of thinking and peculiar way of expressing himself." The "general impression," however, was "bad"—bad enough for Martín to give the article to his assistants to review carefully for a consultation on 3 January. At the meeting, all agreed—"although not all understood well what the author meant"—that the article was offensive and in danger of being condemned by the Sacred Congregation of the Index.[62] On 7 January, therefore, Martín wrote sternly to that effect to Charnley, who was acting provincial while Gerard was visiting a foreign mission. The article, Martín warned, "does not even have to contain heresies or errors to be condemned. It is enough that it be dangerous to the faithful." Besides that, he had received complaints about some of Tyrrell's earlier writings, particularly his *Notes on the Catholic Doctrine of Purity*, "which seemed dangerous to not a few." And after complaining once again about the Lucas articles, Martín pointed to this latest offense of Tyrrell's as evidence that the English censors had come away from their previous upbraiding "not better and stricter, but more remiss and lax." Therefore Charnley was to investigate at once and inform Martín (1) whether or not Tyrrell had submitted his article to censors, and, if he did, (2) who the censors were, (3) what judgment each had rendered, and (4) why the article was published in that liberal-Catholic *Weekly Register*. Meanwhile he was to forbid Tyrrell to publish anything outside the *Month*, and then only after rigorous censorship, until Gerard had received a final decision on the matter.[63] Martín then gave the article for censorship first to Josef Flöck, rector of the German College (where Martín lived and his curia was housed), then to Giuseppe-Maria Piccirelli, assistant to the Neapolitan provincial, but formerly and latterly a professor of dogmatic theology at schools in France, Spain, and Italy.[64]

Charnley replied that Thurston was the only censor for Tyrrell's article, that the censorship consisted of a simple reading with some slight observation made about the use of language, and that this process was customary with articles for such journals. As to the *Weekly Register* itself, Charnley explained, even though the tone was regarded as rather liberal, the English fathers found publishing in it useful for reaching a certain class of young Catholics who read no other Catholic journals, and so the provincial had approved the article's publication in it. As to Tyrrell, although he was exceedingly sensitive, he was much esteemed and able to do much good among educated and influential people.[65] Charnley followed that letter with another excusing Tyrrell and testifying that even Cardinal Vaughan had found nothing disturbing in "A Perverted Devotion" and had professed his great regard and appreciation for Tyrrell.[66]

Vaughan's testimony, however, counted for little with Martín, as the cardinal had already been discredited for his softness in dealing with the Dreyfus affair.[67] Furthermore, new complaints about Tyrrell began to arrive from a much more creditable quarter, namely the now *Bishop* Merry del Val. The latter protested to Meyer about "A Perverted Devotion" and the potential evil from Tyrrell's ideas after he had learned from a chat with Tyrrell himself the previous summer in England that the ideas expressed in that article were indeed the author's own. Merry del Val was particularly dismayed at Tyrrell's brag "that this [Americanism] was not so bad, that he himself was an Americanist, but that he knew how to express himself about such ideas."[68]

Tyrrell's reputation incurred further damage by a letter from a house consultor at St. Beuno's Jesuit theologate impugning Tyrrell as a preacher of retreats. Apparently Tyrrell had conducted a retreat for that community at the beginning of the previous school year and had—so the charge went—"disturbed the consciences of not a few." "His prudence and orthodoxy are disputed," the consultor reported. "What [Tyrrell] said about the presence of our Lord in the Most Holy Eucharist seems less than sound, and what he said against eternal punishment was at the very least audacious. He said almost nothing that could not stand correction."[69]

Armed with these testimonies and the censures of "A Perverted Devotion" by Flöck and Piccirelli, Martín called a consultation with his assistants on 24 January. All agreed, after having seen the censures, that they had to prevent such a situation from recurring, and so Tyrrell would have to be forbidden to publish either in the *Weekly Register*, or in the *Month*, or in any other medium that he found convenient. Further, the censors in England would have to be changed and the new ones approved by the general—the implication again being that the English fathers could not be trusted to monitor themselves. Liberal Catholicism, so manifest in the writers of the *Month* and even in their provincial, had to be expunged.[70]

Within a day or so of this consultation, Martín received a letter from Charnley dated 23 January, in which the latter first defended Tyrrell by citing Cardinal Vaughan's support, then inquired about publishing two prefaces that Tyrrell had earlier committed himself to write.[71] The full contents of Charnley's letter are unknown, as it seems to have disappeared after Martín used it. But perhaps it contained the interesting note recorded in the minutes of the meeting of the English Province consultors on 8 February 1900: "The Cardinal, who called especially to see Fr. Tyrrell after having heard from Rome of the affair, was desirous of engaging Fr. Tyrrell in writing articles in connection with Dr. Mivart's case."[72] Such a commendation would not have squared with Martín's view, and in fact Martín replied on 5 February that the views of his censors in Rome "differ by the widest possible margin from the opinion of His Eminence Cardinal Vaughan" and that "in these matters the opinions of externs are to be disregarded, as are even the opinions of Ours who are not censors. Only the judgments of officially appointed censors are to be considered." At an opportune time, Martín said, he would send the censures and inform Gerard of his final decision. Meanwhile Tyrrell was not to publish anything except the two prefaces, and those not until the English censures of the prefaces had been cleared in Rome and permission granted.[73]

Three days earlier, Sydney Smith, head of the Farm Street writers, had addressed to Meyer a lengthy and sympathetic explanation of Tyrrell's style and outlined the genesis of "A Perverted Devotion." He pointed out that he had given Tyrrell leave to publish that article, which had been solicited by the editor of the *Weekly Register*, but that no one in England would regard a contribution to the *Register* as an endorsement of its editorial leanings. Smith then tried his best to explain Tyrrell's effective apologetic style by pointing to his own recent failure to satisfy a young man's difficulties about inspiration and certain narratives in the Old Testament.

I wished I had let him rest content with the position that he believed what the Church taught on the subject but found it most difficult to understand. . . . In stating this I know that I am stating what Fr. Tyrrell feels strongly, and it needs to be borne in mind that he is precisely the one amongst us all who is sought out by these earnest inquirers, Catholic and non-Catholic. He holds that they are repelled by the harsh unsympathetic way in which their very real mental difficulties are pooh-poohed by so many of our priests and apologists, in books and conversations, who expect them to be satisfied with solutions taken out of the textbooks which seem to them to explain nothing. The article on a <u>Perverted Devotion</u> was, as he explains it to me, written with a special view to his personal experience of how this method was being injuriously pursued. The passage, for instance, in which he depicted as useless the attempt to meet a scientific difficulty regarding the nature of fire by distinguishing between the <u>per</u>

modum combustionis and per modum alligationis, was of this nature. To a remote reader the passage might naturally appear to be aimed at St. Thomas, and this, I freely acknowledge was a defect in it [the article] . . . but in fact it was aimed at a use made of St. Thomas's distinction by a priest here who had been doling it out in a very wooden way to an inquirer who could not find rhyme or reason in it. Hence Fr. Tyrrell's feeling that it is more practical to bring this class of inquirers face to face with the Church's teaching and our Lord's words, about Hell & similar subjects of difficulty, & explain to them the reasonableness of believing even if they cannot understand.

I feel that what I am trying to explain is difficult, at least for me to describe clearly, though it is clear enough to many of us who are in the midst of the complications of English thought. But if I may now conclude, my feeling is that, whilst the admonition given by Fr. General may do Fr. Tyrrell much good, by making him more careful, it would be a great loss to our apostolic work over here if he were not allowed to continue his writings both in the Month & in other ways as hitherto.[74]

Martín quoted much of this letter in his Memorias, but omitted most of the above quotation containing the heart of Smith's apologia. It is instructive to see what Martín selected as the point of the letter that told with him. He interpreted Smith's description of Tyrrell's (and Smith's) standpoint as this: "the intention is not to impose on the understanding more truths than ought to be imposed and so to reject many answers which the manuals give to certain difficulties."[75] Martín clearly jumped to a conclusion unwarranted by Smith's words. Neither Smith nor Tyrrell had said anything about rejecting answers given in the manuals. Rather, as Smith tried to explain, they tried to encourage faithful affirmation of the authentic tradition even when certain doctrines could not be rationally explained; it was a question of using the manuals wisely, interpreting and adapting them for different times and cultures. Obviously Martín disagreed with the English assessment of what wisdom required, and it is difficult to see how he himself transcended the Saxon–Latin polarization that he so passionately discountenanced.

Smith's apologia, far from brightening Rome's view of the English scene, only made it dimmer. Indeed, Martín acknowledged that Smith's confession "carried much weight in coming to conclude that there was excessive condescension to the heterodox and Catholic liberals,"[76] and that he himself could not afford to wait for Gerard's return from the missions before taking decisive counter-measures. He might even have seen Gerard's absence as an opportunity to effect a change unhindered, as he was coming to conclude that Gerard himself was tainted with liberalism and so would not or could not act effectively on mandates from Rome. On 12 February 1900, therefore, Martín sent the censures of "A Perverted Devotion" to Charnley, along with a very long letter for Gerard, and instructed Charnley to read everything carefully and to execute at once what pertained to Tyrrell and Thurston.[77] The following course was to be taken: Since Tyrrell's article had perpetrated a public scandal, the scandal had to be publicly repaired both by the writer and by the censor who had so casually approved it. Tyrrell was therefore to compose a new article deploring the misunderstanding or misreading of his previous article and expounding the true doctrine according to the censures—this article to be sent to Rome for approval prior to publication. As to Thurston, he was never again to serve as sole censor of anything; nor was anything to be published that he had approved if other censors had disapproved.

The lengthy instruction to Gerard contains most of Martín's complaints and suspicions about the English Province and proposed remedies. It is a letter that Martín recalls repeatedly as programmatic but as having had little effect. Its critical importance demands that it receive a full exposition here.

Martín began by complaining about how upset he was over "A Perverted Devotion," that it was published in the *Weekly Register*, and that, "since it seemed scandalous enough to deserve to be referred to the 'Index of forbidden books,' it was delated to me by ecclesiastics in high places who are most devoted to our Society." Other writings of Tyrrell's too were suspect, for he combines a "certain audacity with I do not know what obscurity of style, which usually leads to serious dangers." All this was by way of preface. Martín then launched into the heart of his criticism, which, simply put, was that behind all the trouble lay Americanism or liberalism. These, for Martín, were of a single piece.[78]

Worse than that article were two grievous complaints recently received: one from a certain Father, "whom you all admire for his sound doctrine and great moderation," about Tyrrell's imprudent, if not unorthodox, words while preaching a retreat to the Jesuit community at St. Bueno's the previous autumn; the other, not from a Jesuit, "*sed fide dignus*"—Martín did not tell Gerard that "*fide dignus*" was Merry del Val—who reported that Tyrrell, "in speaking about that form of Liberalism which is now customarily called 'Americanism,' had said of himself, 'Americanism can be held; I myself am an Americanist, but I know how to use the words.' "[79]

It is instructive to note how here once again Martín has slightly twisted his previous account of this conversation.[80] In that account, he has Tyrrell saying that "Americanism is not so bad." Now he has him saying that it "can be held"—words which quite possibly suggested to Martín's mind that Tyrrell had been positively promoting Americanism/liberalism. Indeed, Martín's suspicion soon turned to conviction that Tyrrell was guilty of such a promotion.

Apparently by now Martín had accumulated enough evidence against the English Province in general and Tyrrell in particular to convince himself that he had a "situation" on his hands and that he had to take swift and concrete action. So he gave Tyrrell's article to two "experts in theology to criticize, neither of whom is Roman," he assured Gerard, "or has anything in common with our Roman writers." Their censures "confirm in all aspects the judgment which both ours and externs who have read the article hold in common here in Rome."[81]

It must be noted here that Martín was overstating his case on two points. First, only in some very literal sense might it be said that the two censors, Flöck and Piccirelli, were not Roman and had nothing in common with the Roman writers. Flöck had been in Rome since 1887 and was the rector of the house in which Martín himself lived and worked. Piccirelli was the assistant to the Neapolitan provincial and was well known to Brandi, the editor of *La Civiltà Cattolica*, himself a Neapolitan and thoroughly Romanized. Even if Piccirelli was not, strictly speaking, Roman, the Italian Jesuits were quite well aware of their proximity to the Roman curia and tended to comport themselves accordingly. Second, Martín seems to want to convey the impression of a wide reading and consequent groundswell of disapproval of the article. Evidence suggests, however, that Martín was speaking of the views of only Merry del Val and perhaps half a dozen Jesuits, his appointees, whose thought largely mirrored his own.

The censorship process in England was, for Martín, decidedly below standard. To improve it, Gerard was henceforth annually to send the names of proposed censors to the general for approval, and only then to publish their names in the province catalogue. Gerard was also to admonish the censors to read and heed all the prescriptions about censorship in the Jesuit traditions and to bear in mind that they would be condignly punished should they approve a manuscript out of cowardice. As to the writers, Martín's main complaint was that they favored a temperate style, facilely attributed good faith and good will to non-Catholics, and cleverly accommodated themselves to the prejudices of dissidents. Such tactics, Martín observed, were acceptable as long as truth and the interests of the church were "vigorously upheld," as the Supreme Pontiff has rightly demanded of Jesuits:

For which reason I must tell you not without sorrow what some are saying, namely, that the English Fathers have sometimes shown themselves to be too weak or too laggardly. And indeed in these past years there has been no lack of occasions offered to them spontaneously [to prove themselves otherwise]. Now to pass over in silence the overt enemies who write in English, whether they publish from or originate in England—so many pseudo-Catholics or men who scarcely think as Catholics—who, either under their own or assumed names, calumniate and insult the most holy institute of the Church, the Supreme Pontiff himself, religious orders, and the Society by name. Such men among the laity are Dillon, Gibson, Bagot, Mivart etc.; and among priests, Barry etc.;[82] especially, however, the writers for several journals which are falsely called Catholic, e.g., "The New Era," "The Weekly Register" etc. These men are known not only to our Fathers, but also to the Cardinals and the Supreme Pontiff. So they are not only not surprised by the apostasy [i.e., Mivart's] which has recently so disturbed your souls, but they fear still worse apostasies unless the new ultra-liberal doctrines, which have most assuredly sunk deep roots in England, are forcefully resisted.

In the past, Martín recalled, the English fathers had a reputation for valor in service of the truth. But now some, perhaps not knowingly,

have given their hands over to the enemy. Certainly Fr. Lucas gave his hands over to the enemy when he wrote his articles clearly in accord with the mind of the liberal school, which excited complaints from so many Cardinals and other men of the highest standing. So too did they give their hands over to the enemy who yielded our London hall to a certain conference or who attended that conference even though Cardinal Vaughan prudently absented himself. All of which must sadden not only our Fathers in other parts of Europe but even more so our American Fathers.[83]

Finally, Martín complained,

Fr. Tyrrell gave his hands over to the enemy, not only because he wrote an article according to the mind of the liberal school which had already abused his other writings, but also because he published that article in a liberal journal. For although the English Fathers might laudably contribute articles to non-Catholic periodicals, or rather to periodicals of no particular color, there can be no doubt about periodicals which abuse the Catholic name. It will not do to publish in such journals, except vigorously to impugn their false assertions. For otherwise, by our presence in those pages, we cooperate in propagating error; which ought to be as far removed from us as possible. For that Liberalism, with which the above-mentioned pages are more or less infected and which your Cardinal Newman calls "that deep, plausible scepticism," is the heresy of our age.[84]

Martín concluded with the strongest possible language of condemnation by quoting biblical texts about incest and the Antichrist and the true Christian comportment toward them:

Last year YR [Your Reverence] denied that the English Fathers fostered those false doctrines. Nor would I dare to believe or suspect anything of this sort of the Province as a whole; otherwise it would have to be said that the Province had fallen utterly from the genuine spirit of the Society. But YR has since discovered from sad examples that some Fathers not only foster those doctrines but are deeply imbued with them. "They went out from us, but they did not really

belong to us; for if they had belonged to us, they would have remained with us." Let us give thanks to God that they have gone out
from us. For such men are the "leaven that" can easily "corrupt the
whole mass"; nor is there any other remedy but completely to "purge
out the old leaven," in obedience to the Apostolic words.[85]

Perhaps not coincidentally Merry del Val had appealed to the
same text from 1 John in a letter to Wilfrid Ward of 5 June 1899:
"There exists unfortunately in England as well as France, Germany, the United States and over here, a group of traitors in
the camp, and it would be better were they to quickly go 'out
from us' for they are 'not of us.' 'That they may be manifest,
that they are not all of us.' "[86]

Martín enjoined Charnley to communicate his programmatic
letter to the provincial consultors and to those writers and censors to whom it pertained. But Charnley judiciously chose not
to show it to Tyrrell, as Martín's allusions to the Antichrist and
the most heinous of crimes against community would have
been a red flag to a raging bull.

Thurston's Intervention

Thurston, however, was alarmed by the potential danger and
wrote at once, not to Martín or Meyer, but to his fellow Englishman Peter Chandlery, Meyer's secretary, to impress on him
the seriousness of the situation and to gain his intervention. It
is an extraordinary letter of seventeen quarto pages and requires lengthy quotation. It begins "For God's sake, <u>for God's
sake</u>, <u>for God's sake</u> persuade Father General somehow or
other to withdraw that injunction to Father Tyrrell about his
article in the Weekly Register. I am not an alarmist or given to
panics, but I venture to say that no one realises even faintly the
harm that may and probably will come of it all, if nothing is
done." If Tyrrell were provoked to leave the Society, Thurston
warned, the potential for damage all round was enormous.

I know his Irish combativeness and I know his quite extraordinary
gifts. He has a number of influential friends. He is the one man in the
Society in England who has really won the respect of thinking men,
within and without the Church—men like Professor Sidgwick, Sir
Mountstuart Grant Duff, Mr. Wyndham and Mr. Balfour members of

the Government whom he meets at the Synthetic Society.[87] All the reviews will be open to him, and if he leaves the Society and the Church, he will certainly write to justify himself. He will explain in his own caustic way his experiences in the Society, the efforts made to suppress all originality of thought. He knows so many scandals. He has been in the thick of all sorts of delicate matters (in giving retreats to Ours etc.), some of which even superiors do not know of. He has had all Father Cornelius Clifford's (the one who left not long since) stock of experiences to draw on of the things which he has seen in the Society in America. It would not be pleasant to find public references made to a story of the Master of Novices in one of our Provinces committing unnatural crime with some of his novices (of course, I do not know how much truth may be in this story, but I know that Fr Tyrrell heard it and credits it), the shock of which is supposed to have killed Father Anderledy.[88]

Thurston explained that Tyrrell had already been depressed because of the problems submitted to him in connection with the Mivart affair, but "N.B. He has absolutely no sympathy with Mivart."[89] Then Tyrrell began to have health problems,[90] on top of which came this blow regarding his article.

And the thought I know in his mind is that the situation is intolerable, that he cannot breathe in an atmosphere so stifling. That if he cannot even say that the doctrine of God's punishments is a grievous difficulty which we believe as one of the <u>mysteries</u> of our Faith, without being pelted with censures "<u>scandalosum, offensivum piis auribus, haeresi proximum</u>" and all the rest of the mediaeval terminology, that then it is best to end it all at once.

You see what makes it all so sad, is that Fr Tyrrell, as you, my dear Father, know very well, is a man <u>integerrimae vitae</u>. He has never been in any sort of sense a black sheep.[91] He is observant and mortified and spiritually minded.

His Celtic imagination may carry him a bit too far at times in his writing, Thurston continued,

but he writes always honestly and sincerely. . . . He is no humbug, posing and acting and laughing in his sleeve at the folly of those who believe him. Therefore should it ever happen that Fr Tyrrell leaves the Church it will be a blow far worse than the fall of some such man as Klein or Dr Sullivan.[92] He is the chosen spiritual guide of some of the noblest characters I have ever known both in religion and out of it. He has the confidence of more of our scholastics—I speak especially of the more gifted of these scholastics—than any other father of the Province. His books are literally scrambled for in convents . . . and are read by good people of all classes in the Church and out of it.

Having cited testimonies to Tyrrell from such influential figures as Randall T. Davidson, the Anglican bishop of Rochester, Lord Halifax, and Wilfrid Ward, Thurston pointed out that Tyrrell had been chosen to deliver two courses of lectures to the Catholic undergraduates at Oxford—"as the appointed guardian in some sense of their faith.[93] What a shock to the Catholic cause if such a man six months afterwards should be found writing in the Nineteenth Century the reasons why he has found his position as a Jesuit, a priest and a Catholic untenable." In that case, Thurston speculated, someone as unsparing of his epithets as Fr. Richard F. Clarke would be told to reply. And Tyrrell would undoubtedly strike back. He would never be libelous or untruthful, Thurston observed, but, lacking discretion, "he easily goes further than he means to."[94]

Certainly, Thurston continued, Tyrrell has ample reason to be incensed by the Roman censors who "qualified" his article. "The first is not so bad, but the second I consider simply atrocious. Whether the writer is insufficiently acquainted with English to understand the article, or is unable to follow Fr. Tyrrell's drift, or what not I am unable to say, but he utterly perverts the writer's meaning. He attributes to Fr. Tyrrell propositions which not only he never held or insinuated but which no reasonable person could suppose him to insinuate." The censor not only completely misapprehended Tyrrell's meaning, but he used inverted commas professedly to quote Tyrrell's words, whereas in fact he quoted his own misleading summary and passed it off as Tyrrell's. The basic error of the foreign censors from the outset was their inability to perceive and enter into Tyrrell's ironical and humorous style. Nor did they grant—if they even grasped—Tyrrell's explicit distinction, that he was dealing not with the *doctrine* of hell, but with certain extra-doctrinal and quasi-devotional *elaborations* of the doctrine. "Yet the censors take this all quite solemnly and test it as a theological proposition." As far as positive assertions about the doctrine of hell are concerned, Tyrrell had said it all before in *Nova et Ve-tera*.[95] "In many places," Thurston noted vehemently,

the article does no more than repeat in other words what will be found in Nova et Vetera second edition pp 151–154. That work has been printed for three years. It is in its third edition. It is read by Catholics all over England and America. It is used by Fathers for their meditation book in many of our houses. It appeared after careful censure, Fr C Blount and Fr Roche both as you know most pious men as well as ex-professors of Theology being amongst the number of the censors. It had and still has the imprimatur of the Cardinal Archbishop. What is more, I happen to know that those pages were not overlooked but were carefully read by the censors, and more changes were made in them in accordance with their suggestions. And yet these very propositions are now branded with scandalosum, temerarium, ecclesiae injuriosum etc etc, in fact the first censor says of a proposition which appears almost in identical words in Nova et Vetera "certe haereticum censeri debet."[96]

No doubt, Thurston continued, Father General was wondering what possible justification there could be for such an article in the first place. Thurston then alluded to the Latin–Celtic antithesis as a plausible source of this wonderment and misunderstanding—which allusion could not have pleased Martín.

I submit with all respect that it is very hard for those who live among Catholics in such countries as France, Italy or Spain, to understand the tone of thought of Catholics here in England and the deplorable change which is coming upon us so fast. . . . Such articles as those of Mivart, or of Verax etc. in the Times are read by all Catholics without scruple.[97] One finds the laity now urging their difficulties against all revelation at the luncheon table and in drawing rooms, condemning the action of the Church right and left, and these are good people, mind you, who wish to be known as practising Catholics.

On the very issue of eternal punishment, Thurston related a recent encounter at a luncheon where he was seated next to the Lord Chief Justice, Lord Russell of Killowen. The latter remarked that he considered the prayer at the end of Mass about "thrust down into Hell"

a most atrocious prayer; and he added calmly that he could not believe that God in His Goodness could punish people through ages and ages of the sort of eternity which is described in mission sermons. It is no good telling such men that there is no difficulty about the doctrine, that you only have to remember that God is infinite and that the malice of sin acquires a quasi-infinity and the matter is plain. If you take that tone, your friend will simply tell you "well, sir, we live in different worlds and talk a different language; you may tell me that it is no difficulty to you, but that does not make it the less a shocking and a horrible thing to me; and the priest who will help me will be the one who understands what I feel about it, and does not attempt to put me off with words and explanations which explain nothing. I believe it, if I have to believe it, but I believe it as a mystery." I have had such things said to me by nuns in convents, nuns of absolutely innocent lives and blameless religious. The number of such is growing every day and personally I must confess that all my sympathies are with them. The only thing that helps me is precisely such a view of the case as is presented in Fr. Tyrrell's Nova et Vetera. I do not wish to condemn the old Hell Fire sermons and the old ascetical treatises. They were good for the state of feeling which prevailed then, they are good even now for the crowds who flock to missions but with an educated audience my experience is that here in England they do far more harm than good. . . . Formerly when a person came to say that it seemed to him cruel for God to punish one act of passion or of lust with inconceivable torment for ever and for ever, if he did not understand the explanation given him, he went away thinking that he was stupid, and that the priest was wise and understood it all. But now people, at least educated English men and women, insist on thinking for themselves and they say that in such a matter there is question not of an abstruse science but of the fundamental principles of justice. And if the priest sees differently it is the priest and his system are wrong not they.[98]

These are the sort of people, Thurston explained, with whom Tyrrell regularly dealt and for whom he was writing. His thesis was not what the censors made it to be. Rather it was to admit that the doctrine of eternal punishment *is* a difficulty for every humane and reflective person, in fact a difficulty of such proportions that the wiser method of meeting it is not to attempt to reduce it to "reasonable" explanations but to recognize it as a mystery of faith.

In substance Fr. Tyrrell meant to say nothing more than he has already said in Nova et Vetera but he introduced his article with a certain amount of persifflage [*sic*] of those teachers who find the doctrine of Hell so easy and natural that they seem to take a positive content in the thought of it. Such people, he says love to make the most of the number of the lost, to dwell and insist much upon the fire being like our own kitchen fire, to heap up comparisons about the endlessness of eternity. They make Hell the key-note of their piety, just as other people take up the devotion to the Sacred Heart or to the Blessed Virgin. Now this may be exaggerated or indiscreet but it is most of it obviously a kind of grim satire. You have to know the writer a little to understand his cast of mind.

But, Thurston continued, what really distressed Tyrrell were two grievances: (1) the fact that he was ordered by the general to write a reparative article in accord with censors who had misread his article and who would require him to affirm theological formulations that he does not accept and are not *de fide*; (2) and probably worse was the inflammatory, insulting language, particularly of the second censor.

The dogmatic tone of the censor, without a shade of misgiving that what he pronounced to be erroneous and scandalous was really and infallibly erroneous and scandalous, just as if he embodied in himself the whole Catholic Church, has done more mischief than anything. And then he goes on to read Fr Tyrrell a lecture on his parva scientia, as if he were a little boy not old enough to understand the mysteries of theology. Surely when a theologian is asked his opinion of certain propositions he might confine himself to the question before him and abstain from insulting the writer.

Thurston concluded with an urgent plea to let the matter drop. "People have forgotten all about the article here in England. No individual has been attacked or offended. Whatever the censors may say the article has given no grave scandal and cannot be described as openly heretical or offensive to pious ears." The article had been read and passed by Fathers Charnley, Smith, and Humphrey. Gerard too, Thurston thought, had also read it before he sailed for Guyana and made no adverse comment on it. And Cardinal Vaughan himself told Tyrrell that he found nothing much to complain of in it—except perhaps for some indiscreet wording—"and he showed his confidence in Fr Tyrrell by naming him as one of the two theologians whom he suggested to Mivart to discuss his difficulties with." Finally,

Thurston warned, it would not do to have another celebrated case on their hands. "We have had Dreyfus and Mivart and the effects are <u>very very</u> serious to the Church in England." He assured Chandlery (and, of course, Martín) that he had no knowledge that Tyrrell would attack the Society if he were "to cut adrift. . . . He is not malicious or untruthful, but I know his character and I know how a man gets led on from one thing to another, when anything like controversy begins. I only hope it may not already be too late." Thurston ended by giving Chandlery permission to show his letter to all concerned, meaning, of course, primarily the general.[99]

It is curious that Martín, in his *Memorias*, quoted Thurston's momentous letter only down to the mention of Tyrrell's threat to use the Clifford stories, perhaps indicative of how that threat stuck in Martín's mind and blocked out the heart of Thurston's apologia. Indeed, Martín concluded that these words "appeared to be written to alarm me," but he portrayed himself as calm and in control—compared to Chandlery, who was "very agitated" by the letter. "I tried to calm him down," Martín reported, "saying that in a few days he would reply for me . . . and that meanwhile he should do nothing else."[100]

But Chandlery got little respite. Thurston followed his first letter with one that was even more urgent. He was alarmed that Tyrrell had stopped celebrating Mass and was apparently committing himself to a hopeless position. Martín, he suggested, could save the situation by telegraphing a promise to review the whole case. This move would commit him to nothing, but it would give Tyrrell

a ray of hope that a way can be found out of the impasse. He simply <u>will</u> not unsay many of those things which he has seriously said. They are not contrary to the faith, and they are not scandalous and offensive to pious ears merely because some professor of theology who knows absolutely nothing of the philosophy and thought of the day chooses to pronounce them so. . . . A man's vow of obedience does not and cannot bind his intellectual convictions in matters which no one pretends to be of faith.

Thurston hastened to add that this intervention of his should be kept secret, as Tyrrell would be furious if he found out.[101]

Alarmed as he was, Thurston again could not wait for a reply but wrote a third time to Chandlery on 21 February to justify Tyrrell's loss of confidence in the church and the Society. The previous August, Thurston said, Tyrrell had preached a retreat to the clergy of the troubled Salford diocese, and, as an ear of last resort and absolutely trusted, he came away with all their woes. Subsequently a diocesan priest complained to Tyrrell that a certain Jesuit was giving grave scandal by frequenting a brothel in the priest's parish. Tyrrell was already feeling utterly wretched about the state of the church and of the Society, so that this story simply broke his spirit, and he could not keep it to himself. Thurston explained that he was taking the liberty to pass on this information both to help officials understand several very important truths about Tyrrell: first, how invaluable he was to the church in England as that rare priest so completely trusted; second, how seriously committed he was to the Society; and therefore, third, how deeply hurt he was to find his integrity called into question by the general himself, whereas superiors seemed somnolent in the face of other real scandals.[102]

Chandlery had just completed his response—drafted by Martín (considered below)—to Thurston's first letter when this third letter arrived and apparently moved him to respond at once in his own name. A brief and seemingly heartless reply, it treated the story about the philandering Jesuit as a product of Tyrrell's imagination and credulity in the face of disillusionment. This and other stories about the English Province, Chandlery alleged, could be dealt with easily. For one thing, they were nearly all based on hearsay, so that "it is sufficient to say that these stories . . . are either true or false. If they are false, (as I firmly believe they are) the English Fathers should find no difficulty in refuting them: if they are true, they may prove the occasion for correcting abuses, that otherwise could not have been corrected; & so God will draw good out of evil."[103] The threat about Tyrrell's possibly divulging Clifford's stories, Chandlery said, was dealt with in his just-posted lengthy reply to Thurston's first letter.

But before Thurston had received either of these replies, he had sent a fourth letter to Chandlery, this one breathing a sigh of relief. Martín had apparently sent the telegram Thurston wanted to defuse the situation, and indeed it had the desired effect. Tyrrell was again celebrating Mass, but leniency was still urgently needed so that Tyrrell might not resort to desperate measures. Thurston could not insist enough that his earlier letters had not exaggerated the danger.[104]

Meanwhile Martín had drafted a reply for Chandlery to Thurston's momentous letter of 18 February. Dated 24 February, it crossed Thurston's last to Chandlery. Both the Chandlery/Martín letter and Martín's reflection on it in his *Memorias* depict the general as tranquil in the face of the dangers to which Thurston had alluded. Indeed, Chandlery reported, the general had taken such dangers into account when he prescribed to Charnley on 12 February the action to be taken. About censures in general, Father General's duty was to seek competent censorship, not approve it. But about Tyrrell's article specifically, Father General wanted to distinguish two points: the matter of fact (the scandal given) and the matter of doctrine (the veracity of opinions set forth). On the former point there was no doubt. He had it as a fact both from men of distinguished learning and from men of high standing in the church that scandal had been given. As to doctrine, he had never accused Tyrrell of heresy. In his letter to Charnley and Gerard, Father General merely expressed the hope that the censured passages were "not attributable to bad faith, but in part to too great a desire on the part of the Father to temper the difficulties of dissidents, and in part to the error of his readers or hearers." But the article, because of how it read, was liable to be misunderstood and to arouse suspicion about Tyrrell's orthodoxy—as was clear both from the complaints of intelligent and highly educated men and from the censors, all of whom knew English perfectly well. Neither of the censors, Chandlery argued, had ever heard of Tyrrell; nor had they any reason for prejudice against him. Neither of them was a Roman theologian; nor had they any connection with the Roman writers. He went on to explain the general's proposal in his letter to Charnley and Gerard of 12 February for Tyrrell's reparative article and observed how benign the general was in giving Tyrrell the opportunity of clear gain both for himself and for Catholic truth. Then came a blow directly to Thurston:

Fr. Genl regrets that you, dear Fr. Thurston, should have been t.[the] occasion of so much trouble and anxiety to himself, and now to Fr. Tyrrell, by giving your approval to his article too readily. He regrets it all the more for the very reasons you now allege for letting the matter drop. You say that Fr. Tyrrell had said and written substantially the same things as in the article, in other works; that these works have been approved; that they are used by Ours for spiritual reading & even meditation; that through them Fr. Tyrrell has acquired an influence, such as no other Father has, over the brighter young men of the Province etc.

All this, Fr. Gen. says, is a matter of special regret to him.

The reason being, of course, that such ideas—substantially the same as in "A Perverted Devotion," which had scandalized people abroad as well as in England—had been approved by English censors. A subject of still deeper regret and anxiety to the general was "to hear that the brighter young men of the Province are fascinated by such publications."[105]

Then came another swipe. Thurston had confessed to sympathizing with the kind of dissidents who were helped by Tyrrell's way of putting the truths of faith, and he had cited the example of Lord Russell and his difficulty with the prayer prescribed by the pope for the end of Mass. The general took umbrage:

If he [Lord Russell—and by implication Thurston] knew what he was saying, the man would have been guilty of blasphemy. The idea of thinking God cruel for punishing Satan in hell, who has an eternal hatred of God. What else cd. God do? Hell is Satan's proper place. The proper answer to such a man would have been: "You are horrified at God's justice in the case of a creature who is unrepentant, & who cherishes eternal hatred. Suppose a man had out of malice murdered the Sovereign of the land. Would you regard it as cruel to condemn him to death, even if he were repentant of the deed? Now capital punishment, as far as human law can make it, is eternal punishment. In the case of Satan, too, there is no repentance". . . [sic].

If this be an instance of what is meant by English thought at the present day, it is by no means confined to or peculiar to England: it is to be found in other countries: it is simply uncatholic thought, liberalistic thought, rationalistic thought, in fact out & out liberalism.

Here Chandlery quoted Martín's 12 February letter to Gerard: "Liberalismus ille . . . quem Cardinalis Newman vocat scepticismum profundum et speciosum, haeresis est nostrae aetatis, a qua Nostri quam maxime abhorreant oportet."[106] As Chandlery continued, the depth of Martín's fear and the reasons for it become apparent:

Thought of this kind, His Paternity added, must not be encouraged or dallied with, but corrected: it constitutes the heresy of modern times, & unless it is corrected, it developes, as in all preceding ages has been the case, into regular formal heresy. No heresy starts up at once full fledged: it is in a half developed state in the minds of the people perhaps for years & years before it fully shows itself in its true form. And here precisely is where, as Fr. Gen. added, the Fathers in England are found fault with, viz for being too gentle[,] conciliatory, accommodating, minimizing in dealing with these men of "liberal" views, — too ready to sympathize with them, or to believe them in good faith etc. Unless firmness & courage is shown, the false opinions will gradually get the upper hand, &, as a consequence, you will have apostasies (like Mivart's) & such miserable attacks on the Church & things sacred, as those of Mivart, Dillon, Gibson, Bagot, Verax, etc.[107] These men may pose as Catholics, but they are nothing more than rationalists, out & out enemies of the church; & harm, not good, is done by dealing with them & their views in a minimizing, accommodating spirit.

The fatal result of not upholding Catholic Truth boldly, is precisely what you state: Catholic laymen, women, nuns even, are beginning to express doubts about the truths of faith, to discuss, to criticize, to question v.g. God's Justice (considering only the rights of man, & not God's side of the question,) & in general to assume in some way man's independence of God. . . .

What you say about Fr. Tyrrell writing his article as a newspaper skit, not as a serious theological essay, such as the censors took it to be, in some sense rather aggravates the matter, because it shows how irreverently, before a promiscuous reading public, such sacred & delicate subjects are handled, at the risk of giving very false ideas to people who are already perplexed.

Finally, Chandlery told Thurston, Father General enjoined him in conscience — since he had most influence with Tyrrell and had "unhappily been the occasion of his present trouble" — to do all he could to induce Tyrrell to comply with the general's wishes. Such a compliance would not entail adopting all that the censors said, but only writing an article " 'according to the censures' ie. accordg to the suggestions & on the lines there traced out: for these suggestions show where Fr. Tyrrell, consciously or unconsciously it matters not, expressed himself in a way that puts him in a bad light before well meaning intelligent Catholics. . . . He need not compromise himself." As to Tyrrell's arsenal of Clifford stories, there was no reason for concern.

It would be enough to mention the reason why he (Fr. Clifford) was dismissed from the Soc. some 8 years ago, & his stories will be thoroughly discredited. This is perhaps the reason why Fr. Clifford has written nothing against the Society. Fr. Gen. adds that Fr. Clifford deceived all his Superiors in England, beginning with Fr. Purbrick, who specially befriended & recommended him: but he didn't deceive Fr. Gen. who was all along convinced the man would leave the Society after his second admission: & for this reason, he would not allow him to be readmitted for three years, nor allow him to be ordained before he had completed the required time, though Superiors pleaded continually in his favour.

Chandlery concluded by advising Thurston to take up any further representations directly with Meyer.[108]

Thurston, however, replied again to Chandlery on 28 February, to impress on him that he (Thurston) had indeed used all his influence to prevent Tyrrell from doing anything foolish, but that no one should be surprised if he does. After all, "he is quite aware of what St. Thomas and other theologians have written and when censors treat him as if he were a little child writing of what he does not understand, but at the same time shamefully perverting and misquoting . . . his article, it is not surprising that a man of his sensitive character gets perfectly sick of the whole thing and reckless of what he says." Furthermore, Thurston said, he regretted not having vetoed the article from the outset only because of the trouble it had brought upon Tyrrell, not because it contained unorthodox teachings.[109]

Chandlery's reply is missing, but it prompted an expression of deep sadness from Thurston.

What seems to me so hopeless is the disinclination in your letter to admit that the censors can possibly have made a mistake. . . . If I stood alone in my view of Fr. Tyrrell's article and its meaning I should perhaps be rash in persisting in my opinion against the better judgment of others. But I do not stand alone. Every single person here whose judgment I in any way respect thinks substantially as I do. Fr. Provincial, Fr. Charnley, Fr. Smith, Fr. Roche, Fr. Blount, even Fr. Humphrey. . . . Those who condemn it are men like Fr. Slater and Fr. Tepe, whose narrowness and woodenness are notorious, and who never in their lives have had the least experience in dealing with the difficulties of doubting but quite conscientious Catholics. . . . There are thousands and thousands of people here starving for want of bread (intellectually I mean), but the [party-line] theologians for all the help that they give them might be in another planet. "If you don't see the arguments for revelation you are eaten up with intellectual pride, or you keep a mistress." That is practically what they tell them, and when any rash person tries to enter into the difficulties of these agnostics or troubled Catholics, the theologians shut their pious ears and scream "heresy!"

Thurston was further saddened by the realization that an earnest man like Tyrrell, whose faith was "bled by causes within and without," who "meets with respect and courtesy" by world-renowned intellectuals "even when they differ from him," should receive such shabby treatment from his own religious brothers.

Surely if such a man perpetrates an indiscreet article it would have been easy to write him a friendly letter asking if he could not manage in this respect or in that to correct a false impression. To friendly treatment of that sort Fr. Tyrrell is always amenable, and I know that in all this business he is most grateful for the consideration shown to him by his immediate superiors. But instead of persuasion we have a brutum fulmen.[110] There comes a condemnation in the most wounding language which treats him as a perfect ignoramus, a perfect torrent of ecclesiastical Billingsgate.[111]

Chandlery did not answer this letter.

On 17 March 1900 Gerard, having returned from Guyana, addressed a lengthy review, explanation, and defense of Tyrrell to Martín, enclosing Tyrrell's twelve-page typescript, "A Reply to My Censors," along with a covering letter from Tyrrell to Gerard dated 14 March 1900. In his letter Tyrrell took a hard stance against the kind of qualifications that the censors seemed to want and complained acerbically that, as his "Reply" made clear,

my censors have failed altogether to appreciate the purport & spirit of the article as a whole, and thus, bring in a wrong key to unlock the meaning of the parts. In dealing severally with these dismembered parts they display a purely destructive and therefore uncritical spirit; and above all, a patent unfamiliarity with idiomatic & literary English—a defect common even to English-speaking ecclesiastics whose saturation with Church Latin disposed them to render theological terms by their nearest English assonant, irrespective of current usage. For these, and for other more obvious reasons, I repudiate and protest against these censures in their entirety and in their details.[112]

Tyrrell's "Reply," Gerard's Support, Martín's Dismay

A brief look at Tyrrell's "A Reply to My Censors" is in order here because it highlights the "readings" of Roman theologians, displays their fears, biases, and resultant epithets, and thus provides important data relevant to the background of the modernist crisis. Tyrrell's "Reply" dealt primarily with the objections of the first censor, "who is also the more temperate and measured . . . and therefore merits more careful handling."[113] The second censor, Tyrrell averred, "offers little matter for special notice beyond the marvellous method of his procedure." But the principal objection of both was to Tyrrell's use of the term "devotion." They understood it within the framework of scholastic theology, whereas Tyrrell used it in its current idiomatic English sense. Not having grasped the nuance, the censors missed Tyrrell's irony and so misquoted him as holding that the doctrine of hell ought to be explained on the basis of divine goodness rather than divine justice. Tyrrell's argument was, of course, just the other way around.

The strongest charges against Tyrrell were fideism and sheer positivism, because he advocated "a certain temperate agnosticism" as "one of the essential prerequisites of intelligent faith when using analogies to describe divine mysteries." Tyrrell defended this advocacy by pointing out that he had borrowed the argument from Pope St. Leo's ninth sermon on the Nativity. "Temperate agnosticism," he explained, was "a sense of the limitations of our mind,—that child-like disposition which

Christ insists upon as one of the elements of faith." And in saying that the mind must fall back on revelation in the matter of the church's teaching on hell, he meant only that the doctrine was not accessible to pure reason, though it was in some degree accessible to reason as the Vatican council spoke of it, that is, *ratio fide illustrata* (reason illumined by faith). But the censors again misunderstood and charged Tyrrell with blatant agnosticism because he argued that the doctrine was not accessible to pure reason.

The censors also scored Tyrrell for criticizing the traditional explanations of the nature of hell-fire and particularly for rejecting Thomas' theory of *alligation* (the pain is not that of combustion but that of "bondage" of the free spirit to matter) by which the action of fire on spiritual beings is supposed to be rendered intelligible. Tyrrell had expressed doubt that material fire was defined by the church as the agent of torment, and this doubt his second censor found "proximately heretical," since "nothing but the definition of the Church is lacking to make the point <u>de fide Catholica</u>." Which, of course, was Tyrrell's point: the definition was lacking, and for good reason.[114]

Tyrrell ended by excoriating his second censor's method of stringing together bits and pieces of text interpolated with the censor's own words and presenting this conflation in quotation marks as Tyrrell's words to be roundly condemned as " 'illsounding, offensive to pious ears, & not only injurious to the faithful and to the Church, but blasphemous to the most Sacred Heart of Jesus'. This," Tyrrell commented wryly, "needs no comment."[115]

Gerard, in his 17 March letter to Martín, while attempting to be as conciliatory to the general as possible, said little negative and much positive about Tyrrell. He advised the general to proceed with great caution to avoid a disastrous miscalculation, as the matter was extremely complex. He expressed regret that the article had been published in the *Weekly Register* and conceded that he had been negligent in his responsibility as overseer of the censorship process and that the content of the article was not really comprehensible to most readers, especially when treated in such a flippant and sarcastic style. Tyrrell himself, Gerard revealed, now also conceded this, but his desire was to counter the baneful influence of popular preachers who crassly materialized the mystery of hell, even to calculating the temperature of the fire and the number of its victims. As to Tyrrell himself, he is much praised for his work among the well-educated laity as well as among priests and bishops, who prefer him for retreats over all the other fathers. Indeed, he has kept many in the faith who were wavering—something which no one else in England has done. Nor, so far as Gerard knew, did he in any way support "that pernicious liberalism." But, as happened to Cardinal Newman, he has sometimes been mis-understood because of his acute perceptivity combined with a delicate and exquisite style. As to the doctrine of hell, Gerard pointed out that Tyrrell had written superbly on it two years ago in *Nova et Vetera* "(n.n. cxxxiii–cxxxvi, pp. 150–159)." None of the censors had had any doctrinal difficulty with those passages. Nor did any of the English fathers who were consulted about "A Perverted Devotion" find in it any propositions that were theologically indefensible, however much the publication of the article might have displeased them.

Gerard then denounced the two Roman censors, particularly the second, not only for misreading Tyrrell, erroneously para-phrasing him, quoting words not his, and omitting others crucial to his sense, but also for an "unconscionable acrimony that seeks rather to condemn the proposition of his brother than to save it—contrary to the very well known dictum of S.P.N."[116] Gerard explained that he was underscoring this last point because it had precipitated the gravest difficulty of the entire affair. The severity of the Roman censures had thrown Tyrrell into extreme depression—indeed into such a state of despera-tion—that one could not predict his actions. "He is, as they say, thin skinned and moreover Irish and therefore irascible."[117]

Gerard ended on an inflammatory point. The style and method of the English fathers in handling controversies with non-Catholics and pseudo-Catholics, he explained, tends to be more temperate and conciliatory than some believe to be con-sonant with Catholic zeal because experience had shown that nothing is gained and much lost by the violent approach so often found in the *La Civiltà Cattolica*. This could well have been the moment when Martín decided to remove Gerard from office.

Martín replied at length on 27 March. He first strung together the few remarks in Gerard's letter that were in any way critical of Tyrrell: his sarcastic and levitous style which virtually guarantees misunderstanding, and the imprudence of publishing such an article at all, let alone in the *Weekly Register*. Martín then cited an English priest, not a Jesuit, "but a theologian of the greatest possible competence, as is granted by all," who characterized "A Perverted Devotion" as dangerous and its author as "a man of undoubted ability who in his writings aims at a sort of mysticism, which deals in vague generalities and broad assertions, so that he seems to say a good deal that nobody ever said before, but on examination, the originality of thought is found only to be apparent."[118]

Martín again explained his own role in the censorship process—that it was his place, first, to seek competent censors, not to pass judgment on the censures, and, second, to see to appropriate reparation if scandal or even the danger of scandal had resulted from a work already published. That Tyrrell had in fact given scandal was evident from the denunciations of two English prelates, the testimony of an outstanding English theologian not of the Society, the testimony of an outstanding Jesuit theologian who knows English like a native, and the two censors appointed by himself who are eminent in theology and completely competent in the English language. So the only remaining question was how to repair the damage.

The two options Tyrrell had suggested—publish a separate article or include it in a forthcoming volume of articles—were unacceptable because both entailed primarily a refutation of the censures, and since the censures were private, they were not to be publicly debated. It would be sufficient for Tyrrell to say that some people wrongly understood the doctrine of eternal punishment and then go on to expose the Catholic doctrine in a simple, direct style. But whatever Tyrrell wrote, it was not to refer to the censures, and it was to be vetted in Rome prior to publication.

As to Tyrrell himself, Martín observed that in general he was "moved by a certain dangerous spirit toward audacious expression and was inclined toward novelties." These defects were apparent from his manner when he was teaching philosophy, his published articles and books by which many readers reported being scandalized, the disturbance he caused to some Jesuit scholastics when he gave them a retreat, his audacious and sometimes sarcastic style of talking and writing about delicate matters, his dangerous article "A Perverted Devotion," and his own defense against the censors.[119]

Martín was particularly appalled "that a Father of the Society . . . would simply by-pass a theological definition (v.g. of devotion) given by St. Thomas and theologians of the Society and appeal instead to a popular definition in Webster." And then, because the censors either do not understand or will not accept such a definition, he says that they do not know English. The general concluded by ordering Gerard to forbid Tyrrell ever again to preach retreats to Jesuits until he had given "clear evidence of remaining firm in the imitation [of Christ?] and in prudence."[120]

It is instructive to note, as Martín himself did in his *Memorias*, the points in Gerard's letter that he avoided responding to and why: (1) Gerard's argument that Tyrrell had already written excellently and with ecclesiastical approval on the doctrine of hell—because Martín knew of Gerard's too-exalted opinion of *Nova et Vetera*; (2) Gerard's criticism of the censors and his refusal to admit the fallaciousness of "A Perverted Devotion"— for two reasons: (*a*) Martín himself agreed that the second censor was extreme, and (*b*) he did not want to exacerbate Tyrrell's desperate condition; (3) Gerard's apologia for the English writers—because he suspected that the reason behind the English writers' irenic style was not the reason Gerard alleged but rather "the tinge of liberalism" about which Chandlery had written to Thurston, and the moment was not right to deal with that issue; (4) the points Tyrrell had made in his "Reply"—because "although they can be absolutely explained and defended according to the author's assumptions, they could not help but make a bad impression on Christian people, so . . . I restricted my response to insisting that they were scandalous, which I proved."[121]

But the matter did not end there. The general's reading of

the whole affair raised two questions in the minds of English Jesuit and ecclesiastical officials: exactly to whom was Tyrrell's article—and other similarly styled writings—scandalous? And would Martín's proposed cure be worse than the disease he diagnosed? The rub was simply this: Roman officials did not trust the reading and testimony of English officials—Cardinal Vaughan, himself narrowly orthodox, and the Jesuit provincial John Gerard, among many other witnesses—about Tyrrell's works specifically and about apologetics for England in general.

On 1 April two further attestations were sent from England. John Gerard replied to Martín's letter of 27 March, suggesting, without actually saying so, that the prescription by which Tyrrell was to write a reparative article without alluding to the censures was unfair. For his own part, he urged that the matter be simply dropped—on two counts: one, hardly anyone in England was talking about or even remembered the article any more; and two, raising the issue again would run the very real risk of playing into the hands of the Society's enemies, whose calumnies find ready ears even among the most devout Catholics. Furthermore, publishing the proposed article in the *Month* would lay it open to the charge that it was nothing more than a mouthpiece for Rome. He added that his own excellent theologians, "who are in no way inclined to liberalism, with whom I have communicated the entire affair—such as Frs. John Moore and Sydney Smith, were astonished and quite indignant that [the censors] . . . who had so poorly grasped the author's meaning, should have so boldly and unrestrainedly passed judgment on his doctrine." In a word, Gerard said, Your Paternity's proposed solution is fraught with difficulty.[122]

On the same day Sidney Smith addressed a nine-page typewritten critique of the censures to Rudolf Meyer, decrying the numerous and substantive misreadings as everything from "grossly unfair" to "absolutely monstrous." But Martín scarcely alluded to Smith's compelling apologia, and instead focused on the concluding paragraph in which Smith referred to his own assessment of Tyrrell's article in his previous letter to Meyer of 2 February 1900. There, amidst another staunch defense of Tyrrell, Smith had interjected a minor criticism of

Tyrrell's "tendency to use occasionally expressions which, to say the least, are liable to be misconstrued into hits at orthodox theologians and their teaching, though usually not incapable of being theologically defended."[123] Here too, after more than eight pages of defense, Smith in his conclusion gave Martín a handle of criticism to grasp:

What is my own judgment of Father Tyrrell's article I have already said in my former letter, and I need not repeat it here, and will only remind your Reverence that I find in it much that is regrettable, in the many obscure phrases that read as if they might be meant as hits at the common disparagement of many rationes theologicae which are certainly helpful in understanding the truths of faith. But what has moved me to write this letter is that Censor II attributes to him many things which he does not say, things vastly more objectionable than what he does say, and that it is on the basis of these superadded charges that he founds his sweeping and far-reaching censures. It seems to me that Father General could not be aware of the nature of this censura.[124]

But the general was very well aware of the nature of the censures, particularly the second one. Of primary concern to him, however, was not the injury to Tyrrell but the injury that he judged Tyrrell had done to traditional apologetics. Thus he fixed on just a few words from Smith's final paragraph as validating the reprisals against Tyrrell and the English writers, and therefore he concluded his annual letter of assessment of the English Province: "These expressions appeared to me to be reasonable, and I believe, put things in their proper place; and so there was no reason to change anything in my letter to Fr. Gerard."[125]

That letter, based on reports from consultors in each of the religious houses, was dated 1 April 1900 and probably crossed the urgent letters from Gerard and Smith of that same date. In this letter Martín anonymously quoted two complaints—whether from one source or two, he did not say—about Tyrrell regarding the retreat he had preached the previous autumn to Jesuit scholastics at St. Beuno's: "There is some debate about his prudence and orthodoxy"; and "What that Father said about the presence of Christ in the Most Holy Eucharist seems less than sound; and what he said against the eternality of punishments is at least rash. He said almost nothing that was not wanting some correction." On the basis of these two remarks, and no doubt also taking into account all the recent allegations—without, however, being swayed by the many testimonies in support of Tyrrell—the general drew the following conclusions:

I am deeply grieved that the spiritual formation of Our Scholastics is committed to such Fathers. . . . Of course, I have no doubt about Father Tyrrell's orthodoxy, but since these complaints come not only from that quarter but also from elsewhere, I cannot be moved concerning this matter and must make the following observation: that a man who speaks and writes in such a way as to give occasion to many people to make such judgments is not a man who writes and speaks as befits men of the Society, nor therefore can superiors allow that man to have such an office without taking great precautions. Therefore, since I know for certain from reliable written testimonies that Father Tyrrell both in speaking and in writing has disturbed the consciences of many of Ours and of externs, and also has scandalized some, Your Reverence is not to allow that Father to preach the Spiritual Exercises either to Ours or to the secular clergy or to nuns, nor to hold conferences for students at Oxford and Cambridge.[126]

Gerard pondered his dwindling options for several days before deciding to appeal through Rudolf Meyer. Martín's latest prescription regarding Tyrrell, Gerard confided to Meyer on 9 April, "completely upset me, & filled me with consternation." Did the general realize that he was effectively imposing total silence upon Tyrrell?

For a man, especially such a man as he, thus branded as dangerous will inevitably shut up altogether, & as his best defense adopt an attitude of absolute silence. But this will cause many inconveniences. He has more power amongst *men* by a long way, than any of our Fathers in London, being sought not only by those whose Faith is weak, many of whom he alone—as I know—can retain, but by educated Catholics of the old-fashioned sturdy school who declare that he does them more good than any director they ever had. So with the Secular Clergy. He is more sought for to give their retreats than any one else, it being precisely the better & sounder men that ask for him, and those who have made retreats under him declare that they have learnt more from him than from any other. Now if he is to be suddenly withdrawn from public offices, & it comes to be understood that he is not available for such work, there will be excited an amount of wonder & vexation that it is not easy to realise. Of course it is only those who criticise that make themselves heard:—those who approve & admire say nothing and may easily be unnoticed, although undoubtedly they are far the more numerous party.

Gerard then put himself entirely on the line and proposed a condition that would cost him dearly. He urged that the

embargo laid upon Fr. Tyrrell be removed, on condition that I go bail for him and undertake that nothing shall occur henceforth to which any just exception can be taken. I feel sure that I can secure this. Throughout this painful period, as Fr. Charnley also found, in spite of his extreme sensitiveness, & the distress he undoubtedly suffered, he has behaved exceedingly well, & shown himself as tractable & submissive as could be desired. I think that he is particularly disposed to take in good part whatever I say to him, & to accept any condition from me, & if what I ask should be conceded I will take care to lay down such as shall obviate all peril—making myself personally responsible for the result.[127]

The general took Gerard at his word, held him personally responsible, and would soon remove him from office.

Meanwhile, on 7 April, Martín drafted a reply to Gerard's letter of 1 April, that crossed Gerard's of 9 April to Meyer. Martín told Gerard not to fear. If slanders arose because of a sincere and clear explanation of Catholic truth—such as the new article that Tyrrell was to write—then the English fathers ought spontaneously to embrace them, after the example of the English Jesuit martyrs of old who would not have been borne to glory had they let fear of persecution deter their defense of truth.[128]

As we are about to see, however, the intertwined issues of Tyrrell's writings—particularly his "A Perverted Devotion"— and liberalism among English Jesuits were to become even more complicated and alarming to Roman authorities.

NOTES

1. Cardinal Herbert Vaughan and the Bishops of the Province of Westminister, "The Church and Liberal Catholicism: A Joint Pastoral

Letter," dated 29 December 1900 and published in the *Tablet* 97 (5, 12 January 1901) 8–12, 50–52. The "liberalism" condemned in this pastoral refers to theological liberalism—more specifically to that liberty taken by such recent "troublers of the household" as the layman St. George Jackson Mivart (on whom see n. 62 and pp. 131–40 below) to theologize and publish without prior ecclesiastical censorship. But the reader's attention is called to the discussion in the previous chapter on the connection drawn by official Vatican documents between theological liberalism and the various other liberal-isms of the nineteenth century.

2. Reported by Maisie Ward, *The Wilfrid Wards and the Transition*, vol. 2, *Insurrection versus Resurrection* (London: Sheed & Ward, 1937), p. 134.

3. My 1975 doctoral dissertation, "The Foundations and Genesis of George Tyrreli's Philosophy of Religion and Apologetic"(St. Louis University), revised and published as *George Tyrrell: In Search of Catholicism* gives a full account of the joint pastoral episode from then-available sources. See *George Tyrrell*, pp. 143–65. See also Mary Jo Weaver, "George Tyrrell and the Joint Pastoral Letter," *Downside Review* 99 (January 1981) 18–39. On the connection between liberalism and modernism, Gabriel Daly, *Transcendence and Immanence*, p. 4, contends that "there remains no convincing reason for distinguishing between 'modernism' and 'liberal Catholicism' or between the 'modernism' of Tyrrell, Blondel, or von Hügel in respect of neo-scholastic orthodoxy as it was then understood and practised." Daly's probably will not be the last word on the argument, but I regard it as substantive and accept it for purposes of the present study.

4. George Tyrrell at this time was banished to a country mission at Richmond-in-Swaledale, having been removed from the staff of the *Month* for his literary indiscretions. See Schultenover, *George Tyrrell*, pp. 91–112.

5. See obituary notice of James Hayes, LN 168 (July 1907) 202–206.

6. Hayes to Colley, 5 October 1902, AEPSJ, V/8.5.

7. Hayes himself had been an object of such a slanderous report. Thus the obvious feeling in his question. In a letter of 13 May 1899 to Martín, Hayes's then provincial John Gerard wrote from a Jesuit parish in Liverpool: "Fr. Rector (James Hayes) has given up all alcohol bc. of accusations against him (which were too strong)." ARSJ, ANGL 1017.II.54 (my paraphrase of Gerard's nearly illegible Latin script). The issue of excessive drink comes up repeatedly in the correspondence to and from Rome over the years covered by my research,

1880–1914. Some cases of alcoholism were definitely involved, but the correspondence points up what the English were complaining about: inability on the part of the Latins to understand the non-Latins.

8. Hayes to Colley, 5 October 1902, AEPSJ, V/8.5. How extreme Martín's oversight of the English Province was can be judged by the following example regarding the use of alcoholic beverages. Every Jesuit province kept a book of customs observed throughout the year—regarding such practices as daily order and how feast days are celebrated. These custom books were regularly revised and sent to Martín for approval. In 1900 at the height of proceedings against Tyrrell and the other writers of the English Province, the English provincial John Gerard sent the general the revised custom book. The minutes of the next consultors' meeting of the English Province contained the following telling entry: "2) <u>Custom Book</u>. The General approved the new Custom Book, but suggested a few alterations. As his Paternity did not seem to be aware of the wine measure in use in the province it was decided to send him specimens of wine & liquor glasses in use" [!]. Meeting of 24 April 1900, Minute Books, in the care of the provincial of the English Province of the Society of Jesus, London.

9. John Gerard (1840–1912) served as provincial superior of the English Province from 8 September 1897 to 1 January 1901.

10. *Memorias*, fl. 33r–47r, 78r–v, 83v–84v. The issue of Martín's character and personality is dealt with at length in the last chapter.

11. Hayes to Colley, 25 September 1902, AEPSJ, V/8.5. Meyer was from the Missouri Province.

12. Hayes to Colley, 5 October 1902. Emphasis added.

13. How political and ecclesiastical elements combine and confuse issues is recounted smartly in Fogarty, *Vatican*, pp. 115–94. A key figure in the formation and control of opinion, as well as in the confusion of such issues as political liberalism, theological liberalism, and Americanism is the Neapolitan Jesuit Salvatore Brandi (1852–1915). Brandi studied theology at Woodstock College in Maryland under Camillo Mazzella (1875–1878), then, after several years in pastoral work, taught theology there (1884–1891). In 1891 he was appointed to the staff of *La Civiltà Cattolica*, a semi-official organ of the Vatican, entrusted to the Jesuits. He enjoyed a close relationship with Leo XIII and Pius X, beginning in 1893 when Leo appointed him advocate for the then Cardinal Sarto (soon to be Pope Pius X), whose *exequatur* as Patriarch of Venice had been refused by the Italian government, which claimed the right of nomination as formerly exercised by the emperor of Austria. Partly due to Brandi's pleading, Sarto eventually entered Venice. Brandi's obituary notice in *Woodstock Letters* 44 (1915)

433–35 (reprinted from *America* [2 October 1915]) notes: "from that day dated a close friendship between Father Brandi and the future Pope, which grew in intimacy owing to the fact that every second Monday, Father Brandi, after he had assumed the direction of the magazine in 1905, had to take to the Holy Father the advance sheets of the coming number." Brandi was an ardent partisan of monarchists and opponent of liberals of any color. As editor of *La Civiltà*, he was an intimate of Vatican circles in general and of Mgr. Rafael Merry del Val in particular. He was a chief source of information and opinion for Luis Martín. In this connection, it is important to note Martín's early and furtive attachment to *La Civiltà*. As a seminarian in Burgos in 1864, he became intensely interested in political history and, contrary to rules, began reading in Spanish newspapers articles translated from *La Civiltà*. "The Civilta cattolica was at the time for me the most incontestable authority about politics, and consequently its opinions and suggestions were received . . . like articles of faith." *Memorias*, fl. 101r.

14. The one used for the present study is titled *Select Letters of Our Very Reverend Fathers General to the Fathers and Brothers of the Society of Jesus* (Woodstock, MD: Woodstock College, 1900), pp. 501–46.

15. *Renovation Reading*, rev., enl. ed. (Woodstock, MD: Woodstock College, 1931).

16. On 16 August 1773 Pope Clement XIV yielded to extreme pressure from the Bourbons—the threat of schism of France, Portugal, and Spain—and issued the brief *Dominus ac Redemptor* dissolving the Society of Jesus. On 7 August 1814, upon the collapse of the Napoleonic Empire, Pope Pius VII restored the Society with the bull *Sollicitudo omnium ecclesiarum*. See Bangert, *History of the Society of Jesus*, pp. 302–303, 366–410, 422–28.

17. *Select Letters*, par. 2–3.

18. Ibid., par. 3.

19. Ibid., par. 7–8.

20. Ibid., par. 10.

21. Ibid. Note the similarity of tone between this letter and what Thurston complained of in one of the censures Tyrrell received: "The dogmatic tone of the censor, without a shade of misgiving that what he pronounced to be erroneous and scandalous was really and infallibly erroneous and scandalous, just as if he embodied in himself the whole Catholic Church, has done more mischief than anything. And then he goes on to read Fr Tyrrell a lecture on his parva scientia, as if he were a little boy not old enough to understand the mysteries of theology. Surely when a theologian is asked his opinion of certain propositions he might confine himself to the question before him and

abstain from insulting the writer." Thurston to Chandlery, 18 February 1900, ARSJ, ANGL 1021.IB.7. Although Martín was piqued by those who injected the Latin-*vs.*-Saxon polarization into issues (see above, pp. 77–78), contemporary researchers suggest that there is more to that polarization than rhetoric—although rhetoric plays a large part in the expression of cultural differences. See Walter Ong, S.J., *Orality and Literacy: The Technologizing of the Word* (London and New York: Methuen, 1982). What I am suggesting here is that the source of some of the difficulty between Roman curial officials and non-Mediterranean peoples is the cultural characteristic of machismo which determines rhetoric. Non-Mediterraneans who are ignorant of the rhetoric of machismo find it insulting, while Mediterraneans who are ignorant of northern European rhetoric do not understand why offense is taken. See the illuminating essays in *Honor and Shame and the Unity of the Mediterranean*, ed. David D. Gilmore, a special publication of the American Anthropological Association, no. 22 (Washington, D.C.: American Anthropological Association, 1987), esp. Gilmore's introductory essay, "The Shame of Dishonor," pp. 2–21; also Margaret M. and David D. Gilmore, " 'Machismo': A Psychodynamic Approach (Spain)," *Journal of Psychological Anthropology* 2 (1979) 281–300, and George R. Saunders, "Men and Women in Southern Europe: A Review of Some Aspects of Cultural Complexity," *Journal of Psychoanalytic Anthropology* 4 (Fall 1981) 435–66.

22. Martín was current on the criticisms from around the world of the Jesuit formation program, because in 1891 he was summoned by the then-General Anton Maria Anderledy to the curia and given the special assignment of analyzing and summarizing the voluminous reports from all the provinces on the proposed changes in the course of studies for young Jesuits. Chandlery wrote: "To Father Anderledy's surprise he [Martín] did the work in an incredibly short time, and it is said that he summed up the results on a single slip of paper— *negative*." Chandlery, "Biographical Sketch," LN 167 (April 1907) 73.

23. *Select Letters*, par. 21.

24. Ibid., par. 24.

25. Ibid., par. 25. Martín wrote of these matters with such passionate conviction because, as we shall see below (pp. 207–16), he himself had endured many years of personal torment from indulging a morbid curiosity.

26. Ibid., par. 28.

27. Ibid., par. 30–31.

28. Ibid., par. 34–35.

29. Ibid., par. 36. Had Martín been at all sympathetic to what the

majority of the Western world was fighting for, he would have realized that their complaint was precisely against "that atrocious maxim" as invoked by repressive monarchies.

30. Ibid., par. 37–39.

31. Ibid., par. 46.

32. *Memorias*, fl. 2280r.

33. *Memorias*, fl. 2280r. It is interesting to note that Lucas' articles are not listed in either of the large Jesuit bibliographical sources that ought to list them: Edmund F. Sutcliffe, s.j., *Bibliography of the English Province of the Society of Jesus, 1773–1953* (Roehampton [London]: Manresa Press, 1957), and Carlos Sommervogel, s.j., *Moniteur bibliographique de la Compagnie de Jésus*, vols. 11–20 (1894–1899). The latter are bound supplements to the Jesuit journal *Études*.

34. See above, p. 59, n. 33.

35. Martín to Gerard, 16 May 1899, Rome. ARSJ, Registrum Epistolarum ad Provinciam Angliae (hereafter, Reg. Epp. Angl.), vol. 5 (1897–1907), p. 59. It is unclear whether or not Martín received this account from Turinaz personally or from his account published in his diocesan paper *Semaine réligieuse* and reproduced as a curiosity by *Le Temps*, when Félix Klein reproduced his very similar account in *Americanism*, p. 262 n. 1.

36. To give one example: on 30 August 1899, Martín replied to a report by Gerard on the state of affairs in the English Province: "Concerning the journal 'The Month' edited by Ours. The following have been reported by a certain Father of the Province: 'In the July issue there is a 12-page article by a certain woman on poetry. And even though Fathers Rickaby and Tyrrell are excellent writers and highly qualified and deal with most serious issues, they seem to be lazy. A certain writer in the journal 'Weekly Register' recently stated that the readers of the 'Month' are laid low by boredom and somnolence." Martín to Gerard, ARSJ, Reg. Epp. Angl., vol. 5, p. 73. Although Martín reported this delation without comment, the clear implication for the provincial was that he was to remedy the situation at once.

37. A full exposition of events surrounding a crucial letter of 12 February 1900 from Martín to Gerard is given above, pp. 88–92.

38. Gerard opposed Martín on numerous issues, on which see above, pp. 66 and 75–113, and below, pp. 134–38, passim.

39. Minutes for provincial consultors' meeting of 10–11 June 1897, AEPSJ, Minute Books.

40. Joseph Reinach, a lifelong student of the Dreyfus affair, from the very beginning credited and propagated the myth of a Jesuit plot against Dreyfus. His views were broadcast by Yves Guyot, editor of

Le Siècle, and picked up by the Oxford historian (and graduate of a Jesuit college) Frederick Cornwallis, who, under the pseudonym Fred Conybeare, wrote *The Dreyfus Case* (London: Allen, 1898). It was the first English treatment of the Affair and exercised considerable influence on subsequent English studies. Conybeare's conclusion indicates how perilous Jesuit standing was in England as well as in France—a standing that weighed heavily on the Jesuit general: "Thus a larger problem awaits the French than the mere rehabilitation of Dreyfus and the retrieving of their national character. . . . They must reform the army itself. . . . The first step will be to emancipate the army from the Jesuits who have fastened their teeth into it: and this can be done by enforcing the decrees of 1880 and so obliging the Jesuits to quit France. We hope that no more of them will drift into England. Secondly the Jesuit military schools in the Rue des Postes and elsewhere must be closed and a law made that no young men shall be admitted into St. Cyr and the Polytechnique who have not been educated up to the moment of their admission in the national lycees, which are not confessional schools. Thirdly the state must look after the military clubs provided for the common soldier, and see that they are not mere centres of Jesuit propaganda, where such sheets as those of MM. Maurras, Drumont and Judet are alone set before him . . ." (p. 317). The Jesuit journal *Études* and French church officials in general maintained a hands-off policy, which left them open to the Dreyfusard accusation that they at best tolerated and at worst instigated the anti-Dreyfus movement. The failure of French Jesuits to speak out, complained their English confreres, led to a general suspicion that Jesuits everywhere were involved in sedition against Jews and due process. Certain articles by Salvatore Brandi and others in *La Civiltà Cattolica*, the Jesuit-run semi-official Vatican journal, would have supplied all the evidence the Dreyfusards wanted for their contention. But some balance has been restored to the historical foundation of the Jesuit myth by the studies of Louis Caperan, published as *L'Anticlericalisme et l'Affaire Dreyfus* (Toulouse: Imprimerie Regionale, 1948). On the prevalence of French Catholic anti-Semitism during this period, see Misner, *Social Catholicism*, pp. 234–36.

41. *Memorias*, fl. 2281r–v. This letter is missing from its proper file in ARSJ. Several other documents used by Martín for his *Memorias* were also not found in their appropriate files in ARSJ.

42. Edouard Jouard Drumont (1844–1917), journalist and anti-Semitic leader, founded the anti-Semitic daily *Libre parole* in April 1892. His unsavory role in the Dreyfus affair is well documented in, among

other places, Guy Chapman, *The Dreyfus Case: A Reassessment* (London: Hart-Davis, 1963).

43. *Memorias*, fl. 2282r. Martín was here probably referring to England's defiance of Rome dating back to Henry VIII.

44. *Memorias*, fl. 2282r–v. When Edmund Sheridan Purcell was about to publish his *The Life of Cardinal Manning, Archbishop of Westminster*, 2 vols. (London: Macmillan, 1895), an alarm was raised among English Jesuits to defend themselves against disclosures about their strained relationship with the cardinal and his dim view of Jesuits. The then-provincial Francis Scoles (1840–1909) held a meeting with his consultors on 12 April 1894 to decide on a course of action. Among the minutes of that meeting are the following remarks: "The very evident spirit of hostility which pervades the late Cardinal's remarks makes them less formidable, and our friends may defend us more powerfully than we can, and will provoke less controversy. F. General could certainly forbid recrimination." AEPSJ, Minute Books. Another intemperate "history," *Black Monks*, by Ethelred L. Taunton, appeared in 1897 and treated the early English Jesuits roughly. Pollen answered temperately but anonymously with "The Rise of the Anglo-Benedictine Congregation," *Month* 90 (December 1897) 581–600, and drew praise from Cardinal Vaughan and the Benedictines. See "Notes," LN 24 (January 1898) 358–60, and letters of Rudolf Meyer to Pollen of 18 November 1897 and 22 February 1898, AEPSJ, RZ/1. So far, archives have not yielded a clear answer to the question why Pollen declined to write a history of the English Jesuits such as his provincial and consultors wanted. But apparently Martín concurred with Pollen, at least for the time being, and Pollen's friend and fellow historian from the Missouri Province, Thomas A. Hughes, wrote cryptically in the preface to his large and scholarly *The History of the Society of Jesus in North America, Colonial and Federal*, 4 vols. (Cleveland: Burrows; London and New York: Longmans, Green, 1907), p. vii, "A number of reasons . . . induced the historian of that [English] Province to seek relief from a piece of historical work, which appeared as dissonant in general tone and temper from English history, as its subject was distant from English soil. Hence, for that first century and a half, it was transferred to the pages of this narrative. . . . So transferred, that portion had to be prefixed. And it now supplies an appropriate and even necessary train of antecedents to the later history of the Order in English-speaking North America."

45. Gerard to Martín, 7 May 1899, ARSJ, ANGL 1017.II.52.

46. Gerard to Martín, 9 May 1899, ARSJ, ANGL 1017.II.53. The bishop of Newport was the Benedictine John Cuthbert Hedley (1837–

1915). The initials "R. D." perhaps stood for "Reverend Doctor." Hedley, though not a strong public leader, was the acknowledged intellectual leader and spokesman for the English bishops on important matters. He was instrumental, for example, in gaining Rome's permission in 1895 for Catholics to attend the Universities of Oxford and Cambridge. See J. A. Wilson, *The Life of Bishop Hedley* (London: Kenedy, 1930).

47. Martín to Gerard, 16 May 1899, ARSJ, Reg. Epp. Angl., p. 59.

48. I found no record of this exchange in the ARSJ. It is recounted in Martín's *Memorias*, fl. 2317r–v. There Martín recalls that it was perhaps in January 1899 that he first learned of Archbishop Ireland's conference scheduled at Farm Street. Martín acknowledges that he was neglectful in this matter, apparently because, having heard about the conference so many months in advance, he failed to take the proper measures to stop it. However, Martín's recollection of these dates seems to be inconsistent with Charnley's. The important point, however, is that Martín felt that he himself had to share the blame for not acting promptly and vigorously enough. He succeeded in preventing Ireland's talking in France, but failed in England, where he thought he had much more advance notice. Doubtless he was all the more frustrated to read the report of Peter Gallwey who, in his official capacity as consultor of the Farm Street residence, wrote that the man responsible for letting the Jesuit Hall (i.e., Charnley himself) was incompetent as prefect of the church. See Gallwey to Martín, 19 July 1899, ARSJ, ANGL 1018.VI.32.

49. Gerard to Martín, 16 July 1899, ARSJ, ANGL 1017.II.61. Charnley to Meyer, 7 February 1900, recorded in Martín, *Memorias*, fl. 2317r–2318v. This letter of Charnley's was missing from its proper file in ARSJ.

50. Martín to Gerard, 6 August 1899, ARSJ, Reg. Epp. Angl., vol. 5, p. 66. Charnley had indicated to Meyer that he, not Gerard, had given the permission but that in fact only three Jesuits had attended—two Farm Street Jesuits (whose names he did not divulge) plus the former provincial from the province of Turin, Giuseppe C. Sasia. Charnley to Meyer, 7 February 1900, quoted in Martín, *Memorias*, fl. 2318r. Gerard, however, reported to Martín, 16 July 1899, ARSJ, ANGL 1017.II.61, that the other two Jesuits were Joseph Bampton and Michael Gavin. Although Vaughan had not attended Ireland's address, he did attend the Duke's *conversazione* later that evening at the Grafton Galleries, an honor given only once before—to Cardinal Newman on the occasion of his investiture as cardinal. James H. Moynihan, in his *The Life of Archbishop John Ireland* (New York: Harper &

Brothers, 1953), pp. 149–50, quotes a letter of Mrs. William Gibson, wife of Lord Ashbourne, to Abbé Klein: " 'The impression at the meeting of the Catholic Union was very good. He [Ireland] met many of the principal men, Lord Halifax, Balfour, the Anglican Bishop of Rochester, and almost all the important Catholics in the world of ideas. One of the Franciscan dignitaries, who had become very reactionary and had read an essay against Americanism at the Roger Bacon Society, at the mere sight of the Archbishop and even without the opportunity of speaking to him, was completely changed in attitude.' " Ireland also spent a night with the Lord Ashbournes. Tyrrell was also a friend of the Lord Ashbournes'. But there is nothing more than circumstantial evidence to suggest that Tyrrell and Ireland met on this or any other occasion.

51. The reference is to Cornelius Clifford, on whom see above, pp. 93 and 98–103, and below, pp. 126 n. 88 and 129 n. 108

52. Gerard to Martín, 13 August 1899, from Stonyhurst, ARSJ, ANGL 1017.II.64.

53. Even Fr. Vincent Hornyold, who lived at St. Aloysius parish in Oxford and favored the rule, complained to Martín. "Archbishop Scarisbrick O.S.B. said to me with a smile . . . Cardinal Ledochowski seems to have the matter much at heart & writes periodically to the English Bishops, to enquire whether they see to the observance of his regulation . . . , but he added, nobody does anything in the matter, and there it remains. I presume it is thought that we [Jesuits] are more likely to obey than other Religious, and hence the reason why nothing is said to enforce the observance of the 'Clausura' except in our case. I am sorry to say . . . that Religious of other Orders, suspect that it is a consequence of abuses having taken place in our residences." Hornyold to Martín, 28 August 1899, ARSJ, ANGL 1017.II.66.

54. *Memorias*, fl. 2283r–v.

55. This letter from Gerard to Meyer was not found in ARSJ, but is quoted by Martín, albeit inaccurately, in *Memorias*, fl. 2283r–v. Whenever Gerard wrote to Martín's assistant for the English-speaking provinces, he wrote in English. Charles Russell, 1st Baron Russell of Killowen (1832–1900), was the first Roman Catholic to hold the office of lord chief justice since the Reformation.

56. Gerard to Meyer, 19 December 1899, not found in ARSJ but quoted by Martín with inaccuracies in *Memorias*, fl. 2283v–2284r. The article referred to was in *La Civiltà Cattolica* for 16 December 1899, p. 793.

57. This letter of Thurston to Meyer was not found in the ARSJ, but is reported in *Memorias*, fl. 2284r. Herbert Thurston (1856–1939)

was a long-time friend of Tyrrell's. See Schultenover, *George Tyrrell*, pp. 32–38, and Joseph Crehan, S.J., *Father Thurston* (London and New York: Sheed & Ward, 1950), pp. 48–72.

58. *Memorias*, fl. 2284v. Martín's reply to Thurston and Thurston's two articles were not found either in ARSJ or in AEPSJ. I found no article by Thurston in the *Month* on the Jewish question, but two by the editor Sydney F. Smith: "The Jesuits and the Dreyfus Case," and "Mr. Conybeare Again," *Month* 93 (February and April 1899) 113–34, 405–12.

59. *Memorias*, fl. 2284v–2285r.

60. *Memorias*, fl. 2285r.

61. On this "Perverted Devotion" episode, see Schultenover, *George Tyrrell*, pp. 91–108.

62. The writings of St. George Jackson Mivart, among others, were currently agitating ecclesiastical officials in England and Rome and undoubtedly influenced decisions made with regard to Tyrrell. On the implications of the Mivart affair for Tyrrell, the English Jesuits, and the impending condemnation of liberalism see below, pp. 131–43.

63. Martín to Charnley, 7 January 1900, Rome, ARSJ, Reg. Epp. Angl., vol. 5, p. 82. Tyrrell's small book, *Notes on the Catholic Doctrine of Purity* (Roehampton [London]: Manresa Press, 1897) was published for private circulation primarily among spiritual directors and confessors.

64. Josef Flöck (1845–1904), born in Koblenz, taught scripture at St. Beuno's Jesuit theologate in North Wales in the year 1875–1876. He was assigned to the German College in Rome in 1878, where he was in turn prefect of studies (9 years), rector (3 years) and procurator (14 years). He taught Oriental languages at the Gregorian University in 1886–1887 and was an examiner of candidates for degrees. He has no publications listed in the *Moniteur bibliographique de la Compagnie de Jésus*, and there is no evidence to suggest that he was a qualified theologian. See Flöck's obituary notice in LN 28 (January 1905) 72. Giuseppe-Maria Piccirelli (1841–1918) had been a professor at Woodstock College in Maryland with Mazzella when Meyer was a student there, 1871–1874. Frail health and the harsh climate compelled him to return to his home province of Naples in 1876. Unlike Flöck, he has a number of publications, mostly on devotion to the Sacred Heart and on the Thomistic/scholastic distinction between essence and existence. See Patrick J. Dooley, S.J., *Woodstock and Its Makers*, Woodstock Letters 56 (Woodstock, MD: College Press, 1927), p. 81.

65. This letter from Charnley was not located in ARSJ. Its contents are reported in *Memorias*, fl. 2286r.

66. Ibid. This letter too was not found in ARSJ. It is perhaps the one dated 23 January 1900 and referred to in Martín to Charnley, 5 February 1900 (see below, n. 71).

67. See above, pp. 81–83.

68. *Memorias*, fl. 2286r–v. See also Martín to Gerard, 12 February 1900, Reg. Epp. Angl., vol. 5, p. 86.

69. This letter was not located in ARSJ. Martín quoted it in Latin in *Memorias*, fl. 2286v, as it was no doubt written in Latin. Martín did not identify the sender.

70. *Memorias*, fl. 2286v.

71. Charnley to Martín, 23 January 1900, not found in ARSJ; reported in *Memorias*, fl. 2287r.

72. AEPSJ, Minute Books, 8 February 1900.

73. Martín to Charnley, 5 February 1900, Reg. Epp. Angl., vol. 5, pp. 83–84.

74. Sydney Smith to Meyer, 2 February 1900, from Farm Street, London. ARSJ, ANGL 1021.I^B.5.

75. *Memorias*, fl. 2288r.

76. Ibid.

77. Martín to Charnley, 12 February 1900, Rome, ARSJ, Reg. Epp. Angl., vol. 5, p. 85; Martín to Gerard, 12 February 1900, ibid., pp. 85–88.

78. Martín to Gerard, 12 February 1900, ibid., pp. 85–86. Per custom the letter was in Latin. The translation here and below is mine.

79. Ibid., p. 86.

80. See above, pp. 84–85.

81. Martín to Gerard, 12 February 1900, p. 86.

82. Émile Joseph Dillon (1854–1933) was for 33 years correspondent of the *Daily Telegraph* (London) in Russia. A constant traveler, he was friends with Loisy and Bishop Eudoxe-Irénée Mignot and a regular but anonymous contributor on religious affairs to the *Contemporary Review*. See Loome, *Liberal Catholicism, Reform Catholicism, Modernism*, pp. 273–74, and Alec R. Vidler, *A Variety of Catholic Modernists* (Cambridge: Cambridge University Press, 1970), pp. 166–67. The Hon. William Gibson (1868–1942), from 1913 2nd Lord Ashbourne, author of *The Abbé de Lamennais and the Liberal Catholic Movement in France*, was a "modernist" and friend of Tyrrell's and a regular contributor to newspapers and journals; see Vidler, *Variety of Catholic Modernists*, pp. 176–77. Richard Bagot (1860–1921), novelist and journalist, spent most of his professional life in Italy. He published in

Italian and British reviews usually on political and literary subjects but occasionally also on religious matters. His recent novel, *A Roman Mystery* (1899), caused a flap. On St. George Jackson Mivart see below, pp. 131–40. Dr. William Francis Barry (1849–1930), priest and professor of theology at the major Roman Catholic seminary at Oscott, authored several articles on the Americanist controversy, particularly for the *Catholic Times*; but see especially his "An American Religious Crusade," *National Review* 193 (March 1899) 115–28. Barry was one of the first to see and declare that Americanism was neither American nor theological but political.

83. American Jesuits opposed Ireland on most questions and in general were in league with Ireland's chief rival, Archibishop Michael Corrigan of New York. See Fogarty, *Vatican*, pp. 42–43, 60, 75, 128, 142, 157–59, 171, 176, 185.

84. Martín to Gerard, 12 February 1900, pp. 87–88. The quotation from Newman is found in his *Apologia pro vita sua* (London: Oxford University Press, 1913), p. 352.

85. Martín to Gerard, 12 February 1900, p. 88. The biblical references are 1 John 2:18–19 and 1 Cor. 5:6–7, 13.

86. Ward Family Papers, St. Andrews University Library, VII, 205a (3). Note that Merry del Val did not mention Spain. Gary Lease, in "Merry del Val and Tyrrell: A Modernist Struggle," *Downside Review* 102 (April 1984) 133–56, here p. 137, quotes this passage and observes that "Merry del Val, however, does not tell Ward that it is he whom he has in mind, among others, when he makes those remarks."

87. Arthur James Balfour (1848–1930), statesman and philosopher, is considered by Alec Vidler (*Scenes from a Clerical Life* [London: Collins, 1977], p. 172) to have been "the most interesting Prime Minister of this century" and by Owen Chadwick (*The Victorian Church*, 2 vols. [London: Black, 1966 and 1970] 2:424) as "a Christian philosopher of the first rank." See John David Root's fine historical essay "The Philosophical and Religious Thought of Arthur James Balfour (1848–1930)," *Journal of British Studies* 19 (Spring 1980) 120–41. George Wyndham (1863–1913), statesman and man of letters, became Balfour's private secretary in 1887 and was a member of the House of Commons from 1889 until his death. Both he and Balfour were much involved in the governing of Ireland and were instrumental in the passage of two much-disputed Land Acts (1891 and 1903). See *Dictionary of National Biography*, vol. 24. (1912–1921). Henry Sidgwick (1839–1900) is the well-known agnostic professor of moral philosophy of Trinity College, Cambridge, who earlier in his career resigned his fellowship at Trinity rather than sign the Thirty-Nine Articles of Relig-

ion. He married Balfour's sister Eleanor in 1876. See ibid., vol. 22, Supplement. Sir Mountstuart Elphinstone Grant Duff (1829–1906), statesman and author of numerous memoirs and articles mostly on politics, traveled broadly and cultivated a wide circle of socially and politically prominent figures. See ibid., vol. 23, Supplement. Balfour, Wyndham, and Sidgwick were members of the Synthetic Society. Grant Duff was not.

88. Thurston to Chandlery, 18 February 1900, ARSJ, ANGL 1021.IB.7, pp. 1–2. Cornelius Clifford (1859–1938) entered the Society of Jesus from Fordham University in 1879. He studied theology at Innsbruck (1891–1892) and Louvain (1892–1893) but was dismissed from the Society on 2 January 1893, the reason for dismissal being stated cryptically in *Dimissi ex Societate* (1811–1965), Archives of the Maryland Province, Georgetown University, p. 39, as "contra 6 m~." (i.e., "contra sextum mandatum" = "against the Sixth Commandment," with emphasis placed on *dismissal*, rather than leaving of his own accord, as noted in the Maryland provincial consultors' book for 17 January 1893, p. 45). He re-entered the Society in the English Province in 1894. After having studied and worked in various Jesuit houses on a trial basis, he was ordained to the priesthood in February 1898. But in the summer of 1899, completely disillusioned with the governance of the Society, he requested and was granted dismissal. Gerard to Martín, 13 August 1899, ARSJ, ANGL 1017.II.64, indicates that Clifford had secretly requested incardination in Archbishop Ireland's diocese. Ireland agreed pending satisfactory resolution of Clifford's dimissorial process. Martín must have found this news greatly disturbing. Clifford's request for release from the Jesuits was summarily granted, and he seems to have gone directly to St. Paul, Minnesota, where he taught very briefly at St. Thomas College, before returning to the East Coast and eventually settling down as pastor of Our Lady of Mercy Church, Whippany, New Jersey (29 years) and part-time lecturer in philosophy at Columbia University (27 years). There is no record in the St. Paul archdiocesan archives that he was ever incardinated in that diocese. See Matthew Hoehn, ed., *Catholic Authors: Contemporary Biographical Sketches, 1930–1947* (Newark, NJ: St. Mary's Abbey, 1948), pp. 143–44. Anton Maria Anderledy (1819–1892) of the German province was the general of the Society of Jesus from 1883 to his death. Martín succeeded him. See also below, n. 108.

89. Tyrrell was apparently importuned by Cardinal Vaughan himself to assist in the Mivart case. See above, p. 85.

90. The problem was first regarded rather casually as nothing more than a case of dyspepsia, but Tyrrell learned in May 1900 that

he was suffering from a kidney or liver disease or both. He eventually died in 1909 of renal failure—or of what was then called "Bright's Disease." I have treated at some length the speculations about the effect of his health problems on his life and thought. See my *George Tyrrell*, pp. 348–49, 354–55; chap. 6, nn. 95, 114, 117; chap. 7, n. 200.

91. "Integerrimae vitae" = "of utmost integrity." Apparently, Thurston was passing over the dispute about Thomism *vs.* Suarezianism between Tyrrell and other faculty members at Stonyhurst four years previously that got him transferred to London. This confrontation certainly made Tyrrell a marked man among very influential members of his province, and subjectively it marked the beginning of his disaffection from the Society of Jesus. On this dispute see ibid., pp. 36–37. ARSJ, ANGL 1021.I contains twelve documents on the dispute.

92. Thurston's reference to a "fall" makes the identification of Klein and Sullivan puzzling. As to the former, Thurston was doubtless referring to Abbé Félix Klein (1862–1953), professor at the Institut Catholique in Paris, over whose head the Americanism controversy broke in 1897 because of his editing and prefacing of the French translation of Fr. Walter Elliott's *Life of Father Hecker* (1891). But however heated and vicious the Americanist controversy became, it seemed not seriously to have damaged Klein. At the height of the controversy, he was nominated for advancement to assistant professor, and the Institut's entire board of directors save one (Bishop Turinaz) voted for him. As to Sullivan, one might expect Thurston to have been referring to the later American modernist William L. Sullivan (1872–1935), but at the time of Thurston's writing, Sullivan was scarcely a year from his ordination, was working as a missionary in Kansas City, and had not yet written anything of note. For the best assessment of Sullivan, see Appleby, *"Church and Age Unite!"* On Turinaz, see above, pp. 40–41, 55 n. 6, 75, and 118 n. 35.

93. Thurston was not politically astute. Testimony from the figures mentioned would only have counted against Tyrrell. A recommendation from Anglicans would have convicted Tyrrell of liberalism, and Wilfrid Ward was regarded in Vatican circles as even more dangerous than avowed liberals because he was tainted without knowing it. Merry del Val told Cardinal Vaughan that Ward's thought was "in some respects . . . more harmful than Mivart's, because it steadily weakens all the screws and prepares the way for many more Mivarts in the future. It is very insidious and among converts it does incalculable harm." Merry del Val to Vaughan, AAW, Vaughan Papers, V.1/14/28. Merry del Val was a key figure in Rome's condemnation of

Anglican orders. See John Jay Hughes's excellent study, *Absolutely Null and Utterly Void: The Papal Condemnation of Anglican Orders, 1896* (Washington, DC: Corpus, 1968).

94. Thurston to Chandlery, 18 February 1900, pp. 3–6.

95. George Tyrrell, *Nova et Vetera: Informal Meditations for Times of Spiritual Dryness* (London: Longmans, Green, 1897).

96. Thurston to Chandlery, pp. 6–10. "Scandalosum, temerarium, ecclesiae injuriosum" = "scandalous, rash, injurious to the church." "Certe haereticum censeri debet" = "It ought to be censored as certainly heretical." Charles Blount (1855–1931) had completed a biennium in dogmatic theology but at that time was prefect of studies at St. Stanislaus College, Beaumont. See his obituary notice in LN 46 (1931) 148–54. William Roche (1856–1945), described by Maude Petre as "perhaps the best-loved of all his [Tyrrell's] Jesuit friends," was on the faculty at St. Mary's Hall, Stonyhurst, with Tyrrell in 1895 but was replaced in 1896 by Charles Coupe, who was less than congenial to Tyrrell. Tyrrell and Roche were also together for a time on the staff of writers for the *Month*. There is no known extant correspondence between them. See Maude D. Petre, *Autobiography and Life of George Tyrrell* [hereafter AL], 2 vols. (London: Arnold, 1912), 2:33, and *Our Dead*, Part III, January 1944–December 1945, a special volume of LN, printed for private circulation (copy at Farm Street Jesuit community library), pp. 376–84.

97. "Verax" was the pseudonym of a letter writer to the London *Times*. I have been unable to identify this figure.

98. Thurston to Chandlery, 18 February 1900, pp. 10–14. ARSJ, ANGL 1021.I^B.7, pp. 14–17.

99. Thurston to Chandlery, 18 February 1900.

100. *Memorias*, fl. 2290v.

101. Thurston to Chandlery, 20 February 1900, London, ARSJ, ANGL 1021.I^C.1.

102. Thurston to Chandlery, 21 February 1900, London, ARSJ, ANGL 1021.I^C.2. The story was not a case of conscience or a confessional matter. It was told to get the information to those who could remove the scandal and help the priest involved.

103. Chandlery to Thurston, 25 February 1900, ARSJ, Reg. Epp. Angl., vol. 5, p. 93.

104. Thurston to Chandlery, 23 February 1900, London, ARSJ, ANGL 1021.I^C.3.

105. Chandlery to Thurston, 24 February 1900, ARSJ, Reg. Epp. Angl., vol. 5, pp. 89–91.

106. "That Liberalism . . . which Cardinal Newman calls that deep,

plausible skepticism, is the heresy of our age and must be utterly rejected by Ours." Cf. above, pp. 88–92, esp. p. 91.

107. On Richard Bagot see above, pp. 90 and 124 n. 82. On "Verax," see above, p. 95 and n. 97.

108. Chandlery to Thurston, 24 February 1900, pp. 91–93. It is true that superiors pleaded continually in Clifford's favor, but it is difficult to know what Chandlery meant by Martín's insistence on the "three years" required before readmission and "the required time" before ordination. Clifford's timetable was actually this: He was dismissed on 2 January 1893 (see above, n. 88); petitioned re-entrance to the Society in England on 21 June 1893 (Clifford to Martín, 21 June 1893, ARSJ, ANGL 1006.VIII.4, one of five items in a file titled "Diversorum externorum epistolae et negotia [Cornelius Clifford aliique] 1882–1893)"]; was admitted to the English Province on 30 July 1894 after successive petitions, first by the former provincial Edward Ignatius Purbrick, who had been assigned by the current provincial John Clayton to be Clifford's confessor (Clayton to Martín, 25 November 1893, ARSJ, ANGL 1006.VIII.5), then by Clayton himself in a letter to Rudolf Meyer of 27 April 1894 (ARSJ, ANGL 1006.II.73), and finally by Richard F. Clarke, rector of the College of the Sacred Heart, Wimbledon, where Clifford was employed (Clarke to Martín, 2 July 1894, ARSJ, ANGL 1007.VII.17). Martín granted permission to readmit Clifford in a letter to Clayton of 5 June 1894, Reg. Epp. Angl., vol. 4, pp. 93–94. Clifford was ordained on 12 April 1898, less than four years after readmission—a surprisingly brief interval for a man who had once before been dismissed from the Society. It is a curious anomaly for the Jesuits at that time in their history that Clifford should be listed for the first time in the *English Province Catalog* for 1895, p. 18, as a novice at *Stonyhurst*, since the novitiate house was at Roehampton. Tyrrell was on the faculty of St. Mary's Hall, Stonyhurst, at that time.

109. Thurston to Chandlery, 28 February 1900, ARSJ, ANGL 1021.I^C.4.

110. "A brutal thunderbolt."

111. Thurston to Chandlery, 9 March 1900, ARSJ, ANGL 1021.I^C.5.

112. Tyrrell to Gerard, 14 March 1900, ARSJ, ANGL 1021.I^B.8—a 2-page handwritten covering letter to a 12-page typescript titled "A Reply to My Censors," ANGL 1021.I.^{B}.9, pages numbered 2–13.

113. As explained above, Tyrrell did not know the identity of his censors. The first was Josef Flöck; the second, Giuseppe-Maria Piccirelli. See above, pp. 84–85, 89–90, and 123 n. 64.

114. "A Reply," pp. 9–11.

115. This was a swipe at Piccirelli, who wrote on devotion to the Sacred Heart. "A Reply," p. 11.

116. S.P.N. = Sancti Patris Nostri, i.e., Ignatius of Loyola.

117. Gerard to Martín, 17 March 1900, ARSJ, ANGL 1017.II.77.

118. Martín to Gerard, 27 March 1900, ARSJ, Registrum epistolarum ad missiones assistentiae Angliae, vol. 2 (1891–1912), pp. 111–13, here, p. 111.

119. Ibid., p. 112.

120. Ibid.

121. Martín, *Memorias*, fl. 2294v–2295r.

122. Gerard to Martín, 1 April 1900, ARSJ, ANGL 1021.I^B.11.

123. Smith to Meyer, 2 February 1900, ARSJ, ANGL 1020.I^B.5, p. 2. Incidentally, Gerard to Martín, 1.10.99, ARSJ, ANGL 1017.II.67, indicates that a catalogue of books published in the English Province from June 1896 to July 1899 was sent to Rome along with two copies of each book. Included would have been Tyrrell's *Nova et Vetera, Notes on the Catholic Doctrine of Purity, Hard Sayings,* and *External Religion.*

124. Smith to Meyer, 1 April 1900, ARSJ, ANGL 1021.I^B.12, pp. 8–9.

125. Martín, *Memorias*, fl. 2295r.

126. Martín to Gerard, 1 April 1900, Reg. Epp. Angl., vol. 5, pp. 98–99. Martín, *Memorias*, fl. 2296r, alleged that Gerard's urgent letter of 1 April 1900 was precipitated by his own of that date. There appears to be a discrepancy here. Even in those days, the mail did not move so fast.

127. Gerard to Meyer, 9 April 1900, ARSJ, ANGL 1021.I^B.13.

128. Martín to Gerard, 7 April 1900, Reg. Epp. Angl., vol. 5, pp. 107–108.

4

The Joint Pastoral Affair

While the row over George Tyrrell's "A Perverted Devotion" was cooling down, the official ecclesiastical condemnation of "liberalism" was heating up. The Mivart affair—the condemnation of his writings, his excommunication, his untimely death and burial outside the Catholic Church, and the ensuing controversy, all fully and sensationally covered in the press—was a staggering blow to Catholicism in England. It is important here to note the critical parallel developments regarding Mivart's writings, among others, that were currently agitating ecclesiastical officials in England and Rome, because they influenced Rome's decisions regarding Tyrrell and the other English Jesuit writers.[1]

In late summer of 1899 St. George Jackson Mivart learned that his name appeared in the new edition of the Index of Forbidden Books. He protested at once to the Jesuit Cardinal Andreas Steinhuber, prefect of the Sacred Congregation of the Index (and resident in the same community as the Jesuit general), demanding to know the identity of his accuser and the specific charges. Steinhuber declined to reveal Mivart's accuser,[2] but merely referred to the 1893 decree condemning his infamous article "Happiness in Hell" and his two subsequent rejoinders to critics.[3] Incensed at this reply, Mivart rescinded his earlier submission. From August 1899 on, therefore, Mivart weighed heavily on the minds of church officials, all the more so now that he lately entered into the rekindled Dreyfus affair.

We have already seen how the Dreyfus affair in France had influenced the Americanist controversy and recoiled on the

Catholic Church in many places but particularly in England where critics—among whom, Mivart—pointed the finger at Jesuits and church officials either for engineering the affair or for failing to intervene.[4] When the French court upheld Dreyfus' conviction at his second trial in September 1899, Mivart published a shrill attack in the 17 October London *Times*, decrying the duplicity, if not complicity, of a hierarchy that tolerated "the vilest newspapers" and bestowed "their *imprimatur* on publications the iniquity of which is only exceeded by their marvelous absurdity."[5]

Mivart followed that attack with two more in the first week of January 1900—"The Continuity of Catholicism" and "Some Recent Catholic Apologists"[6]—regarded as intemperate by almost everyone, including Tyrrell and von Hügel. Church officials could not let such public indictments go unanswered. Thus an equally intemperate, unsigned retort appeared in the 6 January *Tablet*, the newspaper of the Catholic Archdiocese of Westminster. That article, incitingly titled "Dr. Mivart's Heresy," was almost certainly the work of Cardinal Vaughan's theological adviser, Canon James Moyes. Seething with personal invective, it summarily declared Mivart "an outsider and an opponent of the Catholic faith."[7] Mivart was furious and demanded an apology from Vaughan before he would even consider any sort of retraction. At this point Vaughan, who rarely acted in substantive matters without consulting Rome, sent Mivart's file to Merry del Val.

"I hope Mivart's heresy," Merry del Val replied on 10 January, "may serve to open the eyes of some Catholics to the logical conclusions of certain theories and of certain sentiments in regard to the Holy See"—no doubt a veiled reference to Mivart's inevitable excommunication.[8] Merry del Val assured Vaughan that the Holy Office would deal with the matter, but he also personally took it to the pope. That very day, 10 January, the Holy Office took up the case, and the next day Merry del Val informed Vaughan of their conclusion, writing that Mivart's "errors with which some liberal Catholics sympathize in greater or lesser degree must be met." He then quoted Cardinal Lucido Maria Parocchi's triumphal exclamation, "At last!" uttered upon receiving Mivart's file at the Holy Office—to which

Merry del Val added the marginal note, "Rebellion to the authority of the Holy See exercised through a congregation is a grievous act."[9] Supreme authority was behind this judgment. A satisfied Merry del Val reported to Vaughan on 13 January that the pope "spoke very energetically against Mivart . . . and will not allow any hesitation in dealing with him or with any of those who may sympathise in some degree with him. The matter has already been considered by the Holy Office and I expect you will hear from that quarter."[10] On 16 January both Parocchi and Cardinal Mieczyslaw Ledóchowski, prefect of the Vatican Congregation de Propaganda Fide, sent Vaughan authorization to proceed against Mivart at once.[11]

Two days later a printed declaration of Mivart's excommunication, dated St. Peter's Chair, 18 January 1900, was issued, and the very next day Vaughan sent a copy of it to his friend David Fleming, consultor to the Holy Office, with the words, "We have a group of ill-conditioned Catholics to whom it will serve as a warning. . . . We shall clear the air in the course of a few months and be all the better for conflict with heresy & sedition."[12]

By 22 January newspapers throughout England headlined Mivart's excommunication, and a lengthy and anguished commentary ensued in both the religious and the secular press. Alarmed by the publicity, Cardinal Vaughan issued a pastoral, dated 22 February, that defined firm boundaries:

Catholic journals are perfectly free to take any line, in literature, science, art . . . and other subjects which have not been decided by the Church. . . . But when it comes to questions directly concerning religion, such as the policy of the Church, the character and conduct of the Sovereign Pontiff, of the Roman Congregations, or of the Cardinals *in curia*, of Bishops in their official capacity, of the laws and discipline of the Church, . . . the case is altogether different. This is holy ground.[13]

TYRRELL AND ENGLISH JESUITS IMPLICATED

Sudden death on 1 April mercifully delivered St. George Mivart from the scene, but his stigma passed to George Tyrrell, whose censors had explicitly linked the two.[14] Coincident with Mivart's death, the *Nineteenth Century* published the obstreperous Robert Dell's "A Liberal Catholic View of the Case of Dr. Mivart," in which he upbraided the Jesuits, neo-scholastic theologians, and narrow church politicians while complimenting Tyrrell as "an English Jesuit father whose views seem to be as much out of harmony with the spirit of his Society as his abilities are superior to those of his *confrères*."[15]

To Luis Martín this coupling was simply tragic and indicated that affairs in England were out of control. He reflected in his *Memorias*:

The saddest part was that not a few liberal Catholics, who until now had been contained by the iron hand of Card. Manning . . . now no longer respecting the ecclesiastical authority represented by Card. Vaughan, placed themselves at Dr. Mivart's side. . . . The Cardinal, who was a sincere Catholic, if a little weak, as he showed himself the year before on the Dreyfus affair, became frightened when he saw that movement of rebellion against the Church and tried to stem it by gentle means and to win over Mivart and his followers. To that end he figured on using Fr. Tyrrell because of his influence and prestige among those Catholics, but I was opposed because of the fear which Fr. Tyrrell stirred up in me with his rather liberal and strange ideas.[16]

The danger, Martín told Gerard on 12 April, was that Tyrrell would be regarded "as a Jesuit imbued . . . with liberal ideas, who does not agree doctrinally with the rest of the Fathers of the Society." Certainly such a suspicion about Tyrrell's orthodoxy, Martín believed, could not be left unresolved; it was time for him to publish an article that would eliminate all the ambiguity of "A Perverted Devotion."

Indeed this is a most opportune moment for producing that article which I have so often requested in the past, for, apart from the censures, we now have a compelling motive that necessitates issuing that article for the general public. Thus Fr. Tyrrell can say that he . . . had been wrongly understood by not a few: that therefore he now wants to declare openly that he dissents on no point from the common teaching of the Society and that in clear, indubitable, and easily understood language he will expound his and the Society's doctrine on eternal punishment.

With these or similar words Tyrrell was to introduce his article and send it to Rome for review without further delay.[17]

But Tyrrell was currently lying ill in a hospital and was in no condition to comply. Gerard tried to soft-pedal the Dell connection by telling Martín that Dell had merely signed the article, that it seemed to have been authored by William Gibson, "probably with the assistance of a priest well enough versed in theology and hostile to us," and that Dell had broken off with Tyrrell months ago over a disagreement about the *Weekly Register*'s editorial policies.[18]

This news, Martín reflected, "consoled me considerably."[19] Gerard then wrote to Tyrrell and urged him to comply with the general's wish, arguing that although "A Perverted Devotion" was theologically defensible, the general's position was understandable since harm had been done where the article had been misapprehended.[20]

Tyrrell, however, was not consoled. From his hospital bed on 22 April he executed a letter to Meyer, objecting in the most biting language to Martín's "new suggestion of a 'conflated' article." As to the delay in complying with earlier demands, Tyrrell explained that, among other reasons, there were the moral and mental difficulties of writing an article which no one in England was trusted to censure and which had to satisfy foreign censors who had already displayed "a profound ignorance of literary English, of theology, and of the first principles of truthfulness and candour. I doubt if Christ Himself could satisfy such a request." Finally, Tyrrell roared, "whatever I write must be above all things sincere and *ex corde*," something that no one will believe "unless I can *state explicitly* that I have been left a perfectly free hand in the matter. But if His Paternity does not trust the English Province, I cannot expect that he should trust me—indeed, the idea of 'trust' in the Society has no place—hinc illae lac[r]ymae."[21]

Meyer rendered a faithful Latin translation of this letter—no doubt for Martín and his consultors—then drafted a reply to tell the general's side and to depict him as Tyrrell's protector rather than enemy. The general, he said, was moved not by any personal feelings against Tyrrell nor by the censures, but by the danger that the article would be placed on the Index, because several articles "by very orthodox writers"—none of them Jesuits—had been sent to the general's attention, one of which severely censured a number of propositions taken from Tyrrell's writings "and apparently so formulated that they might at any time by [*sic*] denounced to the Holy Office." So the general had to act. As to the censures of "A Perverted Devotion," the general "wished them to be a guide to you, in as much as they showed how you might be—and as a fact had been—understood." His reason for wanting the reparative article censored in Rome was "that no exception might be taken to the censorship, as was the case with the article on A Per D ["A Perverted Devotion"]. It was a measure . . . meant to protect you as well as [save?] you immediate & Fr Genl himself from future vexation." He did not intend this stipulation to "tie your hands, or compell [*sic*] you to hold views that you are not bound to hold, or to retract views that you are free to hold. You need only give expression in words *incapable* of being misunderstood [as contrary to the common(?)] teaching of the Church. By doing so you have nothing to lose, but everything to gain."[22]

On 28 April, Martín held a consultation on Tyrrell's letter of 22 April to Meyer. The proceedings again betray the Roman tendency to link Americanism and liberalism. They also betray a decidedly harder line to be taken toward Tyrrell—and toward Gerard—than did Meyer's letter:

The serious business of Father Tyrrell . . . is all the more serious in that recently some Liberal and Americanist opinions are flourishing among certain English Catholics. The question therefore is what would seem best to do. It was decided that the Provincial should be forcefully urged . . . to see to it that the scandal given by Fr. Tyrrell be satisfied, then that he [the provincial] exercise all diligence in completely repressing and entirely exterminating new opinions of this kind. Father Tyrrell may be allowed to write his defense openly and sincerely, so long as it is sent to Rome and the scandal is removed. If he refuses, action can be taken toward his dismissal. Indeed action can be taken even toward removing the Provincial, if he seems to be moving more slowly than is appropriate.[23]

At this point an unforeseen intervention by the Jesuit Richard F. Clarke, superior of the new Jesuit scholastics' residence—

named "Clarke's Hall" after its Master as was customary—at Oxford University, hastened the removal of Gerard from office. As a longtime editor of the *Month* and predecessor to Gerard in that post, and as originator and editor of the widely used Stonyhurst Philosophical Series, Clarke's views counted in Rome. On 3 May 1900 he sent Meyer a copy of the recently published *The Testament of Ignatius Loyola* with preface and epilogue by George Tyrrell, and commented, "I am afraid there must be something very wrong with our system of Censorship, if such sentiments as F. Tyrrells are allowed to pass. There is a sort of clique of quasi-Liberals among the present House of writers & to speak plainly, I fear that F. Provincial backs them up. . . . It is the Preface which will compromise us."[24] Meyer replied with two queries for Clarke, the first about possible replacements for the *Month*'s staff, the second about a replacement for Gerard.[25]

Meanwhile Gerard forwarded to Rome Tyrrell's second effort toward satisfying the general's demand, but this essay fared no better than the first.[26] Indeed it was so caustic that Tyrrell could only have composed it to exorcise his rage.

On 9 May Martín held another consultation on the two articles Tyrrell had sent and decided to forbid Tyrrell through his provincial "to write anything again," even at the risk of his seeking dismissal from the order.[27] By now the general was convinced that he was not going to get the reparation he wanted and would have to settle for a brief statement from Tyrrell professing theological orthodoxy. Accordingly, on 17 May Meyer prevailed on Gerard to "induce" Tyrrell to compose a statement similar to the one enclosed and to forward it to Rome at once.[28] Tyrrell complied—after his fashion—Gerard forwarded it on 23 May,[29] and Martín approved it against Meyer's objection to its equivocation.[30]

On 27 May Martín announced to his advisers "that the question was thought to be terminated,"[31] and on 1 June Tyrrell's statement appeared in the *Weekly Register*—"an absolutely fatuous and unmeaning letter," Tyrrell wrote to Baron von Hügel. "Of course they will never forget or forgive."[32] Nor would Tyrrell. Indeed, this experience irrevocably soured him toward the Society of Jesus.[33]

The broader issue of liberalism throughout the English Province, however, had still to be addressed. Here, too, Richard Clarke's advice proved decisive. "The present troubles," he commented to Meyer on 18 May, "seem to me to proceed, as you say, from the mistaken policy of minimising differences. It is well intentioned, but most pernicious. . . . I have found out how that Preface got into print. The members of the House of Writers got leave from F. Provincial to submit what they wrote to one censor only, chosen from among themselves."[34] That this letter weighed heavily with Martín is indicated by the fact that he quoted a large section of it in his *Memorias* and followed it with the resolve,

that the remedy for the evil was not to retire this or that writer or to change him, but in other more radical means—changing the provincial, so that in the college of writers as well as in the rest of the province this tendency to liberalism which was raising its head in diverse quarters might be arrested with a severe hand. This was agreeable to all the Assistants, and so from that time on I determined to bring this about with gentleness but at all costs.[35]

On 1 January 1901, Reginald Colley replaced Gerard as the English provincial. Hardly anyone in the English Province would have described that move as gentle.

Preparing the Official Condemnation of Liberalism

Fall-out from the Mivart affair was felt all round. George Tyrrell was worried that church officials, "elated with success" in that case, would try to bring all his own past writings under censure. On 10 March he wrote to von Hügel in Rome, "I hear that Merry del Val is not satisfied with 'External Religion,' etc. etc.; and even the cardinal tells me complaints have been made." At least, he said, Mivart would be "a useful object lesson to me on the necessity of keeping one's temper." Then in typically droll understatement he remarked, "Vaughan is beginning to be dimly conscious of something wrong and is puzzled by the almost complete drying up of the stream of conversions. At Farm Street our returns are but one to five of this time last year."[36]

Tyrrell of course knew that Vaughan was more than dimly

aware. The Mivart affair had shocked him into realizing that he had to do something decisive to counter the liberal influence. Exactly what, he was not sure, but he knew he could count on sure advice from Merry del Val in Rome.[37] In fact, that advice would engage the machinery that produced the ominous joint pastoral condemnation of liberalism, harbinger of the 1907 condemnation of modernism. Although much of the story surrounding the joint pastoral has already been told—the part accessible in public documents—the critically important inside story has until now remained secret. To this aspect of the story we now turn.

Upon Mivart's refusal to sign the profession of faith drawn up for him, Vaughan sent a note of distress to Merry del Val along with a copy of the profession and Mivart's letters of reply. By 21 January Vaughan had also distributed printed copies of the profession to his clergy along with a letter declaring Mivart inhibited from the sacraments. Merry del Val replied to Vaughan:

I have your letters and I need hardly say how sadly impressed I am by what you tell me of the number of liberal-Catholics, priests and laymen, who would refuse to sign the profession of faith you put before Mivart, and which as you say contained nothing that is not found in the Creeds, etc. I am not surprised but I had suspected the existence of this state of things for some time, but it is dreadful to thus see one's worst fears confirmed. It is something more than liberal Catholicism tho' this is bad enough. There is a lot of trouble in store and we must be ready to face it bravely. We shall lose a certain number but the Church in England will gain by their withdrawal, I am convinced, no matter who they are. You do not mention names, but I should not be intimidated by anybody in such matters.[38]

Precisely what Merry del Val meant by "It is something *more than* liberal Catholicism" is unclear, but certainly he meant that "it" was *worse than* liberalism and so perhaps needed a different name (*modernism?*). The names of liberals did not need mentioning, as they were on everyone's minds these days—Mivart, Dell, Wilfrid Ward, and Tyrrell. Ward, self-styled apologist for both parties to the dispute but irritating to both, felt compelled to answer Dell's contentious article, "A Liberal Catholic View of the Case of Dr. Mivart." His answer, "Liberalism and Intransigeance," appeared in the June *Nineteenth Century*. It was an answer that Tyrrell found curiously parallel to his own ideas,[39] but it was also an answer that apparently incited church officials to move vigorously toward an official and decisive condemnation of liberalism.

Vaughan wrote to Merry del Val about Ward's article and about a tentative plan of action. Merry del Val replied that Ward had already sent him a copy of his article with a triumphal note about its wholehearted endorsement by his Jesuit censor—"evidently . . . to draw an expression of opinion from me." But that, Merry del Val told Vaughan, Ward would not get. He distrusted Ward and would not let himself be "drawn into the network of his action." Merry del Val knew that to do so would be to vitiate his value to the Holy See—it had been less than a month since his elevation to archbishopric, and he was keenly alive to his call to serve the church in a central executive capacity. "I need hardly tell you what I thought of the article," he continued.

. . . I was horrified to see the eulogy of it in the Tablet. . . . He is very presumptious [*sic*] and any praise turns his head. He really does not understand his subject, he gives things away and assumes a great deal without a shadow of proof. . . . I fancy W. W. will come to grief unless he is humble enough to acknowledge his mistake and allow himself to be taught by the Church instead of trying to be the "Ecclesia docens" himself. He will not satisfy the extreme liberals because as yet he does not go far enough, and he falls out with the orthodox feeling by going much too far. . . . In some respects I consider W. W's action more harmful than Mivart's, because it steadily weakens all the screws and prepares the way for many more Mivarts in the future. It is very insidious and among converts it does incalculable harm.[40]

Merry del Val then alluded to the fact that he had contacted Jesuit authorities about this crisis—Martín and/or Meyer. That contact, we shall see, would rapidly become collusion to exterminate liberalism in the English Catholic Church. "The S.J. authorities," he assured Vaughan, "feel entirely as you do and you can reckon on their support. They are concerned and distressed by the action and behaviour of a small group of their English members. I am very glad you are seriously taking the matter up. I will see what I can do to help you as you suggest."[41]

Two weeks later Merry del Val wrote again to Vaughan—"in compliance with your request" to suggest a line of action—and confided that just two days earlier he had had an audience with Leo XIII, who "spoke of the condition of things in England and of the evil results of the liberal-Catholic movement now in progress." The pope was "entirely of the opinion that you should make the stand in a full doctrinal pronouncement upon the whole subject, clearly expounding Catholic doctrine without any regard to persons, whoever they may be. He will be quite ready to follow on and express his approval." Then, to ensure the efficacy of the proposed document, Merry del Val suggested a scheme that had to be kept secret:

It is essential that your letter or declaration should be unassailable in its force and that you should be able to issue it with the certainty that every word of it will be supported here as expressing the teaching and mind of the Church. To attain this end, I hardly think that under the circumstances you can reckon upon much help in England, especially as it will not be easy to obtain absolute discretion before and afterwards from the persons who might be called upon to cooperate with you in the drawing up of the document. And if anything transpired as to the persons who have worked with you, your statements will be set aside by many as simply the expression of the opinions of individual teachers. Would it not be well then, either that you should draft the document and then send it here to be revised by competent persons with the knowledge and approval of the authorities; or that you should allow such persons to draft the document and send it to you for your sanction, and final publication? I could get this done for you without any one appearing in the matter, and if you accept the suggestion I would set about doing so at once, for there is no time to be lost if the document is to be got ready within a reasonable time. Of course it would be your declaration and none of the cooperators would appear at all. Your task would thus be facilitated and you would speak with the assurance that the Holy See was entirely with you. You need not be afraid of coming in conflict with Father Tyrrell, who is quoted as the leader of thought on the other side, nor indeed of any one else. The S.J. authorities are just as anxious as you are on the subject and are most desirous to help and back you up. This I know positively. They will bring their men into line whether they like it or not. I submit this proposal to you, 'tamquam minus sapiens' and without any desire but that of assisting you if possible, and I need hardly add that I leave it, as is my duty, in your hands to settle as you think best under God.[42]

In fact, Merry del Val had already discussed the idea of a pastoral condemnation with Jesuit authorities—Rudolf Meyer, to be exact, who took the matter to Martín, who "fully approved."[43]

Vaughan accepted Merry del Val's offer. The scheme was now in operation and developed very quickly. Merry del Val informed Martín, who "induced Fr. Meyer to offer himself to Bishop Merry del Val for this purpose." Martín then appointed two Jesuit writers to draft the initial document: Salvatore Brandi, editor of *La Civiltà Cattolica*, and Thomas A. Hughes, student of Jesuit history from Meyer's own Missouri Province, who was assigned as a writer to the Roman curia and whose birth in Liverpool gave him an English connection. After conferring with Meyer on the specific points to be covered in the pastoral, Brandi and Hughes took the project with them on their July vacation at the *Civiltà*'s villa outside Poppi in the Tuscan Apennines. There they wrote the English bishops' joint pastoral condemning liberalism.[44]

Martín approved their work, and Meyer delivered it to Merry del Val just before Martín left Rome on 2 August for his own summer holiday. "My idea," Martín recalled, "was to assist not only the Catholic people of England but also our Fathers who would see themselves obliged to support the Cardinal's pastoral with their writings."[45]

For his part, Merry del Val was intending to holiday as usual in England and personally to deliver the approved draft of the pastoral to Vaughan, but the assassination of King Umberto on 29 July kept him in Rome for the funeral. Martín seized the opportunity to invite Merry del Val to preside over the Roman Jesuits' celebration of the feast of St. Ignatius on 31 July. *Post hoc*, if not *propter hoc*, Merry del Val contracted typhoid fever and had to delay his trip to England for many weeks. In fact, it is uncertain that he went to England at all that summer. And so, Martín grumbled in his *Memorias*, the archbishop "was not able to urge forward the business of the pastoral as he should have. Thus the entire autumn passed without my hearing a word about it, so that I began to suspect that it would not be published at all. But not so. It was just that C. Vaughan had taken all this time to mull over the points presented by Bishop Merry del Val and to edit it [the pastoral]."[46]

CONTINUING VEXATIONS IN ENGLAND

That summer other developments in the English Province heightened Martín's anxiety about any hitch in the publication of the pastoral. He was rapidly reaching the conclusion that he had on his hands a province rife with liberalism and governed by a provincial he could not trust. Clearly Gerard was to blame for the failure to exhort, cajole, or even coerce the kind of reparative article from Tyrrell that was required. But what alarmed Martín all the more at the present juncture was that he received confirmation of his views on the English Province in general and on Gerard in particular from three of the province's patriarchs: Richard F. Clarke; John Clayton, former provincial; and Peter Gallwey, former provincial and former novice master.

Clarke, as rector of the house of studies at Oxford, had complained to Martín in March that Gerard was prejudiced against the Jesuits there, was interfering even in minor decisions, and thus was undermining his authority.[47] On 20 May Martín brought these charges to the attention of Gerard, who replied on 5 June that his appointing a substitute for a recently deceased member of the Oxford mission was not an interference in Clarke's office but a necessary requirement of his own, and that, as far as he was concerned, the only real bone of contention between them was the number of altars to install in "Clarke's Hall." He suggested that perhaps Clarke was being spiteful, because more than once as editor of the *Month* he had had to tell Clarke, the former editor, the galling news that an article of his had not passed censors.[48]

A brief lull ensued while Martín considered his options. Then on 22 July he sent Gerard a stern rebuke to attend to the long list of long-standing defects in the province that were still being ignored. Among other things, Martín called for strict adherence to the Society's rules for censorship to prevent a recurrence of an affair like the one with Tyrrell. And, by the way, where was that list of new censors for the English Province that was to be submitted for his approval? To reinforce his point, Martín appended a postscript about Fr. Ernest Hull, a recently ordained student at St. Beuno's, who was reported to hold dangerous views—for example, that John's gospel contains interpolations and transpositions, that Christ could not have spoken as portrayed in that gospel, and that the encyclical *Providentissimus Deus* should be abandoned. "Are our men taught to hold such opinions? Are there any teachers of Sacred Scripture . . . whom the Society can trust?"[49] An obviously irritated Gerard retorted that he was finding it impossible to govern the province because some members were taking criticisms directly to the general without first giving him a chance to deal with them, and that such a practice was contrary to charity and to the Institute.[50]

One such member was Peter Gallwey. Since the day of his ordination in 1852, he had occupied important posts in the province, including master of novices and provincial, so he was well practiced in writing letters to Rome. Currently, as consultor to the rector of Gerard's own community, he posted letters on 25 July and 23 August that cited, among other issues threatening the province, the "danger to doctrine under two professors of the College of St. Beuno," their softness on Protestants, and the provincial's record of ignoring his consultors' advice. Gallwey also delated Tyrrell for having told a nun, whose brother's conversion was balked by the doctrine of original sin, that the historicity of the Genesis account had not been established and that some Catholic theologians regarded it as allegorical. While this information cleared her brother's way, it disturbed her, and she laid it at Gallwey's door, who brought it to Martín who thanked him and promised to investigate.[51]

Martín was loath to ruffle Tyrrell now in exile at Richmond, but several weeks later he sent queries to St. Beuno's,[52] and to Gerard he replied at once, sharply and at great length, that it was not contrary to the Institute for consultors of the province and houses to write directly to the general at the appointed times about the state of the province and their houses. Nor was the general bound only to those consultors for his information or only to those points that they had first brought to the provincial's attention. Nor do they sin against charity who denounce particular faults that the provincial does not think need correcting, especially faults pointed out in the general's previous letter. Martín then chided Gerard for repeatedly and injudiciously charging that his delators "have no official authority. . . . Perhaps Your Reverence would be surprised and would weigh his words more carefully if I were allowed to disclose the names of those who write such things."[53]

Martín then took up specific points for reform, and it is interesting that he began with and let out his frustration at great length on perennially intractable problems not at all peculiar to Gerard's tenure—abuse of alcohol, the excessive commitment of manpower to parish work contrary to the Institute, and the disposition of an inheritance.[54] Not until his adrenalin was nearly spent did he bring up—almost as an afterthought—the burning issue of recent delations: namely, doctrinally suspect teaching and writing. "Perhaps something ought to be added on other points," Martín averred, "but the letter has already become too long." Still he went on about the case of Ernest Hull, asserting that there was indeed foundation—and "in a matter of the gravest importance"—to the charges against him, and warning that "elsewhere not long ago a certain scholastic of the Society lost his vocation and his faith and went over to the German rationalists." Nor, Martín continued, did Gerard's letter allay the suspicions against Fr. Lucas. That man was to be resolutely investigated and watched. He then instructed Gerard and his consultors to meditate on this and his previous letter of 28 March 1899. In conclusion he protested that the length of his letter showed how much he loved the English Province, and that he did not have time to be forced to deal again with issues on which he had already made up his mind.[55]

Gerard did not jump. Several weeks passed before he met with his consultors on 18 September to take up the general's concerns. When they did meet, either they defended their previous stance (on reported alcohol abuse) or they agreed that something ought to be done but not quickly (on withdrawing from some parishes). They said nothing on the cases of Hull and Lucas.[56]

Meanwhile two letters critical of Gerard were sent in quick succession from John Clayton to Rudolf Meyer. The first alleged that "the ordinations of Very Rev. Fr. Anderledy had fallen or were falling into desuetude." The second gave two instances of Gerard's laxness compared to his predecessors: his allowing Jesuits to spend time—sometimes weeks—with externs, and his reported permission for laywomen to return to work in two Jesuit parishes.[57]

On 21 September Martín initiated his inquiry into the charges brought by John Clayton against the two professors at St. Beuno's, Herbert Lucas, professor of Sacred Scripture, and John Rickaby, professor of dogmatic theology.[58] The inquiry was sensitive, in that Martín had to address his letter to the rector of St. Beuno's and the prefect of studies, who in both cases was John Rickaby, one of the accused. Martín began by telling Rickaby that the case of Father Hull and the testimony of several fathers of the province had given him reason to fear that "sound doctrine was suffering harm" at St. Beuno's. The professor of Sacred Scripture was reported to entertain a "propensity for some modern opinions, such as are disseminated by the School of 'Higher Criticism'." And the professor of dogmatic theology was said "to be making light of ecclesiastical traditions, lecturing in the historical method rather than the scholastic, raising doubts in the minds of students without providing solutions, and causing scandal by debating dangerous questions among them, etc." Martín then instructed Rickaby to carry out the responsibilities of his office by keeping strict watch "that the doctrine of the Society and its method of teaching it be most diligently preserved according to the Institute; and that all lax opinions, or 'liberal', as they say, be crushed with a firm hand, so that positive Scholastic Theology is handed on with consummate care and diligence; and so that the studies of the College are returned to the true norm of the Society."[59]

In Martín's view liberalism pervaded the church and the Society of Jesus in England, and by now he was convinced that he could not count on Gerard to help him fight it. Indeed, Gerard himself was proving to be an obstacle that had to be removed. Thus on 22 September, after lamenting the recent and sudden death of Richard Clarke, "a true son of the Society," Martín asked Gerard for a *"terna"*—a list of three candidates for provincial, agreed on by him and his consultors and given in order of preference. From this list Martín would select Gerard's replacement or ask for a new *terna*.[60] A month later, Gerard replied that the list would follow soon, as he would not be meeting with his consultors until 23 October.[61]

The day after that meeting Tyrrell reinserted himself into the picture with an inflammatory letter to Meyer. He wrote that he could block a forthcoming publication about Jesuit obstructionism to the spread of Catholicism in America if Meyer could categorically deny the truth of one of the author's stories, "that some years back a novice-master was removed from his post on account of alleged immoral conduct with his novices."[62] Tyrrell's motives in raising this issue are unknown, but Meyer, although busy preaching a retreat at the North American College in Rome, brought Tyrrell's letter at once to the general. Martín recalls, "I told Fr. Meyer that he should reply that he knew nothing of it, and at the same time that he should write to Fr. Purbrick, who had just returned from America and who could commit an indiscretion with Fr. Tyrrell if the latter asked him the same question."[63]

The next day, 28 October, Meyer answered Tyrrell with a denial that was as close to categorical as honesty would allow: that is, he was certain that the charge was untrue of his own province from its beginning to the present. As to the other six novitiates in the United States, it was certainly untrue from the inception of his official relations with them (1893). About the previous period, he had never heard "even so much as a breath of suspicion from any quarter." Moreover, if it were true, the offending party would have been "visited with the severest chastisement—probably immediate expulsion. This well-known severity ought to be a sufficient vindication of the Society when charges are brought against individual members.[64] Meyer's denial, therefore, was for the most part a denial of *knowledge* of, rather than the *truth* of, the charge—this deft distinction accorded by Martín. Apparently this answer set Tyrrell at rest on the question, and for two whole months Martín did not have to deal with him, except indirectly.

On 2 November 1900 Martín wrote to inform Reginald Colley that he was to replace Gerard as provincial, on the condition that his health would stand the strain of the agenda: (1) halting the abuse of alcohol, (2) turning over the small Jesuit parishes to the local bishops, and (3) curbing the liberal ideas and imprudent styles of writing that had caused so much trouble both to the province and to superiors in Rome.[65] Colley accepted the challenge, and one month later Martín informed Gerard that he was to be replaced.[66]

Michael King, Gerard's assistant, protested to Martín on 20 December that, despite what he thought, Gerard "was most loyal to the wishes of Father General," that he "chafed considerably under the representations made to Rome about his government and about the state of the Province, which he did not think just or correct," and finally that his chief faults arose not out of incompetence or defiance but out of lack of experience as a superior.[67] Martín replied that he had never doubted Gerard's zeal or loyalty, but that "*relationes*" made by "Fathers of the highest authority and prudence in the province" and by prelates outside could not be ignored.[68]

On 1 January 1901 Reginald Colley assumed the office of provincial. He wanted to keep Michael King on as his own assistant, but Martín ordered him to appoint Arthur Knight, the previous provincial's assistant, who was notoriously disciplined and attentive to detail.[69]

The Joint Pastoral Condemning Liberalism Goes to Press

By early November 1900 Merry del Val, his health restored, returned to his post at the Accademia and braced Martín's spirit with the news that the revised pastoral would arrive in Rome shortly.[70] He also arranged an audience with the pope to discuss the pastoral and on 7 November sent the following account to Vaughan:

I saw the Holy Father who at once spoke of the Pastoral and the evil it is intended to counteract. He emphatically said that he would like it to be a joint Pastoral signed by all the Bishops.

He went on to consider the causes which have given rise to these liberal tendencies and the evil effects upon Catholics of living in a Protestant and rationalistic atmosphere where almost in spite of themselves they must gradually assimilate so much that is wrong. . . .

If you do not object I think it would be as well to let Father David [Fleming] see the draft of the Pastoral, confidentially of course. He might make some useful suggestions and then be in a position to keep the Holy Office informed of its contents. You will tell me when you send the document whether you think it advisable or not.[71]

Whether or not Fleming had a hand in the final editing is not known. Martín certainly did. On 18 November Merry del Val notified Meyer that the page proofs had arrived. Two days later the pastoral was in Martín's hands. "I read it carefully," Martín recalled, "and, although in general it pleased me, I noted two or three quite defective points and notified Fr. Meyer of them. He met with Frs. Hughes and Brandi on the 24th and discussed the corrections that ought to be made in the pastoral, and these with unanimous accord were sent by Bishop Merry del Val to Card. Vaughan. He received them gratefully and, having approved the new redaction, sent the pastoral to Rome."[72]

Strategy for publication then required careful attention. Cardinal Vaughan was planning his *ad limina* visit to Rome at the end of December. Should he issue the pastoral before, during, or after that visit? And what about papal approbation? Should that be given before or after publication? Merry del Val presented both questions to Martín. On the latter question, Martín argued for papal approbation *prior* to publication, as that would add leverage for securing the signatures of all the bishops of England. On the former question, he advised that the pastoral be issued *before* Vaughan departed England for Rome "to avoid creating the suspicion that it had been written under Rome's influence, much less under our inspiration, which would provoke storms."[73]

In the end, who bore final responsibility for authorship of the joint pastoral? Most would say those who signed their names. However, Martín seems to have had another sense of the authorship—at least judging from his *Memorias*. For one thing, he thought that Vaughan himself was so far removed from the execution of the plan that he did not know the identity of the Jesuits "who assisted Merry del Val." For another thing, this last comment suggests that Martín regarded Merry del Val as the chief executor and *sub rosa* author of the pastoral, with *assistance* from Brandi, Hughes, and himself.[74] We have already seen what both Martín and Merry del Val thought of Vaughan's competence for dealing with liberalism and therefore why neither of them would be inclined to consider Vaughan the effective author of the joint pastoral.

"So it was done," Martín recalled. "On 21 December Fr. Meyer told me that Fr. Brandi had given the pastoral to the pope, who had then approved it." The fact of papal approbation was then communicated to all the English bishops and their advisors—"so they all signed it . . . and it was published in the name of all of them at the end of December before the Cardinal departed for Rome."[75]

The pastoral, dated 29 December 1900, appeared in the *Tablet* of 5 and 12 January 1901. By that time Vaughan was making his rounds in Rome. One stop he dared not omit was at the Jesuit curia. Martín was delighted to be able to congratulate the cardinal in person on the pastoral and "on the good which had come from its reception" and to express his hope that it would also "do not a little good for all and for our English Fathers." He also recalled that the pastoral's reception in England pleased him in direct proportion to its offensiveness to liberals. "They did not dare to fight it," he conjectured, "seeing that not only the good Catholics received it well but that many protestants praised it, especially the ritualists, because of the frankness and unity of the bishops on the same doctrine."[76]

Of course, had the public known the true story of the genesis of the pastoral, who really wrote it, how "frankness and unity" had been arranged, and therefore why it all had to be executed with absolute secrecy, the reception even among those who praised it would probably have been not a little different. The pastoral's content and reception by Tyrrell and like-minded readers has been covered at length elsewhere.[77] Suffice it to say that the pastoral harbingered the content and style of *Pascendi dominici gregis*. The similarity is not surprising, now that historical evidence has established Rafael Merry del Val as the principal fabricator of both documents, with executive and editorial assistance on the joint pastoral by Luis Martín.[78]

NOTES

1. For the material on Mivart, I am indebted to the masterful chronicle by John David Root, "The Final Apostasy of St. George Jackson Mivart," *Catholic Historical Review* 71 (January 1985) 1–25.

2. A likely candidate would have been Merry del Val who, as a confidant of Cardinal Vaughan's and a consultor for the Sacred Congregation of the Index, kept a close watch on English affairs.

3. St. George Jackson Mivart, "Happiness in Hell," *Nineteenth Century* 32 (December 1892) 899–919; "The Happiness in Hell: A Rejoinder," and "Last Words on the Happiness in Hell," *Nineteenth Century* 33 (February, April 1893) 320–38, 637–51.

4. See above, pp. 74–83.

5. Mivart, "The Roman Catholic Church and the Dreyfus Case," (London) *Times*, 17 October 1899, pp. 13–14.

6. Mivart, "The Continuity of Catholicism," *Nineteenth Century* 47 (January 1900) 51–72; "Some Recent Catholic Apologists," *Fortnightly Review* N.S. 67 (1 January 1900) 24–44.

7. "Dr. Mivart's Heresy," *Tablet*, 6 January 1900, p. 5. As will be seen in chap. 5, this rhetoric—and especially the denomination "outsider"—is typical of the Mediterranean "mind" displayed in ecclesiastical documents.

8. Merry del Val to Vaughan, 10 January 1900, AAW, V.1/14.23.

9. VP, AAW, V.1/14.23, 24a–b. Parocchi was the commissary of the Holy Office.

10. Merry del Val to Vaughan, 13 January 1900, VP, AAW, V.1/14.26.

11. Parocchi to Vaughan, and Ledóchowski to Vaughan, 16 January 1900, Roman Letters, AAW, VI/3 and 5.

12. Fleming Papers, Franciscan Provincial Archives, Forest Gate, London. As a consultor of the Holy Office, Fleming probably already knew of the excommunication. On Fleming, see above, pp. 57 n. 18 and 60 n. 39.

13. Copy in Rooke Ley Papers, Saint Andrews University Library, MS 36363/15a. Quoted in Root, "Mivart," p. 19.

14. See Piccirelli's censure of Tyrrell's "A Perverted Devotion,"

dated Naples, 22 January 1900, ARSJ, ANGL 1021.I^B.3, p. 1 (of 6 handwritten quarto pages); published anonymously in AL 2:455–58.

15. Robert Edward Dell, "A Liberal Catholic View of the Case of Dr. Mivart," *Nineteenth Century* 47 (April 1900) 676.

16. Martín, *Memorias*, fl. 2297r–v. The Minute Books of the meetings of the English provincials with their consultors includes this entry for 8 February 1900 concerning "A Perverted Devotion": "The article in question was not considered censurable by many of the fathers in the province. The Cardinal, who called especially to see Fr. Tyrrell after having heard from Rome of the affair was desirous of engaging Fr. Tyrrell in writing articles in connection with Dr. Mivart's case." Tyrrell was in no position to participate in such a venture, but when Vaughan wrote to Mivart on 21 January 1900 (VP, AAW, I/2.12) he referred him to Fr. Robert Francis Clarke and/or to Tyrrell, "both of whom would be able to understand your state of mind and to give you counsel and assistance." VP, AAW, I/2.12. See Schultenover, *George Tyrrell*, pp. 99–108.

17. Martín to Gerard, 12 April 1900, ARSJ, Reg. Epp. Angl., vol. 5, pp. 108–109. An account of the ideas for which Tyrrell was censured can be found in my *George Tyrrell*, pp. 97–99. Tyrrell's article first appeared in the liberal Catholic publication *The Weekly Register* 100 (16 December 1899) 797–800, and was reprinted in his posthumously published *Essays on Faith and Immortality*, ed. Maude D. Petre (London: Arnold, 1914), pp. 158–71.

18. Gerard to Martín, 16 April 1900, ARSJ, ANGL 1021.I^B (not paginated).

19. Martín, *Memorias*, fl. 2298r.

20. Gerard to Tyrrell, 19 April 1900, AEPSJ.

21. Tyrrell to Meyer, 22 April 1900, ARSJ, ANGL 1021.I^B.14. Tyrrell seems to be comparing himself before the Society of Jesus to Aeneas at Carthage weeping over the scene of Troy's fall etched in the temple door (*Aeneid* 1.462ff.).

22. Meyer to Tyrrell, n.d. [late April 1900], ARSJ, ANGL 1021.I^B.17, very rough draft—brackets indicate questionable readings.

23. Meyer's note (in Latin) on Tyrrell's file, 28 April 1900, ARSJ, ANGL 1021.I^B.23.

24. Clarke to Meyer, 3 May 1900, ARSJ, ANGL 1021.I^B.21. An indication of Clarke's influence with the Roman curia is the fact that Martín quoted nearly all of this passage in his *Memorias*. Meyer wrote at the top of Clarke's letter: "To the said Preface Fr Tyrrell refers for his conception of 'obedience', in the document which he sent later on

to Fr. General, asking his dismissal." That document, dated 11 June 1904, was published in AL, 2:458–99; reference to the preface, p. 467. For Tyrrell's comment on the preface, see Barmann, *Baron Friedrich von Hügel*, p. 162 n. 1. Clarke had been in regular communication with Rome about the revision of Jesuit studies and just as regularly promoted his idea that scholastic and Catholic philosophy were identical, that the course of studies needed revision to combat modern thought, and that a house of studies at Oxford could serve "to refute the errors of the innovators" and be "a light in the darkness of modern paganism." Clarke to Martín, 27 January 1900, ARSJ, ANGL 1017.V.35.

25. Meyer's letter to Clarke was not found in ARSJ but is referred to in Martín, *Memorias*, fl. 2300v and in Clarke to Meyer, 18 May 1900, ARSJ, ANGL 1021.I^{B}.22.

26. This second effort, preserved in ARSJ, ANGL 1021.I^{B}.18, is a ten-page, handwritten essay intended for the *Weekly Register*. Preserved along with this essay is Josef Flöck's page-and-a-quarter censure of it, dated 13 May 1900, ARSJ, ANGL 1021.I^{B}.19. It was a simple matter for Martín to give Flöck the essay, as the Jesuit curia was at that time housed in the German College where Flöck resided. Martín noted in his *Memorias*, fl. 2298v, that Gerard had sent Tyrrell's essay on 27 April 1900 "without a single observation." On the previous essay, see above, pp. 104–106. Tyrrell composed at least two other essays which did not see print: "Who Are the Reactionaries?", a response to Dell (see Schultenover, *George Tyrrell*, pp. 105–107) and a 21-page handwritten rough draft entitled "A Perverted Devotion. II." preserved in AEPSJ, 39.3.5.1. A third essay was published in part in AL, 2:121–25.

27. Excerpt from the diary of consultations, ARSJ, ANGL 1021.I^{B}.23. That two consultations were held, their dates, and deliberations are indicated by Martín in a footnote in his *Memorias*, fl. 2299r.

28. Meyer to Gerard, ARSJ, Reg. Epp. Angl., vol. 5, pp. 111–12.

29. Gerard to Fr. Assistant [Meyer], 23 May 1900, ARSJ, ANGL 1021.I^{B}.20.

30. Martín, *Memorias*, fl. 2299v. Indeed, Tyrrell, in asserting that on matters of theological opinion he holds "what all theologians hold unanimously & in common," was granting nothing, for the statement is nonsense.

31. Ibid. Meyer made a similar entry on Tyrrell's file and dated it 27 May 1900. Excerpt from the diary of consultations, ARSJ, ANGL 1021.I^{B}.23.

32. Tyrrell to von Hügel, 6 June 1900, Petre Papers, British Library, Additional Manuscripts (hereafter, PP, BL, Add. MSS) 44927.115–17, published in part and with inaccuracies in AL 2:129–30.

33. On this point see Valentine G. Moran's "The 'Breakings' of George Tyrrell," *Downside Review* 102 (July 1984) 174–85.

34. Clarke to Meyer, 18 May 1900, ARSJ, ANGL 1021.I^B.22.

35. Martín, *Memorias*, fl. 2300v–2301r.

36. Tyrrell to von Hügel, 10 March 1900, PP, BL, Add. MSS 44927.107–108. For the story on Tyrrell's book *External Religion*, see Schultenover, *George Tyrrell*, pp. 64–72, 81–85, 150–51.

37. John Root, "Mivart," p. 15, rightly argues: "Minimally, we must conclude that Vaughan was determined to use the case of Mivart to draw a line before what he perceived as a seditious liberalism. We also may conclude that Vaughan solicited and received considerable support from Rome." The succeeding evidence will validate Root's surmise.

38. Merry del Val to Vaughan, [undated, probably late January 1900], VP, AAW, V.1/14.36.

39. Tyrrell said as much to Ward in a letter of 31 May 1900, Ward Family Papers, Saint Andrews University Library. Wilfrid Ward, "Liberalism and Intransigeance," *Nineteenth Century* 47 (June 1900) 960–73. See Schultenover, *George Tyrrell*, pp. 99–112, esp. p. 107.

40. Merry del Val to Vaughan, 17 June 1900, VP, AAW, V.1/14.28.

41. Ibid.

42. Merry del Val to Vaughan, 30 June 1900, VP, AAW, V.1/14.29.

43. Martín, *Memorias*, fl. 2301r.

44. Ibid., fl. 2301r–v.

45. Ibid.

46. Ibid., fl. 2301v.

47. On 12 May 1900, Martín replied to Clarke's letters of 26 March and 20 April (Reg. Epp. Angl., vol. 5, p. 109). Clarke's letter of 26 March is missing from its proper file. It is perhaps the one containing the complaints referred to, because they are not in the 20 April letter (to Meyer, ARSJ, ANGL 1017.V.37). On 23 December 1898, Clarke had sent a similar complaint—see ARSJ, ANGL 1018/2.V.23.

48. Gerard to Martín, 5 June 1900, ARSJ, ANGL 1017.II.80, a reply to Martín's of 20 May 1900, Reg. Epp. Angl., vol. 5, p. 109. Clarke was a narrowly orthodox and much published polemicist. As to his literary style, we find the following anonymous and unflattering testimony in—of all places—his obituary notice: "His literary style was not of the highest quality. . . . Pressure of work often obliged him to write very rapidly, and in such cases he attended to the matter rather

than the form of his sentences." LN 141 (October 1900) 551–52. Gerard objected to Clarke's excessive devotion to a nearby convent and to his justifying it on the grounds that his house did not have enough altars. The Jesuit church had plenty of altars, Gerard argued, and was no farther away than the convent. Clarke died on 10 September 1900 as he finished preaching a retreat to nuns. One of the nuns memorialized him as follows: "He insisted much upon the duty of submission to the Church; it was not the amount of doctrine that a man knew, he said, that made him a good Catholic, but the loyal submission of his will to the will of the Church. For himself he felt, as he had felt at his conversion, that if what he thought black was pronounced to be white by the Church he would believe it to be so." Anon., n.d., AEPSJ, H/1.C.

49. Martín to Gerard, 22 July 1900, Reg. Epp. Angl., vol. 5, pp. 115–18. I was unable to discover who had delated Hull. Some letters to Rome are either missing, misplaced, or contained in files that escaped my search.

50. This letter of 22 August [?] 1900, apparently addressed to Meyer, seems to be missing. Its contents, however, are reviewed in Martín's extraordinarily long reply, dated "Aug 1900" and treated on pp. 144–45. The 22 *August* date is also suspect, because the copyist of Martín's letter over- or underwrote the date with *July* in the *registrum* when referring to Gerard's letter. It would be a simple matter to check the *registrum*'s version against Martín's original letter, but Fr. Francis Edwards, archivist of the English Province, informed me that many records of the English province, including most of the letters from Rome, were destroyed years ago by some form of attic rot.

51. Gallwey's letters to Martín of 25 July and 23 August 1900 are missing or misplaced in the files. Martín referred to them and outlined their contents in his reply of 12 October 1900, Reg. Epp. Angl., vol. 5, p. 129. The part about Tyrrell is related in Martín, *Memorias*, fl. 2302v–2303r. The minutes of the provincial's consultors' meetings indicate that, as a matter of fact, Gerard rarely, if ever, acted contrary to his consultors' advice.

52. Martín to Rickaby, 21 September 1900, Reg. Epp. Angl., vol. 5, pp. 127–28. See below, p. 146.

53. Martín to Gerard, dated "Aug 1900," Reg. Epp. Angl., vol. 5, pp. 118–25. Martín and his consultors dealt with this and related letters at their 18 September meeting (see the Minute Books for that date).

54. The Catholic bishops of England in their private *Relazione* prepared for their *ad limina* visits to Rome designated abuse of alcohol as

the primary evil in the entire Catholic Church in England during the years 1896 and 1906 (the years for which I was allowed to read the *Relazione*). See the *Relazione* in the Archives of the Congregation de Propaganda Fide, New Style [APF, NS], vol. 93, 114, 141, 165, 189, 211, 234, 259. A typical example is the report from Bishop Samuel Webster Allan of the Diocese of Shrewsbury, in which, incidentally, St. Beuno's is located. Under format no. 51 for the principal moral abuses in the diocese, he stated, "senza dubbio l'ubbriaccharezza [*sic*, underlined and misspelled] tra i nostri lavoranti. Sta per la causa di quasi tutti loro altri peccati." Curiously, he advises under no. 55, where he is to list the means for correcting the abuses, that *"senza dubbio"* what is needed above all is a pious and educated priesthood, learned especially in Scripture and philosophy to combat *"lo scepticismo, il razionalismo ed i diversi generi d'agnosticismo."* The connection between drunkenness and a pious and educated priesthood as its cure is obscure. APF, NS vol. 114, rubrica 100–103/1897, fl. 617–29. Even more curious is Cardinal Vaughan's *Relazione*, in which he asserts under format no. 51, that there is *"nessun abuso di questo genere"* (i.e., not a single moral abuse) in his diocese, but then under no. 55 suggests as a corrective to the (non-existent) abuses a band of learned men holding discourses for non-Catholics and writing on Catholic truth. Ibid., fl. 485–501. Abuse of alcohol among the clergy was not rare. Bishop Robert Browne of Cloyne reported in his *Relazione* dated 2 November 1895 on the morals of his priests: "There are a few who scandalize the faithful with drunkenness. . . . Whenever one of our priests is unfaithful to his vocation, the sole cause is drunkenness." APF, NS vol. 93, fl. 703–704.

55. Martín to Gerard, "Aug 1900," esp. p. 125.

56. Minute Books, 18 September 1900.

57. The first letter is missing but is referred to and summarized in the second of 14 September 1900, ARSJ, ANGL 1017.II.80 bis. Anton Maria Anderledy was general from 1887 to 1892. Clayton was provincial from 1888 to 1894 and therefore overlapped Martín's term by two years. Clayton and Anderledy had the vexing task of enforcing a directive from the Holy See through the Vatican Congregation of Bishops and Regulars banning all female employees from Jesuit houses. Presumably the ban extended to *all* religious houses, but Clayton and others complained that of all the religious orders and congregations in England, only the Jesuits were hearing about it from Rome, thus laying them open to vicious rumors. Moreover, they argued, their schools and parishes needed the help and could not afford to hire men; besides, the men who would do that sort of work were not the

sort of men wanted. See, e.g., Clayton to Anderledy, 5 and 23 September, 9 October 1891; to Meyer, 27 April 1894, ARSJ, ANGL 1006.II.19, 20, 73; and John Ross, pastor of St. Mary's, Bristol, to Martín, 22 June 1894, ARSJ, ANGL 1007.VI.9 about the public shame suffered over the court conviction of one of their male domestics on the charge of sodomy.

58. A revelation about Clayton comes in a letter of James F. Murphy, provincial of the Irish Province, to Meyer, 9 March 1904, ARSJ, ANGL 1019.II.5. By Martín's request, Murphy reported to Meyer what he learned on his passage through England from Rome regarding the qualities of various candidates for the new English provincial to replace Colley. In the process Murphy revealed what is obviously a shared secret with Meyer and Martín: "I confess I shd prefer [to] see a man like F. Hayes or—if his appointment did not irritate them— F. Clayton put on at present. He must be a strong man, a man who knows both England & English Province well. F. Clayton is thoroughly sound & is strong. I dont think in England they even suspect it is he who represented to you in Rome in case of F. Rigby or Rickaby or Lucas. They put that down to F. Pope or F. Jagger or F. Slater."

59. Martín to Rickaby, 21 September 1900.

60. Martín to Gerard, 22 September 1900, Reg. Epp. Angl., vol. 5, pp. 289–29. According to custom, Martín would either select one of the three candidates or ask the provincial for another *terna*. The provincial customarily remained in office six years, but the general reserved the option of replacing him after three years. It was therefore a convenient time to replace Gerard. However, Gerard was actually already two weeks into his second three-year tenure by the time he received the request for a *terna*, but perhaps Martín figured that Gerard's removal would cause less comment if the transition occurred on 1 January 1901, when Reginald Colley took office. It is ironic that Clarke's death should coincide with Martín's request for a *terna*, since it was Clarke who was first asked to list and evaluate candidates for Gerard's replacement. See Clarke to Meyer, 18 May 1900, ARSJ, ANGL 1021.I[B].22, and above, pp. 136–38.

61. Gerard to Martín, 19 October 1900, ARSJ, ANGL 1017.II.81.

62. Tyrrell to Meyer, ARSJ, ANGL 1021.I[C].6. See above, pp. 93, 98–103, and 126 n. 88.

63. *Memorias*, fl. 2303r. Edward Ignatius Purbrick (1830–1914), provincial of the English Province from 1880–1888, had become provincial of the Maryland–New York Province in 1897.

64. Meyer to Tyrrell, 28 October 1900, ARSJ, ANGL 1021.I[C].7 (rough draft).

65. Martín to Meyer, 2 November 1900, ARSJ, Reg. Epp. Angl., pp. 131–32.

66. Martín to Gerard, 1 December 1900, ARSJ, Reg. Epp. Angl., p. 134. See also Martín to Colley, 3 December 1900, ibid., pp. 134–35.

67. King to Martín, 20 December 1900, missing from its file, but quoted in Martín to King, 6 February 1901, ARSJ, Reg. Epp. Angl., pp. 141–42.

68. Martín to King, 6 February 1901.

69. See Martín to Colley, 3 and 13 December 1900, ARSJ, Reg. Epp. Angl., pp. 134–36. Martín also appointed two new consultors for Colley—Knight and Frederick O'Hare—while keeping on Joseph Browne and Charnley.

70. Martín, Memorias, fl. 2301v.

71. Merry del Val to Vaughan, 7 November 1900, VP, AAW, V.1/14.30.

72. Martín, Memorias, fl. 2301v.

73. Ibid., fl. 2302r.

74. Ibid., fl. 2301v–2302r.

75. Ibid.

76. Ibid.

77. See Schultenover, George Tyrrell, pp. 143–65, and the sources there cited.

78. I use the term "fabricator" to indicate the one responsible for the production of the document from beginning to end. Gabriel Daly, Transcendence and Immanence, pp. 179–87, 232–34, has established Joseph Lemius as the draftsman of Pascendi. I have now identified the fabricators and draftsmen of the joint pastoral.

III

PERCEPTIONS
OF THE
MEDITERRANEAN MIND

5

Cultural Influences

THE GOAL OF THIS STUDY has been to explore the context of modernism and thereby to broaden our understanding of its origins and dynamic. We discussed the issue of perceptions: how the anti-modernists perceived the threat that they defined and condemned as modernism. In so doing we traced the ideological ancestry of anti-modernism through the papal documents of the nineteenth century quoted by Pius X in his encyclical *Pascendi dominici gregis*. We saw therein that the papacy perceived the threat emerging at the turn of the century to be a direct descendant of liberalism's declaration of independence from external authorities—whether religious, political, or intellectual—which in its turn passed through the Enlightenment back to Luther's initiatory declaration of independence from Rome. It was a broad etiological sweep by Roman authorities. But they consistently pointed to Protestantism as the sword that cut the Gordian knot of Christian unity and so unraveled the medieval synthesis of throne and altar and precipitated the bloody revolutions of the eighteenth and nineteenth centuries. We saw, finally, that in Rome's mind the only hope of restoring the tranquillity of order lay in what Pius X took as his motto, *Instaurare omnia in Christo*, by which he meant what Leo XIII meant in his effort to stake out a claim for papal hegemony over the realm of faith and morals. In other words, earthly order could be restored in Christ only through Christ's earthly vicar, the pope of Rome. An ultimate earthly principle of authority established by God had to be acknowledged if there were to be a secure social order. The existential background to this concern was the revolutions of the nineteenth century, and particularly the loss of the Papal States, with the forcible seizure of church properties and loss of life.

Now, the principal mission of the pope through the ages had been to serve the cause of freedom according to the evangelical promise "You shall know the truth, and the truth will set you free," and "If then the Son sets you free, you will indeed be free" (John 8:32–36). But according to Leo XIII, for the pope to function effectively in this capacity, he himself had to be free. This he could never be, in a position where he could be held prisoner by a secular head of state, and thus the pope must be sovereign over his own state. From that base he could then serve the world as a beacon guiding all who seek direction into the harbor of spiritual freedom—whence might come the struggle for other freedoms but not directly superintended by Rome.

Rome's general perception, therefore, on the eve of the modernist crisis was that virtually all errors—whether theological, philosophical, political, social, or moral—originated from the error of private judgment. In effect, Rome defined private judgment as the originating sin of the modern world. From that sin stemmed all the "isms" of the post-Enlightenment world: rationalism, liberalism, socialism, Gallicanism, Americanism, and finally, as the synthesis of them all, modernism. In Rome's view, the originating sin of modernism was disobedience, a defiance of the church's originating authority.

Although the foregoing chapters only verge on the specifically modernist period, one could legitimately conclude from their argument that what allows a bridging, if not a virtual identification, of "modernism" with "liberalism"—however nuanced their definitions—is the issue of authority. How various parties exercised, dealt with, or reacted to authority depended on their operative model. At this juncture in Western history, two principal models were at loggerheads: the monarchic and the republican/democratic models. The papacy and its ultramontane circle identified with the former; liberals and modernists, with the latter. As theological justification for the papal and ultramontane identification, one could cite Christ's appointing Peter head of the church, which was parlayed through various historical vicissitudes into a papal monarchy with Leo III's deputation of Charlemagne as king of the Holy Roman Empire. (It was hardly Charlemagne who made the empire holy.) That gesture founding "Christendom" was and remains a potent symbol. It could not have been lost on the historically erudite Leo XIII, who deeply regretted the loss of the Papal States and hoped desperately for a restoration of that medieval order.

Up to the final entrance of the republican/democratic model on the world's stage with the American and French Revolutions, papal monarchism received two shattering blows that Rome never forgot or forgave: Henry VIII's self-appointment as head of the Church of England and Luther's individualist declamation mythicized in the words *"Hier stehe ich. Ich kann nicht anders."* Of course, neither challenge would have stood up to Rome's counter-reform had not plausibility structures rooted in the Italian Renaissance already been in place. But stand they did and ushered in the modern era marked by the exaltation of reason alone as the broad basis of all authority vis-à-vis authority from direct and divine revelation.

Thus with the Enlightenment, just as there developed a split between faith and reason, so there developed a split between church and state. And whatever connection there was between the two sides was seen more in opposition than in correlation, more in competition than in complement. For the world of the Enlightenment, reason authorized. Every individual endowed with reason became, in a sense, both pope and king: one person, one vote. It was therefore an easy, indeed compulsory, step intellectually—albeit not socially—from monarchic to democratic social structures. The whole history of the nineteenth century compellingly demonstrates the power of an idea whose time had come: the value of the individual person validated by the internal authority of reason, not by the external authority of religion.

The sad part of this development for religion in general and for Christianity in particular was that the parties to the argument saw the authority issue as black and white, either/or. Rome, more than the reformers, forgot—or never did learn—the lesson of the Hebrew and Christian scriptures, that effective and integral living embraces pluralities, that there is room for Paul as well as for Peter, that revelation and reason authentically correlate with each other, that primacy is not incompatible with parity, monarchy with democracy. The failure to learn that lesson is the engine that drove forward the drama of the modernist crisis.[1]

The all-too-personal experience of the popes in the revolutions of the nineteenth century—being expelled from Rome, being held hostage, losing the Papal States and temporal power to anti-Catholic forces, and the erosion of even spiritual allegiance—precipitated the development of a Vatican counter-offensive. The first step of that offensive was analysis of the situation to its cause: private judgment (= Protestant Revolt). The second step was to devise a strategy to reclaim the spiritual ground threatened by or lost to private judgment. The third step was to execute the strategy. The strategy and its execution were begun by Gregory XVI with *Singulari nos*; advanced significantly by Pius IX with his Syllabus of Errors and definition of papal infallibility; intellectually and spiritually undergirded by Leo XIII with his efforts (*a*) to corral independent modes of thought into the single philosophical system of scholasticism, and (*b*) to provide people everywhere a way out of the social maelstrom by transcending heads of state and appealing directly to conscience, thereby constituting a supranational *populus christianus* led by Christ's vicar; and, finally, the policing of this transcendent state through the measures enacted by Pius X: *Pascendi dominici gregis*, the oath against modernism, and the vigilance committees.

THE POPES AND THEIR JESUITS

Pre-eminent among the forces called on by the popes to execute the strategy against the modern world was the Society of Jesus. This pre-eminence dates back to the foundation of the Jesuits and the decision to add to the three traditional vows of religious life a fourth vow of special obedience to the pope. That vow, unanimously agreed on by the first companions of Ignatius of Loyola, originated in the founder's intense desire to be united with Christ and therefore with Christ's vicar in progressively accomplishing God's redemptive plan.[2] The bond between the papacy and the Jesuits was always close, but historical forces in the late eighteenth and nineteenth centuries, which first pressured the papacy to suppress the Jesuits and then allowed their restoration, made the bond even tighter. Jesuits were always keenly aware that their very existence depended on the will of the supreme pontiff, but at no time was this awareness as keen as in the decades following their suppression and restoration, when the Society became perhaps overweeningly grateful and beholden to the papacy.

Nor was the relationship all one-sided. The popes of the nineteenth century, exceptionally beset by hostile forces, needed all the support they could muster. They counted on the Jesuits for unquestioning loyalty. Leo XIII, while not shy about expressing his affection for the Society of Jesus even in public, was more overt in private.[3] In 1896 at an audience for Jesuits meeting in Rome, Leo spoke with such high praise of the Society that the Jesuit superior general, Luis Martín, forbade the reporting of the pope's words even in Jesuit in-house publications for fear of awakening invidious comparisons and rivalry with other religious orders.[4] In a private letter Leo also confessed that, although as a youth he did not feel called to the religious life, he sometimes prayed that God would nevertheless lead him to become a Jesuit, for he felt unbounded esteem and admiration for the Society. Of special interest is his remark, in an address to the clergy of his home town of Carpineto, which connected Ignatius' Spiritual Exercises with Leo's social agenda: "While my soul was eagerly yearning for a more substantial food, I sought for it in vain in many books; not one satisfied me until I came upon St. Ignatius' Book of the Spiritual Exercises. Keenly did I relish it, and bethought me: here at last is what my soul was craving for. Nor have I ever parted with it since. The meditation on the End of Man alone would suffice to consolidate anew the whole social fabric."[5]

Pius X, naturally less reserved than Leo XIII, was more expressive.[6] On one occasion he gave foundation to the reputation that the Jesuits are the pope's shock troops. To the Jesuit delegates gathered in Rome in autumn 1906 to elect a successor to General Martín he said:

But if indeed we should fall upon evil times, and if bitter war, which is brought upon the Church and her holy institutions almost everywhere, places in jeopardy the eternal salvation of Christ's faithful, while we vehemently deplore this unjust state of affairs, we give the greatest thanks to God, who delivers you to Us as the most select line of soldiers, skilled in battle, instructed for fighting, and ready at the command and nod of the leader even to muster against the enemy where he is most concentrated and to pour out [your] lives.[7]

Rudolf Meyer, Martín's assistant for the English-speaking provinces, recorded the conversation that the Jesuit vicar general and two assistants had with Pius X in 1906 when they sought his permission and advice about calling a general congregation to elect Martín's successor. Toward the end of the audience, the pope said,

"In your congregation, I recommend that you pass decrees in favor of 'Scholasticism' . . . [because] the enemies of the Church fear Scholasticism. . . . [For] when they apply its principles and draw conclusions *according to form*, they have no reply. . . . And if it should be necessary, we will drive the point home as Leo XIII did." Father Vicar replied that the Society wanted to be obedient to the Holy See in all things. And the Holy Father [responded]: "I have never doubted it, I do not doubt it, and I shall never doubt it. I esteem all the religious orders, but I have a special relationship with the Jesuit Fathers. The Society is the Pope's right hand, etc."[8]

The bond between the papacy and the Jesuits, ultramontane from their foundation, was therefore strengthened by the trials of historical events. The Jesuits were identified with the papacy and the papacy with monarchy, and as one was assailed so were they all, and all together retreated into an ideological fastness. To maintain this fastness against the hostilities of the modern world, one virtue was esteemed above all others: the virtue of loyalty. And this virtue was manifest above all by speaking with one mind and one voice.

Luis Martín was one voice the papacy could count on. Indeed, we may take him as a spokesman for the papal-monarchic view. With Leo he sensed very broadly that the foundations of the Catholic Church were threatened. And when he analyzed the threat to its source, he drew a direct line through democracy (as a polity) to liberalism (as a way of thinking) to the Enlightenment (as establishing that way of thinking) to Protestantism (as initiating it); and he saw them all as one unified force battering the ramparts of ecclesiastical authority. And because authority in the church from the beginning was tied — in his perception — rather exclusively to the monarchic model, any threat to "world order" (read "Christendom") or to church order was perceived as a threat to divine order. Consequently, when Martín called liberalism "the heresy of our age," he had only to turn the expression slightly and he was at *Pascendi's* characterization of modernism as "the compendium of all heresies."

That was Rome's carefully considered view of the age and of what was happening in the Catholic Church because of contact with the age. Obviously, the modernists saw things differently. The question of interest here is what accounts for the difference? Was it due to perversity on the part of the modernists — selling out intellectually and morally to the modern world — as papal loyalists alleged? Or was the difference due to tribal intransigence on the part of the papalists, as the modernists alleged? Every answer depends on perspective. In the modernist crisis two seemingly irreconcilable perspectives reached an impasse, with intellectually and morally upstanding people on both sides, at least if they are each granted their separate premises. How does one explain the phenomenon of such intellectually sophisticated and even saintly people as Friedrich von Hügel, Edmund Bishop, Maude Petre, George Tyrrell, Alfred Loisy, and Maurice Blondel lining up (with their admitted differences) over against such figures as Popes Leo XIII and Pius X, Cardinals Désiré Mercier and Merry del Val, and Luis Martín and the writers of *La Civiltà Cattolica*? These people were neither morally nor intellectually perverse. They simply viewed the world, truth, and its pursuit differently. The question is why. The attempt to answer this question will place us at least at the head of the road toward sympathetic dialogue.

Without claiming any sort of complete answer, I would like merely to offer some speculations *toward* an answer. My speculations will be based on the findings of various pioneering anthropologists and ethnologists.[9] I will begin by presenting a composite brief of those findings that seem most pertinent to this study. Then I will try to show how these findings could apply to and illuminate the behaviors and motivations of the principal Roman anti-modernist figures. My hope is that, although brief and needing much qualification, my synopsis will suggest avenues of further investigation toward a fuller, and therefore truer, understanding of the history of modernism.

Two other caveats. First, my brief will draw out the cultural characteristics of the "Mediterranean mind" baldly only to emphasize the differences from, say, the "Anglo-Saxon mind." By no means do I intend thereby to ridicule Mediterraneans or to suggest that one culture is better or worse than another; cultures are merely different, with different consequences of behaviors. Nor, in pointing up a salient characteristic, do I mean to suggest that this particular characteristic is not also found in other cultures. It usually is. I wish to argue merely that it is exaggerated in this particular culture to the degree that it has become typical. People from cultures in which a given behavior is not typical will find such behavior curious or even offensive. Second, it will do modernist sympathizers little good to attempt a sympathetic reading of the anti-modernists if they do not first recognize their own ideological biases.

THE "MEDITERRANEAN MIND": AN ANTHROPOLOGICAL BRIEF

To understand, for example, how Luis Martín, under strictest secrecy, could order two of his men to ghostwrite the English bishops' joint pastoral letter condemning liberalism, edit it himself, and then manipulate its signing by all the English bishops, we must understand the lay of his mind at this point in history and something about the moral justification of behavior in time of war. For war was the context of European secular and ecclesiastical history for over a century now, as the Catholic church in its magisterium was ideologically aligned with an ever-retreating monarchy beleaguered by ever-advancing forces of democratic liberalism. But to understand Luis Martín's mind, one must understand the cultural factors that largely qualified that mind. Thus, we must begin by attempting, however inadequately, to enter into the Mediterranean mind.

That indeed there is such a "mind" with characteristics com-

mon to the many peoples of the Mediterranean basin is cogently argued by the data of numerous Mediterraneanists. My
task here will be simply to describe the salient features of that
"mind" and then outline the argument for the validity of this
construct.

The organizing principle of Mediterranean society is belongingness. The primary social structure of belongingness is the
family. A person's identity depends on belonging to and acceptance by his or her family. But that belonging and acceptance depends on the person's adherence to the traditional rules
of order by which the Mediterranean family is organized and
maintained. Order is a complex, socially transmitted template
to which each family member is expected to conform in order
to belong. To answer the question whether or not one belongs
to the family, one must answer the question, where in the family one belongs. If one is where one belongs (according to the
rules by which family honor is maintained), then one is considered pure and therefore a family member. If one is not where
one belongs, then one is judged impure and is ostracized. In
the Mediterranean world dirt is defined as matter out of place.
And just as dirt is swept out of doors, so a family member who
violates the rules of social order is ejected, at least figuratively
and sometimes literally, depending on the severity and persist-
ence of the violation.[10]

Order in the Mediterranean family is maintained by the com-
plementary codes of honor and shame. Honor is the conferral
of public esteem; shame, the deprivation of public esteem according to whether or not a person upholds the traditional mores of the family. Correlatively, public esteem implies sensitivity to public opinion. What seems peculiar to Mediterranean
society is the rigidly gender-based definition of the order maintained by the codes of honor and shame. All of reality is dyadically defined and organized into male and female categories:
there are "male" times and "female" times, "male " spaces and
"female" spaces, "male" functions and "female" functions
within the social grouping.

The male in Mediterranean society by definition plays the
publicly dominant role because reality is divided between public and private domains, with the former defined as male and

the latter as female. Honor and shame, the codes of reinforcement of order, depend on public esteem and sensitivity to public opinion. Thus it is the man's role to uphold the very system of honor and shame because it pertains to the public domain. In fact, the male person's identity as male depends on his success in his role of upholding and defending the carefully learned purity system.

Shame occurs whenever someone disrupts the purity system, that is, the rigidly defined and learned hierarchical ordering of persons and roles in a family. Generally speaking, therefore, the disruption shames primarily whoever is responsible for maintaining order. Put another way: subordinates are always potential threats to superordinates, and therefore insubordination (disobedience) is the generic disruption of hierarchical order and thus is the generic cause of shame and dishonor.

Relative to the dominant male, therefore, the subordinate female is considered to be the essential generic threat to social order. Women are mythically perceived as Eve, the temptress, who corrupts men and brings disaster (shame) by subverting the social order and hierarchy of values, especially male dominance. Whenever the threat has been successful—that is, whenever male-guarded order has been disrupted—the male guard is shamed, that is, "emasculated" or subverted into the place of the woman.[11]

The Mediterranean concept of authority has little to do with personal talent or charism but is almost entirely defined in terms of the right and power to command, enforce laws, exact obedience, determine, and judge. Authority is exercised by both men and women in their respective spheres, but superordinate authority rests with the man. His primary role of protecting the honor of his family against shame entails a strong exercise of authority. The exercise is generally simple because it is dictatorial according to the learned purity system. Discussion is not in order when one exercises authority by invoking the system rendered sacred by age. Thus the very concept of authority embraces the enforcement of socially accepted mores rather than any power arising from personal, individual, self-authenticating charisms. Indeed, the concept of "personal" (in the sense of individual) has little place in Mediterranean society. Such a notion of authority would be considered foreign and a serious threat to order.

Personal relationships in Mediterranean culture are generally troubled because the purity system inbreeds distrust and ambiguity. Distrust, as suggested above, stems from the requirement that order be hierarchical, with men posted at the top to maintain the accepted and acceptable order. Distrust begins—as the myth of Adam and Eve suggests—when the male–female relationship is perverted by fear from polarity to polarization. In an authentic relationship based on love, the good will of the other can be presumed. But in Mediterranean society, where love is not a primary consideration in male–female relationships but is subordinated to right order and is therefore overshadowed by fear, distrust, and suspicion, the good will of the other cannot be presumed. Subordinates (therefore women) are always regarded with suspicion, since only subordinates can threaten superordinates and their power.

If trust is difficult within the relatively small circle of the family, it is far more difficult in interfamilial relationships. For, as the culture distrusts the virtue and social reliability of its women, so it distrusts the good will of all beyond the family circle and is skeptical and pessimistic about the outcome of events that depend on the good will of others. Mediterranean society, therefore, tends to be xenophobic.[12]

One effect of male–female polarization in Mediterranean society is emotional distance between men and women, even between husbands and wives. The distrust of women in general extends to wives in particular, and since love is seldom a motivating factor in marriage, love cannot overcome the distrust. Moreover, the rigid definition of reality into male and female spheres creates a social climate and opportunity in which intimacy is most commonly experienced with those of the same sex. Men spend most of their time in business and recreation with other men, women with other women, so that a man's best friends are usually other men, and a woman's best friends are usually other women.

Another effect of male–female polarization is a high degree of ambiguity in relationships, often leading to emotional confusion, anxiety, and defensiveness. Here I will deal mainly with male ambiguity since this study is concerned exclusively with males. The majority position among ethnologists and anthropologists on male ambiguity in Mediterranean society begins with the post-Freudian view that all infants, male as well as female, in the pre-oedipal stage identify with their mothers, not (*pace* Freud) their fathers. This early identification with the mother renders subsequent ego-identification for males more problematic than for females, because males must first "dis-identify" with the mother, then counter-identify with the father. This process is difficult in Mediterranean society, compared to northern European societies, due to two interrelated factors: (1) the father's often physical and usual emotional absence from the domestic scene, and (2) the mother's compensatory behavior of keeping her son attached to her through an intense, indulgent, smotheringly affectionate but simultaneously aggressive style of mothering.

Mediterranean fathers are often physically absent (therefore not accessible for male bonding) due to two factors: (1) the purity system itself, which makes the matters of the home (including rearing children through puberty) the virtually exclusive domain of women and the matters of business and public commerce the virtually exclusive domain of men; and (2) economic poverty, which often requires men to leave home for extended periods to find work. The mother's compensatory behavior results from a hunger for intimacy, because frequently the Mediterranean woman's first experience of intimacy occurs not in sex with her husband—normally love is not a motive for marriage—but in breast-feeding her baby. This experience is particularly significant when the baby is male, for producing a male offspring validates the mother socially. The ensuing emotional bond between the emotionally needy mother and the son becomes especially intense and tied to the mother's need.

Because of this intense but skewed bonding, the relationship between mother and son often becomes troubled as soon as the son begins to assert autonomy. The struggle for independence on the part of the male child in turn leads to a dual consciousness of woman in his psyche. When he begins to pull away, the mother reacts with aggressive tactics to keep him dependent, because she lacks other means to satisfy her need for intimacy.

Typically she expresses her counter-rebellion by playing abandonment "games"—for example, saying to her child, "I guess you don't love your mother any more"—and telling him frightening stories of what will happen to him if he leaves his mother's side. Thus he learns that love is precarious even with one's parents, that the world outside is vicious, hostile, and untrustworthy, and that only his mother can truly love and care for him. Of all others he must beware—thus xenophobia.

This aggressive style of mothering is traumatic for the child. It introduces fear, anxiety, and anger into the dependency as the child's natural efforts toward independence are frustrated, and mutual hostility results as child and mother become involved in a love/hate struggle. The upshot is a dual consciousness of woman that ever after rules the male psyche: he perceives woman as a dichotomy of Madonna (the ideal female figure) and whore or demon conniving to usurp his power. Male compensation for this ambiguous relationship to woman and the correlative insecure male identity leads to machismo as a defensive response, which carries over into the way Mediterranean men exercise authority.[13]

Men's ambiguous relationships toward women and correlative ambivalence and insecurity about their own male identity make all relationships troublesome. We have seen how troublesome factors are introduced into the male psyche from infancy. But the purity system itself is responsible and keeps these factors functioning in later life. Here is how.

Honor is regarded in the Mediterranean world as essentially male; shame, as essentially female. Men gain honor by successfully fulfilling their role of guarding their kinswomen's shame (i.e., sexual chastity). Or, as David Gilmore puts it, honor "is the reward for successful power maneuvers in which a man's relationship to other men *through women* is the fundamental axis of evaluation. . . . Honor is everywhere 'closely associated with sex.' " But this constant vigilance of honor against shame renders male reputation or honor dependent on female sexual conduct. When men are unsuccessful in their vigilance, they are said to be "shamed," that is, diminished in relation to other men. Put another way: conceptually, if a man's kinswoman is penetrated, symbolically so is the man who was supposed to be guarding her shame. He is therefore shamed, because by erotic defeat he himself has been diminished, that is, symbolically emasculated or feminized. He has surrendered his masculinity and conceptually rendered himself subject to homosexual assault. Thus in the Mediterranean world the almost universal sign of the cuckold. Thus, too, as Gilmore points out, "women become the 'weak link' in the chain of masculine virtue."[14]

Along with the erotic implications of guarding against shame are economic implications which make male role-success all the more urgent and women's sexual conduct all the more in need of vigilance. For the size and strength of the family patrimony is directly connected with maintaining the family's honor. No one wants to do business with a dishonorable man, but a man's honor depends on his success at avoiding shame by controlling his women.

Furthermore, in the Mediterranean world, which is characterized by competition for scant resources, patrimony is increased and strengthened by marrying within the family—first cousins, if possible. So guarding female modesty against outside intrusion becomes an economic mandate as well. The most effective control mechanism men have to keep their women from wandering and thus endangering the patrimony is to keep them pregnant. Therefore pregnancy—or women's "labor" in re-producing (especially male offspring)—becomes an index of male "performance" and power in relation to other men who could invade the patrimony. Oddly, then, masculine sexuality becomes conceptually broadened into a triadic relationship involving two men (or groups of men) and a woman as arbitrating social index for masculine reputation. We therefore arrive perhaps at some etiological explanation for the sexualized division of time and space in the Mediterranean world into public (as male) and private (as female), and thus the requirement of female veiling and related customs. "There are indeed few societies outside the Latin and Muslim worlds where women must not be 'seen,' as though this amounted to the provocative flaunting of a scarce resource."[15]

To conclude this brief description of Mediterranean social and psychological anthropology, let me recapitulate Gilmore's explanation for why virility in Mediterranean society seems to be peculiarly fragile, beleaguered, and always at risk. Gilmore argues that economic and political factors in the Mediterranean patriarchal society do indeed constitute relevant threats to masculine identity, but that these are external conditions and can become threats only if men's intrapsychic mechanisms allow them to be. Internal psychological conflict stemming from the ambivalence of gender identification (an intolerable unconscious wish to be like a woman and a defense against this wish) renders the reading of external factors as threats to manhood. This ambivalence results from two main factors: (1) the normal pre-oedipal identification of the child with the nurturing parent—usually the mother; and (2) the bipolar split in society between male and female, which renders the oedipal "dis-identification" with the mother and counter-identification with the father troublesome. The father's own sense of masculinity requiring that he be generally both physically and emotionally absent from the private, female environment of home and child rearing, and the mother's consequent compensatory aggressive style of mothering encourage mother–son intimacy and father–son distance, thus making it exceedingly problematic for sons to shift gender identity after puberty.

Two other "external" factors reinforce this problematic. First, the Mediterranean male perception of reality has a contradictory quality that includes as components a distancing dread of the feminine and a phallocentric world view or hypervaluation of the male genital—the former because women are seen as the source of shame, the latter because the penis is at bottom the instrument of subjugation. It is, after all, what women do not have, and male gender identification from the beginning occurs negatively as the antithesis or opposite of femininity.[16] Masculinity has to be won in contradistinction to femininity, but victory is never secure. It is always at risk and so always needs fresh proof and affirmation. A major consequence for personal relationships is competitiveness and correlative defensiveness. Thus, masculinity is simultaneously powerful and fragile, requiring constant vigilance and defense.

Second, the Mediterranean world generally lacks institutionalized rites of passage from boyhood to manhood, so that institutional support for masculine gender identification is lacking at the same time as it is so forcefully stressed. Without this public recognition of a decisive split from femininity and identification with masculinity, each male is left to prove himself in his own way, a lifetime project rendered relentless and always perilous by constant incredulity and suspicion from within and without. Again, the final court of appeal becomes the male genital. Proof of precarious virility rests on demonstrated phallic potency combined with compulsive denigration and distancing of the feminine. As often as not, however, proof reduces to exaggerated claims, joking, and display of machismo.[17]

THE VALIDITY OF THE CONSTRUCT[18]

The very idea of Mediterranean anthropology as a legitimate subspecialty of social anthropology was first broached in the 1950s by Robert Redfield.[19] That suggestion triggered exploratory symposia, some of which organized themselves around tentative themes like "honor and shame," while others lacked any unifier other than geography.[20] A breakthrough in establishing a unifying construct occurred in 1971 with Jane Schneider's article on the origins of the pan-Mediterranean honor–shame complex. To be sure, skeptics challenged the idea and brought its exploration to an impasse. But John Davis' watershed book, *The People of the Mediterranean* (1977), and Jeremy Boissevain's follow-up study, "Toward an Anthropology of the Mediterranean" (1979), helped break the impasse and laid a solid foundation for a discrete Mediterranean subspecialty. It then became a matter for researchers who identified with this subspecialty to provide a unifying definition and construct that would justify their departure.

The effort to justify and define has been advancing for more than ten years now without reaching a final synthesis or agreement. The disagreement is not over whether or not commonalities exist among circum-Mediterranean peoples that would justify an anthropological grouping, but over how to explain the commonalities.

The etiology or historical causes of cultural patterns are notoriously difficult to establish. Some hypotheses point to such factors as uniform climate combined with topography. Others begin with the relatively uniform ecology. Still others simply associate Mediterranean unity with a bundle of socio-cultural traits, described briefly by Gilmore as:

a strong urban orientation; a corresponding disdain for the peasant way of life and for manual labor; sharp social, geographic, and economic stratification; political instability and a history of weak states; "atomistic" community life; rigid sexual segregation; a tendency toward reliance on the smallest possible kinship units (nuclear families and shallow lineages); strong emphasis on shifting, ego-centered noncorporate coalitions; an honor-and-shame syndrome which defines both sexuality and personal reputation. The dynamics of community life also bear many affinities. Most villagers share an intense parochialism or *campanilismo*, and intervillage rivalries are common. Communities are marked off by local cults of patron saints who are identified with the territorial unit. There is a general gregariousness and interdependence of daily life characteristic of small, densely populated neighborhoods. Mediterranean communities also feature similar patterns of institutionalized hostile nicknaming. The evil eye belief is widespread.[21]

Religious and ritual factors also provide correspondences. For example, similar puritanical elements appear both in Maghrebi Islam and in Spanish mysticism; local saints of North Africa parallel patron saints of southern Europe; religions with their priests, saints, and holy men play an important institutionalized political role; and dotal marriage, practiced by only four percent of the world's cultures, is geographically limited to eastern Eurasia and the Mediterranean basin. Governments are inherently unstable—dictatorships alternate with democratic regimes. The former do not survive their leader, and the latter are undermined by competing systems of patronage as a preferred means of dealing with social inequality and as a strategy for political opportunism.

Besides structural, cultural, and ecological continuities as ways to justify the Mediterranean synthesis, some researchers have stressed the history of mutual influences among the peoples of the regions. Davis argues that centuries-long movements of peoples and customs through conquests and reconquests, conversions, trade, and commerce have resulted, certainly not in an area of homogeneous culture, but nevertheless in a unit in some sense. Gilmore is quick to point out, however, that mutual contact, no matter how intense, cannot by itself justify a "unity" label: "Were this so, then the entire Hispanic world would constitute a unity, . . . so would the Sea of Japan or even the North Atlantic. It is rather the combination of historical convergences with synchronic parallels in culture, all within a homogeneous environment, that provides both internal consistency and distinctiveness to the Mediterranean area."[22]

Other researchers analyze Mediterranean distinctiveness in terms of world political economy.[23] They see the various Mediterranean peoples involved in some kind of massive conspiracy against or reaction to their dominant overlords—first Rome, then Spain, then Northern Europe. But this explanation, like all the others cited above, explains too little and cannot account for numerous inconsistencies. Thus Gilmore concludes: "Each dimension is a necessary but not sufficient criterion for defining the Mediterranean construct. In my view, the much heralded unity of the Mediterranean emerges both synchronically and diachronically from an analysis of the unique concurrence of all these multiple factors."[24]

Be that as it may, there is still one other hypothesis that seems to me to come closest to getting at the root of Mediterranean unity. Carol Delaney, in her suggestively titled article "Seeds of Honor, Fields of Shame,"[25] proposes that the honor/shame complex may, after all, be the Mediterranean unifier, even though its manifestation among different peoples of the region varies considerably. She believes that there is both a sameness and a difference about the complex's various manifestations—"in the way that genetically similar seeds sown in different soils produce phenotypically varied fruits." What accounts for these variations-on-a-theme, she suggests, "is a specific theory of sexuality and procreation that produces slightly different permutations in practice depending on the environment in which it takes root."[26] What is common to all the Mediterranean peoples, Christians, Muslims, and Jews alike, is a monotheism that originated in the Fertile Crescent, where a seed-soil theory of "procreation was already a source for the generation and expression of significant symbols by which the world was perceived, ordered, and reproduced."[27] These symbols sprang from a powerful analogy drawn in this agrarian society to account for the mystery of life and its order—the analogy between two subordinate analogues: (a) the potent, life-giving seed sown in the passive, fallow field that results in a superabundant reproduction of the sown seed, and (b) the male semen impregnating the nurturing female to bring forth, it is hoped, a male child to continue the creative line; and these two analogues were elevated to ontology by seeing them mimetically related to monogenesis as their prime analogate, in which the masculine God/Allah/Yahweh is the principle of all created beings and order in the universe. Honor is then necessarily associated with maleness, shame with femaleness, and thus we have the birth of patriarchy.

Patriarchy necessarily defines a masculine God who legitimates all male-defined customs. Not that women in patriarchies do not have their spheres of influence and power to define, but their spheres and powers are strictly subordinate to men's power, which receives approbation from a masculine God and his male priests, prophets, and kings. "A Man is the second god after Allah," Delaney's villagers say.[28] Women have value only subordinately, insofar as they support the system, as a field supports the germination of seed. Thus they are constitutionally inferior (shameful) and gain honor only participatively, to the extent that they remain cognizant of their subordinate and supportive role. Naturally the focus of honor and shame are the genitals. The male's penis is the seat of honor because it has the ability to perpetuate the self in time; the female genitals are the seat of shame precisely because they do not have this ability. "The theory that it is the male who contributes the generative and formal principle [of life] is as old as Aristotle." The ovum was not discovered until 1826, and its function was not understood until genetic theory developed and became widely known only in the mid-twentieth century. Thus it has only recently become known that the woman in fact contributes half of a newborn's genetic material. The conse-

quences of this simple fact are still many years away from playing themselves out.[29]

Muslims, Delaney points out, say that they, along with
Christians and Jews, are "people of the Book." That is, they
trace their common ancestry to Abraham to whom God gave
the covenant "I will multiply your seed as the stars of heaven
and as the sand upon the seashore" (Gen. 22:17). Being "people of the Book," wherever the religions of the Book took root,
so did the ideas of these people. The seed-soil theory of procreation and its manifold implications are as widespread as the
Books' dissemination and assimilation. But, as Delaney concludes, "the intense degree to which they remain in force in
the Mediterranean area is certainly related to the political economy, social structure, education, and ecology of that area."[30]

APPLICATION IN ECCLESIASTICAL STRUCTURES

As we have seen, to the Mediterranean mind, family or belongingness is constitutive of reality itself. To be outside the family
is to be virtually non-existent, or if one first were within the
family and then departed for whatever reason, that one would
be relegated to a status considered worse than non-existence.
The power of discrimination and judgment concerning the
status of one's relationship to the family (and therefore of one's
existence) rests with the paterfamilias, and that power is regarded as virtually absolute, next to God's, for indeed it is considered divinely ordained and guaranteed. It may therefore not
be questioned. To do so is to be rash and insubordinate, and to
persist in questioning is to be defiant and disobedient and subject to a quasi-divine censure, whose declaration carries with it
all the defensiveness and paranoia accruing to the exercise of
insecure male dominance—according to the mechanism and
motivations described above.

If one were to grant some validity to this description of the
Mediterranean mind, and if one were further to grant that the
principal Roman characters of the present study—Leo XIII,
Pius X, Merry del Val, and Luis Martín—were not exempt from
the cultural qualifications of this mind but indeed exemplified

it, one can then begin to read their various behaviors in terms of the anthropological characteristics of this mind and perhaps begin to understand why they responded as they did to various perceived threats—how, for example, they could justify their violent reaction against the designated liberals and/or "modernists" and/or rationalists. It would be instructive to reread the foregoing chapters in the light of this hypothesis, but in the interest of economy, I will highlight just a few of the more salient behaviors of these figures which this hypothesis, I believe, casts into a new light.

For the Mediterranean family model to be applicable to our principal characters, we must accept that they themselves operated, whether consciously or subconsciously, within that model. As celibates for the sake of the Gospel, they had answered Jesus' injunction, "Sell your possessions and give to the poor . . . and come, follow me." Thus they regarded themselves as inheritors of his promise, "Anyone who has left brothers or sisters, father, mother, or children, land or houses for the sake of my name will be repaid many times over, and gain eternal life" (Matt. 19:21–30). In a sense, Leo, Pius, Merry del Val, and Martín had departed from their families of origin, only to be assumed into a new family bound by ties stronger than blood—according to Jesus' words, "'Who is my mother? Who are my brothers?'; and pointing to the disciples, he said, 'Here are my mother and my brothers. Whoever does the will of my heavenly Father is my brother, my sister, my mother'" (Matt. 12:48–50). Ever after, the church and especially its leaders have adopted the language and—inevitably with the language—also the cultural patterns of the Mediterranean family system. For, although all followers of Christ "share in the glorious freedom of the children of God" (Rom. 8:21) as an eschatological reality, none other than Christ himself has attained this freedom. Thus cultural embeddedness is inherent to earthly existence, so that ecclesiology from Paul on down is rooted in the Mediterranean model.[31]

Granted the foundational reality of this model for the church, we need further to specify the operative family roles within this model for our principal figures, roles that take on added significance in the light of the fact that these figures have left their natural families and so now carry out their roles only within the "supernatural" family of the church. Since, from ordination on, they assume the title of "father," their relationship to the church as institution is that of husband to wife—not wife as person and partner, but as signifying patrimony, possession to be guarded—and their relationship to church as community is that of husband to wife and father to children.[32] As they ascend the hierarchical ladder from priest to bishop to pope these relations become even more sharply defined, as responsibility increases for guarding the "wife," "children," and "patrimony" against shame and dishonor. An important aspect of the hierarchical ordering of Mediterranean authority, in which roles are always dyadically gender-defined, the ascendant role is always considered male relative to the descendent role, regardless of the biological sex of the role-players. In other words, subordinates are always considered female. Thus the pope would be considered male relative to the bishops, the bishops male relative to the priests, the priests male relative to their parishioners, and so on. This perception of social order leads to overwhelming feelings of ambiguity, vulnerability, and thus defensiveness, which in turn leads to power struggles with accompanying cross-accusations of domination on the one hand and disobedience on the other.[33]

Before moving on to consider some characteristic behaviors of our principal figures in the light of the foregoing anthropological brief, it would be useful to list typical perceptions exhibited in documents from the Mediterranean world and therefore in many official ecclesiastical documents. The following propositions are typical unexamined presuppositions out of which the typical ecclesiastical official operates.

(1) All that is needed for life (truth) is contained within the boundaries of the social unit (the Catholic Church), which are secured by gender-defined and shame-based rules of order.

(2) This order is perceived as natural, that is, as originating with creation, therefore as divinely ordained, and therefore to be followed without question.

(3) This divinely ordained order is hierarchical, with superiors perceived as male and subordinates as female.

(4) But social (and ecclesiastical) order, security, and identity are always tenuous and needing to be guarded against threats from within and without.

(5) Extreme vigilance is therefore always required.

(6) Therefore there must always be a resolute concern for rules of order.

(7) Order is secured by submission to external authority; internal, personal authority is discounted.

(8) Indeed of primary consideration is not personhood or personality but divinely ordained roles and rules of proper procedure.

(9) Threats are perceived as either male or female, depending on whether they come from above or below the threatened person on the hierarchical social scale. Thus superiors generally perceive threats to their authority as female; subordinates perceive threats as male.

(10) Since self-sufficiency is guaranteed within the enclave, and since personal authority is discounted, challenges to change are perceived as coming from the outside.

(11) Further, due to the perception of self-sufficiency, anything new or different is either forthrightly rejected or belittled as trivial, faddish, and a novelty unworthy of consideration.

(12) What pertains to threats from within the enclave is projected without. Thus, because threats within are perceived as female, external threats are also perceived as female, as coming from effeminate wiles and threatening to gain entrance by stealth and seduction.

(13) Thus all threats are perceived as stemming from a single source: seductive insubordination—a feminine attribute.

(14) Security is maintained by the feminine virtues of humility and obedience to divinely constituted male authority.

The Seamless Robe

The first behavior I wish to exemplify from the evidence cited in the foregoing chapters is the one around which this entire study revolves: the tendency to regard every perceived threat to church order and authority as part of a seamless robe first modeled by Martin Luther. The "seductive insubordination" in this case is the litany of the interconvertible charges of liberalism/rationalism/individualism that stemmed from Luther's stand against Rome.

In the light of this model, it is easy to see why Roman Catholic clergymen characterized the movement set in motion by Luther as a revolt rather than a reform, and why the popes of the nineteenth and early twentieth centuries consistently drew a line through all the "isms" of their day back to Luther. For them Luther was the one who established the social legitimacy of claiming access to truth outside the "family" defined by the Roman Church—which claim in turn led to the social legitimation of separating states from the church. For Catholic ecclesiastics the claim to independent access to truth was represented by individual conscience standing over against the collective conscience of the church as represented and interpreted by the magisterium. Of course, there was nothing theoretically objectionable to posing a dialectical relationship between individual conscience and the church, as the principle of individual conscience and obedience to it was already long established. But to the Mediterranean mind, in the lived reality of this dialectical relationship, conscientiously to stand *over against* the magisterium was to be insubordinate due to a *malformed* conscience. The philosophico-theological reflection on the nature and function of conscience in general and on conscientious opposition to magisterial teaching in particular (which developed in the scholastic and neo-scholastic manuals) laid the cause of such opposition to reason gone astray, that is, to *rationalism*—and this, because the scholastics had reduced conscience to a faculty, power, or act like the faculties of reason and will which played major roles in coming to judgments of conscience.[34] And therefore magisterial figures invariably named rationalism side by side with Luther as the germ from which sprang every evil "ism" that beset the authentic teaching function of the church.

Evidence of this reductive tendency is ubiquitous in the writings of the popes. I will begin my citations of it with salient examples from Pius X and then focus on Luis Martín, the figure of greater interest for this study. The reason for beginning with Pius X is twofold: (1) the reductive tendency is clearest and most programmatic with him; and (2) Martín, as subordinate and especially beholden to the pope, took his cue from him— although obviously not until after 1903 when Pius X became pope. Prior to that, Martín took his cue from Leo XIII, who ratified this reductionism by certifying Neo-Scholasticism as the official thought-form of the Catholic Church over against the outside world—by which was meant primarily liberal Protestantism. In the papal view, after all, it was Protestantism that separated individual reason from the church's authoritative communication of tradition and so enabled the rise, first, of rationalism, then of liberalism, and finally of modernism (that is, liberalism within the fold).[35]

The reductive tendency is already manifest in Pius X in the choice of his motto, *"Instaurare omnia in Christo."* This motto expressed his commitment to restore all things in Christ,[36] for in his estimation—which followed that of his nineteenth-century predecessors—much of the world's reality had departed from the family of the church. As he put it in his inaugural letter, *E supremi apostolatus* of 4 October 1903: "We were terrified beyond all else by the disastrous state of human society today . . . suffering more than in any past age from a terrible and radical malady which, while developing every day and gnawing into its very being, is dragging it to destruction. . . . This disease is apostasy from God"—by which he meant rationalism, individualism, Protestantism.[37] His prescription against the disease was strictly sacerdotal: first, renewal of priestly holiness among the ordained to strengthen those responsible for the church's virtue; second, the "greatest diligence" in "the right government and ordering" of seminaries to prepare those about to assume the mantle of responsibility; but, third and most important, bishops and other ordinaries were to be "co-operators" with Christ's vicar against "that sacrilegious war which is now almost universally being stirred up and fomented against God." As in the Mediterranean family, where the father's authority is virtually absolute, we have here a virtual identification of the papacy and the hierarchy with God. With that identification comes divine sanction of hierarchical action and concomitant divine condemnation of any contrary action. Indeed, opposition to ordained authority is regarded as sacrilegious.

The specific opposition that Pius had in mind—which to him was but a manifestation of the disease of rationalism—was historical criticism. He characterized it as "a certain new and fallacious science, which . . . with masked and cunning arguments strives to open the door to the errors of rationalism and semi-rationalism."[38] Combined in this one remark are several characteristics of the Mediterranean anti-modernist response to opposition (or difference of perception). One that we have just seen is to find all opposition rooted in a single etiology—here, as elsewhere, rationalism. Another is to deal with opposition by belittling, ridiculing, denigrating, or trivializing it—all of which is effected here by the implied feminism of "masked and cunning." One typical way of belittling is to dismiss by epithet. Al Capone's stock-in-trade dismissal of Elliot Ness was "You ain't got nothin' on me. You're nothin' but a punk!"—doubtless intending the sexual derisiveness of that term. Commonly, among the anti-modernists any idea that could in any way be associated with rationalism or liberalism was dismissed both by the association itself ("You're nothing but a rationalist!") and by deprecating the idea as a novelty or as "new" (not approved by tradition). Practically synonymous with "new" was "fallacious." Eventually the error that Pius X defined was reified in the term "modernism."

Why such linguistic usage would characterize the Mediterranean mind is readily seen in the closed, authoritarian, theocratic, and tradition-bound nature of Mediterranean society. All that is conceivably good and true in the world is to be found within the boundaries and traditions of the family (read Catholic Church). What is outside the family and its traditions is to be spurned. It lies outside for a very good reason: it does not belong, it is out of place (= dirt), and therefore it can be readily dismissed as virtually non-existent or even as evil. In Thomistic language (which is, of course, Mediterranean) evil is defined as the absence of good or, by illation, the absence of existence.[39]

A third characteristic response to opposition, allied to the first two, is automatically to regard whatever confronts the family (Catholic Church) as coming from outside the family and as threatening to gain entrance by stealth. It is "masked" and "strives to open the door" through "cunning." Thus extreme vigilance is required. Again, why this language should typify the Mediterranean mind can be seen in its psychology. The Mediterranean city/family/mind is walled around and fortified. Life goes on mainly within the walls, not without. The typical Mediterranean town has a square for negotiating social concerns, the home has a cortile,[40] and the mind mirrors that architecture as well as produces it. In tradition-bound Mediterranean society, the prospect of change is generally greeted negatively and is perceived as happening through some external force. In the sharply dyadic Mediterranean psyche, that force is automatically read as a masculine challenge to another male's feminine preserve. Since the primary duty and preoccupying concern of the paterfamilias is to guard the virtue of his wife, lest he be publicly shamed and his potency and economic value come into question, when he is faced by a tradition-defying challenge, his and his family's honor requires that he mount a counter-attack.

Pius X in *Pascendi dominici gregis* offers a rationale for this preoccupation in his assertion that the remote causes of modernism

may be reduced to two: curiosity and pride. Such is the opinion of Our Predecessor, Gregory XVI, who wrote: "A lamentable spectacle is that presented by the aberrations of human reason when it yields to the spirit of novelty, when against the warning of the Apostle it seeks to know beyond what it is meant to know, and when relying too much on itself it thinks it can find the truth outside the Catholic Church wherein truth is found without the slightest shadow of error."[41]

The language here is that of machismo. Exaggerated claims of the church's (wife's) virtue reflect well on the power of the overseer, particularly if one realizes how prone the church is in her members to the wiles of the flesh. It is best if the overseer can prove his claims, but if he cannot, assertive boasting is the next best tactic. It is no mean feat to keep such a church (wife) under control, when its members are driven by curiosity "to know beyond what it [reason] is meant to know" and to flirt absurdly with what lies outside the church—threatening to yield to "the spirit of novelty"—when inside "truth is found without the slightest shadow of error." "Otherness," what is outside the domain of the paterfamilias, is perceived as female, and therefore as wily and seductive and threatening to bring ruin on the household.

APPLICATION TO LUIS MARTÍN

It should be obvious that, while every representative of the Mediterranean mind is indeed representative, he or she is *uniquely* representative. That is, factors of personality and history qualify each representative's embodiment and expression of the generic mind. Because of our greater interest in Luis Martín, it is in place here to begin by narrating aspects of his personal history which he saw as significant and which I see as characterizing his unique representation of the Mediterranean type. These unique personal factors, of course, could make one either more or less representative. My contention is that Luis Martín did not reach a state of critical freedom from his culture, and that therefore the personal factors made him more representational rather than less, perhaps even a caricature of the Mediterranean personality.

Personal Background

Martín's personal history is replete with suffering from both internal and external causes, the latter of which he attributed to the liberals. Born at Melgar near Burgos in Spain, two years before the upheaval of 1848, Martín grew up in an atmosphere of political and social turmoil. His entrance into the Jesuit order in 1864 (the year of the Syllabus of Errors), far from an escape, was an invitation to greater trials, as Jesuits in Spain at best were tolerated and at worst were targets of assassination.

The question of whether or not Jesuits were even allowed in Spain turned for the most part on the issue of Carlism.[42] Disputes over governmental control raged mainly between two principal but complex factions: the conservatives (comprising monarchists, a majority of the clergy, Basques, and Catalans) and the liberals (comprising the educated bourgeoisie and lower nobility who think like them, laboring classes, separatists, Marxists, and Anarchists). The conservatives sided with the Carlists; the liberals, with Queen Isabella—on condition that she accept a parliamentary constitution in return for the liberals' support against the Carlists. With military aid from England—which the Carlists never forgot or forgave—the liberal coalition prevailed and sent Don Carlos into exile in France in 1839. His cause, however, remained alive throughout the rest of the century and even through the civil war of 1936–1939, as Spain for more than a century was violently jerked back and forth between liberals and conservatives with their unwieldy and unruly constituencies.

Spanish Jesuits, among other religious orders, identified with the Carlists. Jesuit historian William Bangert points out that for nearly a third of the hundred years from their restoration in 1815 to 1915, the Jesuits in Spain were dispersed—1820–1823, 1834–1851, 1868–1875—depending upon which faction controlled the government. Upon the restoration of the Jesuit order following Napoleon's defeat and Pius VII's release from captivity, King Ferdinand VII in 1815 invited the Jesuits to return to Spain. But rebellion against the king sent twenty-five Jesuits to their deaths, and a new anticlerical constitution in 1820 required the expulsion of the Jesuits. Three years later Ferdinand regained full power under Metternich's Concert of Europe, and Jesuits returned to Spain. But when Ferdinand died in 1833 and the first Carlist war broke out, concessions by Isabella's regent mother, Maria Cristina, to gain the support of the liberals meant open season on religious orders. A cholera outbreak in the summer of 1834 occasioned a scapegoat attack on, among other religious institutions, the Jesuit Colegio Imperial in Madrid. In all, fifteen Jesuits, forty Franciscans, eight Mercedarians, and seven Dominicans were murdered, and the Jesuits along with other orders were again dispersed.[43]

During this period of exile, in 1846, Luis Martín was born in the pro-Carlist province of Burgos. Five years later, on 16

March 1851, a concordat arranged between Isabella II and Pope Pius IX restored the Jesuits. Martín entered the novitiate of the Society of Jesus at Loyola near Azpeitia in the Basque province of Guipuzcoa on 13 October 1864. But four years later, a military coup drove Isabella from the throne and again exiled the Jesuits to France. Martín tells of a harrowing escape with fellow Jesuits clad in various disguises. As they passed through railroad stations along the way they met threatening mobs screaming, "Long live the revolution!" and "Death to the Jesuits!"[44]

Less than a year later, still in exile, Martín received the sad news that his only surviving sibling, Hermenegildo, had died of consumption on 11 June 1869. Luis was now the sole surviving offspring of his parents. Absence from his parents in any case meant great anxiety for him. The exile and now the loss of Hermenegildo only heightened it.[45]

The perilousness of Jesuit life in revolutionary Europe, and now particularly in France, was brought home to Martín by horrifying news from Paris in late May 1871. Four French Jesuits, along with the archbishop of Paris, were among twenty-four clergymen executed by the Commune of Paris as the provisional government moved to consolidate power following the defeat of Napoleon III in the Franco-Prussian War.[46]

Martín would have been quick to blame the Liberals, as his political leanings were decidedly royalist—influenced as he was by the Spanish publicist Juan Donoso Cortés (1809–1853), a disciple of the passionate royalist Joseph de Maistre (1754?–1821).[47] In the years 1871–1873, when Martín was in the regency period of his Jesuit formation and was professor of rhetoric and humanities for the junior scholastics at Poyanne, he recalled that the "one exception" he allowed in the syllabus of classical literature and drama "was the reading of Donoso, and especially his speech on the revolution of 48."[48] Although somewhat critical of Donoso's style, Martín contended that "all his defects could be forgiven in the light of his great virtues," for his writings were "filled with sublime thoughts" and "captivating conceptions and illustrations." Martín granted that "most of these great qualities are a gift of God and altogether inimitable" and so were not terribly useful for teaching proper rhetorical style. "Nevertheless it is not useless to awaken in the soul feelings of admiration and to see the eagles of genius fly in order to arouse ourselves and make efforts to follow them in flight even though at a great distance behind." Indeed, he added, the greatness of Donoso "aroused the enthusiasm of the class."[49]

Luis was ordained in 1876 and celebrated his first Mass at Lourdes. His father was present and served the Mass, but ill health kept his mother in Spain. A few months later, Luis received word that his father had died. His mother followed about a year later (1878). Luis was now sole survivor of the Martín family. The forced absence from his parents caused him bitter suffering, especially at such critical moments as ordination, first Mass, and now in their last illness and death.[50]

In 1879 Martín was appointed professor of dogmatic theology at Poyanne. That same year Jules Ferry's decrees for the expulsion of religious from France were passed, and in June 1880 the Jesuits were driven out. Fortuitously, this expulsion coincided with the repeal of anti-religious laws in Spain, so Spanish Jesuits were able to return home.[51] They were never again exiled, but anti-Jesuit feeling ran deep and broke out again as late as 1932 with a decree of exile.[52] During the Bourbon restoration of Alfonso XII and Alfonso XIII, the Jesuits prospered in relative tranquillity, while Spain herself continued to suffer internally from factional disputes and externally from the humiliating losses of her colonies. By 1900, apart from holdings in North and West Africa, the Spanish empire was at an end, and the liberal government was held responsible.

On 12 August 1886 Martín was appointed provincial superior of the Province of Castile, a post he held with distinction until 27 April 1891. His superior general, Anton Maria Anderledy (1819–1892) then summoned him to the curia in Fiesole for a special assignment.[53] Anderledy, now seriously ill, was making arrangements for the care of the Society in the event of his death. Much impressed by Martín, he left instructions to be opened upon his death, that Martín was to guide the order as vicar general until the election of a new general.

Anderledy died on 18 January 1892. Martín called a general congregation and was elected the Society's twenty-fourth superior general on 4 October. Almost immediately he made a tour of all the European provinces, returning to Fiesole two months later. Although full of long days and difficult decisions, life in the Tuscan hills was quiet. That would soon change, however, as one of the tasks urged on Martín by the general congregation was to move the curia back to Rome. He completed that task by 18 January 1895 and had now to deal not only with the burdens of his own office but with those of the papacy as well, as the pope often summoned him for consultation.

Still, compared to the turmoil and atrocities of earlier years, Martín's life in Rome was relatively peaceful. There were only minor insults to endure—government agents regularly monitored his movements; on two occasions during routine walks, boys hurled rocks at him; and once they spat upon him. But the memories of past most painful days remained and cast a shadow of melancholy on his character. Peter Chandlery, his regular companion and biographer, observed that although Martín delighted in God's providence over the Society through the years, he frequently expressed his hatred of the world and his wish to leave it, lamenting the decay of faith and the flood of irreligion and vice rising ever higher and higher. The world's news as recorded in the daily press he never read, except for special paragraphs marked for him by his advisers as containing information necessary for him to know.[54]

These factors of personal history, I would argue, made Luis Martín more rather than less representative of the Mediterranean mind. For one thing, the issue of family was for him a searingly formative factor. The fact that he was the family's sole survivor would probably have intensified his sense of duty to represent all that the family had meant to him. And very likely, as a Jesuit, he would have transferred that sense of duty to his family of adoption, the Society of Jesus, and, as a priest, to the Catholic Church. For another thing, the suffering he endured as a member of the Martín family, as a member of the Society of Jesus, as a priest, and as a religious superior would only have augmented his sense of duty. There were other factors that reinforced the ones already mentioned, which I shall have occasion to explore later in a more appropriate context.

MARTÍN'S FIRST LETTER TO THE SOCIETY OF JESUS IN THE LIGHT OF THE MEDITERRANEAN MIND

One can find no clearer picture of the peculiarly representative Mediterranean mind of Luis Martín as he approached the eve of the modernist crisis than in his first letter as superior general to the whole Society of Jesus. Upon reviewing the exposition of this letter in Chapter 3 above, it will perhaps strike the reader at this remove of time and culture that the language of the letter casts it into the genre of rant. Perhaps. But if one bears in mind the critical personal and political factors operative in Martín's world, one can perhaps see that the man was not merely indulging in histrionics.[55] To understand the letter aright we of course have to read it on its own terms, that is, from within its own cultural milieu. In so doing comparisons might leap to mind between what men of other cultures would have written in the same circumstances and what Luis Martín, Castilian Jesuit general, actually did write; nor should we be surprised to find culturally dependent ways of thought and expression that people from other cultures will curious, puzzling, even unacceptable. These are the features I want to highlight, along with the reasons for them. Scanning this programmatic letter from the viewpoint of the Mediterranean mind can shed light on Martín's motives, rhetoric, and message and on the complaint of the English Jesuits that the Spanish general did not understand them.

One could begin with the foreboding language of the opening paragraphs that gave the letter its title ("On Some Dangers of Our Times"), and ask, what if the general at this moment in history were an Englishman or an American rather than a Spaniard? Is it likely that he would have written such a letter as his first communication to the entire Society of Jesus? Probably not. Such a general would not have been prone to regard the post-Enlightenment and post-Revolutionary world as fraught with dangers for the church and seeking by stealth to gain entrance into the Society of Jesus to destroy it from within. Anglo-Saxon and American Catholics were rather intent on dialogue with the modern world, and they were rather sanguine about possibilities for the future, seeing that they were enjoying new-found freedoms, toleration, and were even gaining respect within representational forms of government. The Mediterranean experience was quite different. For one thing, in Italy the Roman Question was still burning, and in Spain the struggle of liberals and other parties against the monarchists for representational government continued with unabated violence. For another thing, there was the whole ethos of Mediterranean anthropology described above which predisposed Luis Martín automatically to regard "outsiders" as enemies, and, as a defensive tactic, to analyze their program to its root cause (liberalism) and discredit it.

In his analysis of the liberal program, it is interesting that Martín credits its success not to the intrinsic strength of the outsiders but to the intrinsic weakness of the insiders. His basic argument was that the Jesuit order could well have dealt with the enemy had its membership not been weak. But it was weak. Why? Effeminate breeding and rearing:

This levity of mind is fostered and encouraged from early days by that delicacy of body which, in the opinion of men of experience, growing apace and bearing a punier offspring, renders the nervous system more and more excitable. And thus it comes to pass that our youth are becoming indolent, hare-brained and unfit for the battle of life; and far from seeking vigorous mental exertion they shrink from all serious effort of body and mind and are ever looking for relaxation and comfort. Small wonder that this evil propensity of nature brings forth in our day the most lamentable results, since the home-training, which is of paramount influence for good as well as for evil, seeing that it is for the most part soft, inconsistent, mainly bent on satisfying and pleasing the child's whims and flattering his passions that grow apace with the body's growth, only develops levity of mind while debilitating and enervating the will.

The subsequent college discipline and literary education are altogether incapable of remedying the many faults committed in this effeminate domestic training.[56]

A non-Mediterranean could only be amazed at this analysis. In effect, what Martín was saying is that the whole Society of Jesus—insofar as it was rife with liberalism—was composed of "women," because its members were naturally levitous, craved fresh excitement, were "indolent, hare-brained and unfit for the battle of life." In a word, they were cursed with an "evil propensity of nature" that "brings forth in our day the most lamentable results."

Foremost among these results was a rebellious and indulgent nature—created by "effeminate domestic training"—which led to filling the mind with "foolish trifles" from the popular press and to challenging authority and disregarding the rules of religious discipline. His implication was that the former instigates the latter; that is, the outside influence works by stealth to gain entrance and subvert the Society of Jesus from within. The subversion begins first with the mind to produce intellectual levity, which necessarily leads to moral levity. Martín, as we shall soon see, was arguing from personal experience—out of which he went on pointedly to observe that the "vain and ridiculous" notions absorbed from "the habitual reading of such literature" will weaken the soul, and in that weakened state "the imagination, aroused and agitated by so many phantasms," will often obtrude upon the mind and "violently" withdraw one from the taste for spiritual and heavenly things; indeed these latter "will become irksome and produce only disgust and torment."[57]

Ideas absorbed from sources that Martín deemed "utterly foreign to and inconsistent with our religious life" would not only arouse and agitate the imagination but would also provoke dissension and disunity in the ranks. Why? Because by exposure to foreign ideas Jesuits would come to a "diversity of views" and a "difference of opinion," which, Martín argued, are incompatible with "fraternal charity and union." For Jesuits are commanded by rule "to think, to speak, as far as possible, the same thing," after the example of their founder, Ignatius, who was himself, in Martín's view, *a man of few truths* [Martín's italics].[58] For the Mediterranean mind, one mark of unity is uniformity, characterized by a rather literal interpretation and unquestioning execution of rules of order. Thus Martín insisted so forcefully on this point.

Even in the best of times, Martín would have insisted on this point, but in the aftermath of the French Revolution and other subsequent revolutions throughout Europe, he was convinced that the whole world was in the grip of an "ungovernable plague of license," that all nations "have been proclaiming a lawless liberty . . . as a sacred birthright for the individual," indeed that "war is declared against all authority." His model of authority was hierarchical—and this, in accord with "divine law and a natural order," according to which "rights and duties . . . are . . . deduced."[59] God operates, Martín believed, according to one and only one model, the one by which traditional Mediterranean society operated. There was no concept of the possibility of a shared authority, or arrival at truth through induction and dialogue. No, true authority descended directly from God to God's representatives, those duly appointed by ordination. Thus, too, knowledge of God's will also descended through this same chain of consecrated authorities to the people, whose proper virtues were the "feminine virtues" of humility and unquestioning obedience.

This is the perceived ideal order of the Mediterranean family. In practice, however, family order operates, as explained above, with a good deal of ambiguity and defensiveness. There is also, I would contend, an underlying current of violence exercised on all family members due to the gender-defined divisions of life, expressed most sharply in the emotional and even physical dissociation of the father from husbanding and child-rearing. One upshot of these traditional definitions of order is the automatic discounting of personal needs and rights, which often expresses itself in outbursts of rebellion on the part of the person so discounted.

Martín's analysis and description of the present state of affairs takes as its analytical model the Mediterranean family. There, as we noted above, the boys are raised almost exclusively (and, compared to the girls' upbringing, rather indulgently) by their mothers until they reach adolescence. At that point, they are suddenly—and quite absurdly—expected to know how to be men, how to stand on their own two feet in the world of machismo. In such a system, the difficulties of adolescent adjustment to the adult world are compounded. But it was within this system that Martín and most Vatican officials operated, and out of which they judged the rest of the world. In that (hierarchical) view, those in subordinate positions are regarded as either subservient or rebellious. There is no middle ground, no dialogue. The normal methods of coming to truth in the northern Eurpean and North American countries, namely, dialogue and inductive reasoning—influenced as they were by scientific positivism and democratic processes—were in the Mediterranean world at best regarded with suspicion and at worst forthrightly condemned by ecclesiastical officials. Thus, to Martín and other officials in Rome, even in the best of times the world north of the mountains seemed adolescent, self-indulgent, and rebellious. In these times of open and declared revolution, even on home soil, it must have seemed adolescent in the extreme. Thus, while the outside observer might place Martín's letter in the literary category of rant, those familiar with the socio-anthropological factors behind it would have to conclude that, in context, his letter was quite temperate and restrained.

One last point, however, needs to be made about the tenor of Martín's letter. In an agonistic society such as Martín's, honor is hard to gain and easy to lose. Thus, as Peristiany points out, "a true man is always on the alert, constantly prepared to prove himself," indeed "is prepared to stake his 'all' on the throw of a dice." Throw into this requirement the additional factor that in such "exclusive societies where face-to-face personal, as opposed to anonymous, relations are of paramount importance and where the social personality of the actor is as significant as his office," and we have more than enough reason to account for the tone of Martín's letter. Further, Peristiany points out that

when the individual is encapsulated in a social group an aspersion on his honour is an aspersion on the honour of his group. In this type of situation the behaviour of the individual reflects that of his group to such an extent that, in his relations with other groups, the individual is forcibly cast in the role of his group's protagonist. When the individual emerges with a full social personality of his own, his honour is in his sole keeping. In this insecure, individualist, world where nothing is accepted on credit, the individual is constantly forced to prove and assert himself. Whether as the protagonist of his group or as a self-seeking individualist, he is constantly "on show," he is forever courting the public opinion of his "equals" so that they may pronounce him worthy.[60]

If such pressure to perform as protagonist falls on the shoulders of even the ordinary member of a social group, one can imagine how much more pressure would have fallen on Luis Martín as sole representative of his family and now superior general of the Society of Jesus. We can readily see why he would have spontaneously indulged in language that other cultures might regard as intemperate. And my contention that, in fact, Martín actually exercised restraint in writing his letter is reinforced.

MARTÍN ON ENGLAND AND THE ENGLISH JESUITS

Having seen the overall caste of Martín's Mediterranean mind through the lens of his first letter as superior general to the whole Society of Jesus, we may now focus on his mind with respect to England and the English Jesuits. We saw in Chapter 3 how the most representative Jesuits of the English Province, including the provincial superiors, felt completely misunderstood, misrepresented, and mistreated by Martín and his consultors in Rome. Most non-Mediterraneans would be as outraged as Thurston was over the abuse Tyrrell received at the hands of the general's censors, who, with apparently good conscience, misrepresented the text of "A Perverted Devotion" by placing their own words in quotation marks as if they were Tyrrell's and then berated the supposed author of this fallacy as though he were an ignorant and naughty schoolboy; and most would be perhaps even more outraged over the fact that the general could accept such practices without apology. Many would also be puzzled about why Martín seemed unable to trust the highest religious authorities in England—the Jesuit provincial, the cardinal archbishop of London, and numerous other reputable witnesses—in their testimony on behalf of Tyrrell and the good he was doing for the cause of Catholicism in England. Why did Martín have such a ready ear for the disproportionately small number of contrary witnesses? Why did he exhibit such contempt for new ideas, new social, political, and theological movements that other Jesuits found important to take seriously and investigate openly? What seems to account for a siege mentality that to non-Mediterraneans seems dispro-portionate to any realistic threat? How, finally, could Luis Mar-tín in good conscience order two of his men under strictest se-crecy to ghostwrite the English bishops' joint pastoral letter condemning liberalism, edit it himself, and then manipulate its signing by all the English bishops? Enlightenment on questions such as these will come, I contend, when they are considered within the context of Martín's social and psychological anthro-pology.

To deal with these questions, we must first set the socio-po-litical context in which Martín was operating. He himself made the connection between the world socio-political situation and his dealings with the English Province. When he began his re-flections in his *Memorias* on the English Province, he observed that his serious problems with her began with the issue of Americanism. This observation takes on added significance when we realize that the Americanist controversy arose in the heat and aftermath of the Spanish-American War, in which Spain's empire was practically dissolved and the United States emerged as a new international colonial power. That war was a consuming and excruciatingly painful issue for Martín, and to see England ideologically aligned with the United States against Spain made it extremely difficult for him to deal with English Jesuits objectively.

THE EFFECT OF THE SPANISH-AMERICAN WAR

Martín devoted an entire chapter of his *Memorias* to the war, which he preferred to call "The War for Cuba and the Philip-pines" rather than the Spanish-American War. He followed the war's progress with exceptional interest for several reasons. First, he was thoroughly a Spaniard, and Spain was being as-sailed by a foreign power. Second, he was tied by blood to the considerable number of Spaniards and particularly Spanish Jes-uit missionaries on those islands. And, third, as superior gen-eral he had a duty toward the welfare of those men and their missionary enterprises.

Martín described his experience of the war as the most trau-matic of his life, and he blamed the United States and the liberals of Spain for the war's disastrous outcome. But several times he pointedly noted England's alliance with the United States. For example, when the conservative monarchist premier of Spain, Antonio Cánovas del Castillo was assassinated in 1897 by an anarchist, Martín observed without further comment that "England and the United States allowed anarchist meetings to celebrate" the crime—as if to say, "Enough said!" "In effect," Martín wrote, "the year 1898 was for me a year of martyrdom, not only because of what I had to suffer as a Spaniard with the humiliations that followed one upon the other with dreadful speed, but also because of the difficult situation I was in as general of the Society having to deal with the Americans, and my physical infirmity which was aggravated by my moral sufferings."[61]

The first of these humiliations, Martín continued, was "the very disagreeable news" he had received shortly before the United States declared war against Spain—news about Archbishop Ireland's sermon on the occasion of the funeral for the 260 Americans killed in the sinking of the warship *Maine*, and news about a published interview of the American Jesuit Thomas E. Sherman, nephew of Secretary of State John Sherman, "in which he talked like a madman ["*como un furioso*"] against Spain and of the necessity of going to war with her."[62] Then there was the official declaration of war, followed a few days later by the attack on Manila, then the fall of Cavite, the destruction of Spanish ships there, and finally the telegraphed reports of disaster from the waterfront in the first few days of May. All of which impressed Martín "most painfully" (*dolorosíssimamente*) "and did much harm to my health."[63]

His first recourse, he said, was to offer up his pain to the Lord and redouble his prayers. Having done that, he ordered the Spanish provincials to contribute funds to the war effort. He himself was unable to contribute financially, since, as general in Rome, he had no discretion over funds for such a cause. He was delighted, however, to receive a gift of one thousand lire in a gold case from another religious congregation, and this gift he promptly and personally presented to the Spanish ambassador, on the condition that it remain anonymous.[64]

The war occasioned extreme internal tensions for Martín. As

superior general he had to affect exterior neutrality while his heart was anything but neutral. When American Jesuits asked leave to serve as chaplains in the war, Martín seemed disappointed that he "could not be opposed" to this idea, and that he would have to allow it and "content" himself with publishing clear restrictions "to avoid foolish and petty behavior."[65] His relations with his international staff were also extremely sensitive, as "I found myself obligated to be neutral in my political negotiations, despite the great love I felt for Spain and the great hatred for America." When, for example, *La Civiltà Cattolica* wanted to publish a broadside against America, Martín had to veto it, even though "it appeared to me to be just and accurate," because "such an article would be attributed to me, and this would cause very grave damage among the American and English priests who openly supported" the American cause. So he made an heroic effort "to appear exteriorly cold and indifferent," but at the cost of "constant and most painful violence" to himself. "This, combined with the fear and anxiety that I should receive bad news caused me incredible moral suffering; and this moral suffering undermined my health, which soon broke down altogether."[66]

In February Martín was confined to his room for several days and during much of May and June "was constantly ill." To relieve his stress, he had to give up reading newspapers altogether, but the chance remarks he overheard and the oral reports he received from his advisers and others heightened his anxiety, "which because of my sensibility I suffered indescribably."[67] His heroic effort to feign exterior neutrality only aggravated his interior conflict. "At that time I prayed so much and with such determination that I do not remember anything like that in my entire life." Toward the end of June when the decisive battle for Cuba was near, he wrote, "I spent much time and even hours in the chapel or in my room praying with arms extended, asking the Lord to have compassion on Spain and give her victory."[68]

Martín's identity with Spain was so complete that he saw Spain's misfortune as punishment from God for his own sins. When news arrived in early July about the rout of a Spanish squadron, he wrote, "I begged and pleaded with the Lord as never before, but without doubt he accepted my prayers in satisfaction for my sins and to ward off other evils for Spain, but he did not accept them to grant Spain victory." In early May, when Manila was falling, Martín wrote to the three Spanish provincials responsible for the Philippines: "First, I wish that you would assign all our fathers and brothers of the province some prayers and sacrifices, that they might beg God our most gracious Father to grant our most beloved country victory for her troops on both land and sea. Also exhort each and all to ponder with sorrowful heart and weep for their sins, which have brought God's wrath down upon us, and to strive with works of penance to placate God and reconcile him with our country."[69]

When Cuba fell, Martín was no longer able to conceal his anguish. "My grief was indescribable." Even during recreation with the fathers of his community, he said, he could not hide the pain that reports of defeat caused him; nor could he conceal his "antipathy, not to mention aversion, toward Fr. Meyer and all that was American." And because it was very difficult and unpleasant to speak to Meyer at recreation, Martín would ignore him and talk to other fathers nearby.[70]

Martín realized that more was at stake than merely the loss of Spain's honor and position in the world. Defeat abroad could very likely precipitate a revolution at home and put Spanish Jesuits and their property at grave risk.[71] There was also the threat to all the good that Spanish missionaries had done in Cuba and the Philippines.

To illustrate his concern, Martín inserted in his *Memorias* a copy of a summary of conversations he had in late September and early October 1900 with Father José Algué about the future of the Philippines. Algué was an astronomer in the Philippines, but, following the war, was sent to the United States to participate in discussions about the future disposition of the islands, that is, whether the native Filipinos or the United States should assume governance. Algué's view, with which Martín strongly concurred, was that it would be far better if the natives took over, because, Martín argued, even though at first there would be anarchy, order would gradually be restored, and it would then be easy to work with them. But if the Americans assumed control, at first there would be "apparent peace and apparent prosperity in our institutions, but gradually they would be lost by consumption or anemia"—that is, through the gradual Americanization and Protestantization of the islands. Martín based his argument on what happened to the missionary effort in South America compared with North America. In South America, "even amidst great disturbances, the faith was preserved" because "the Protestant spirit had not fully penetrated" these nations; but in North America the missionaries "are reduced to being chaplains for the North Americans, and the Indians are disappearing along with the fruit of the missions."[72]

Martín's Reading of Situations in England

The Spanish-American War severely worsened Martín's already sour disposition toward Protestant America and, by implication, Protestant England. But duty forced him to deal with one unpleasant crisis after another in the English Province just at the time that he was dealing with excruciatingly painful issues of the war. Given his negative feelings toward America and England, we must conclude that he exercised heroic restraint in his dealings with English Jesuits, but at further cost to his health. We return now to review, in the light of the Mediterranean mind, several of the most important confrontations between Martín and the English Province and his personal readings of them.

Given what we now know of Martín's Mediterranean mind, aggravated as it was by church–state crises in many countries but particularly by the Spanish-American War, the opening sentence of Martín's chapter on England in his *Memorias* seems almost a caricature: "The first occasion of displeasure in doctrinal matters regarding the English Fathers occurred over the issue of Americanism, inasmuch as concerning the articles of Father Lucas on Archbishop Ireland they [the English Fathers] were scarcely open to any criticism." In fact, the two opening paragraphs are an effusion of all the issues that troubled Martín about the world, issues which he decried in his first letter to the whole Society of Jesus, and which he found rooted deeply in England. "Lucas' articles were nothing more than a particular manifestation of a rather liberal spirit which was insinuating itself into various Fathers without their knowing it. . . . The *Month* was a rather bland journal, which had no stomach for battling the Protestants and the liberals. I blamed this on the English spirit that is little inclined to break lances over doctrinal issues and is habituated to tolerating Protestant errors." To Martín the Dreyfus affair was more of the same. The English fathers took the liberal line, presupposed Dreyfus' innocence, and railed against the *Civiltà*'s coverage of the affair.[73]

"The issue [of Americanism]," Martín contended in his second paragraph, "becomes clearer in the question of Archbishop Ireland and the articles by Father Lucas." Here, Martín noted, Lucas raised "the issue of the Latin vs. Saxon race." That issue, Martín feared, was a clear indication that Americanism was playing into "a real and dangerous tendency of our English Fathers"—namely, English nationalism—which predisposed them either "to believe many historically false charges against the pope . . . solely because they were contrary . . . to the interests of their nation or race," or to be "afraid to defend sound ideas against Catholics and bishops who were thinking in this way and who were held up as eminent men, representing modern civilization and the glory of the English race." That tendency in the Society was confirmed for Martín when the English Jesuits let their meeting hall be used for a conference by the liberal Archbishop Ireland.[74]

When the English Jesuits responded to Martín's criticisms and mandates with the argument that the Catholic Church in England was so beleaguered by critics that the only sensible tactic for them was to be conciliatory rather than pugnacious, Martín was not at all sympathetic. Conciliation and compromise were simply not in the vocabulary of the Mediterranean mind, especially one that was recently so humiliated (read, shamed) by the Americans. To Martín, having Archbishop Ireland speak in a Jesuit house was the mental equivalent of homosexual rape because he as paterfamilias had failed in guarding the shame of his family and thus was feminized. On the one hand, the English Jesuits simply could not appreciate the depth of Martín's revulsion; on the other, Martín could not comprehend the English Jesuits' lack of concern about this issue and many others that he found so disturbing.

THE TYRRELL AFFAIR FROM A MEDITERRANEAN PERSPECTIVE

Martín's conclusion from the confrontations over the Lucas articles, the Dreyfus affair, and Archbishop Ireland was that the English Province was simply shot through with liberalism, and any lingering doubt about that conclusion was eliminated in the Tyrrell affair. It is quite possible that Martín's reaction to and treatment of Tyrrell would have been considerably more tolerant had not one of the first complaints he heard about Tyrrell—and this from Merry del Val—was his offhanded comment that Americanism "was not so bad, that he himself was an Americanist, but that he knew how to express himself about such ideas." The aftermath of the Spanish-American War was surely not the time to brag about being an Americanist to someone named Merry del Val. Tyrrell's comment burned itself into Merry del Val's memory, because, although the Vatican official was born and spent much of his childhood in England, his parents were both of Spanish origin, and his father was a marquis, long in the Spanish diplomatic service, and in fact from 1898 was the Spanish ambassador to the Vatican.[75] That remark colored the lens through which Roman authorities ever after examined Tyrrell and his writings.

When Salvatore Brandi, the editor of *La Civiltà Cattolica*, delated Tyrrell's "A Perverted Devotion" in 1899, Martín rendered a judgment that to the uninitiate might not seem very serious, but to one who knows the Mediterranean mind, it was very serious indeed. Martín's initial reaction was, "I read it, but some things I did not understand well because of Tyrrell's complex manner of thinking and peculiar way of expressing himself; but I must confess that the general impression was also bad." That impression was reinforced by Martín's assistants. "All found it offensive, although not all understood well what the author meant, but they believed that it was in danger of being delated to the Index and condemned." From this poor reading of Tyrrell's article followed his silencing and all his subsequent troubles, ending in his excommunication and perhaps even precipitating his premature death.[76]

From the viewpoint of the Mediterranean mind, what Tyrrell wrote was probably less serious than the fact that he was in danger of shaming the general and his Society. From time to time Tyrrell would quip that one could write anything for the Roman censors so long as one avoided the *male sonans*. At first glance that remark seems merely clever, but in the present context it looms as remarkably insightful, perhaps more so than Tyrrell himself realized. Martín's ears were endemically tuned to superior voices, and it simply would not do for a subordinate like Tyrrell—suspect on several counts: a convert from Protestantism, an Anglo-Irishman, and an Americanist!—to be bringing criticism from the Vatican down upon the Society of Jesus. It would have meant that Martín had failed to guard the patrimony, that therefore, in a sense, he would have endured the ultimate shame of being cuckolded by one of his subordinates. And therefore the expressed support of Tyrrell by the most substantive authorities in England fell upon deaf ears.

Many observers in England were confused by Martín's reaction and surprised at the severity of Tyrrell's censure. But from the viewpoint of the Mediterranean mind, the response makes perfect sense. To the Spaniard Martín, no Catholic in liberal Protestant England was capable of maintaining the purity of the Catholic faith in the face of their more deeply rooted English nationalism, and therefore no English witness was credible against the charges.

Thus, too, the way the Roman censors and Martín dealt with Tyrrell and his article makes perfect sense. To northern Europeans it seems blatantly dishonest for the censors (1) to place their own words in quotation marks and pass them off as Tyrrell's, then (2) to use these words as an example of the heresy they were condemning; and finally (3) to berate Tyrrell as though he were a culpably ignorant and naughty schoolboy. When Martín accepted his censors' behavior and rendered his own judgment on Tyrrell's article over the opinions of Cardinal Vaughan, Tyrrell's provincial superior, his English censors and readership, he wrote to Charnley, acting provincial in the absence of Gerard, that "the censures by theologians of the Society here in Rome . . . differ by the widest possible margin from the opinion of His Eminence Cardinal Vaughan," and that "in these matters the opinions of externs are to be disregarded, as are even the opinions of Ours who are not censors."[77] In the Mediterranean system, values such as internal, personal identity and authority are subordinated to the integrity of the social group. Thus, relative to the latter value, individual rights scarcely exist. It is of paramount importance to maintain proper social order and thus avoid cutting a *brutta figura* in the eyes of superiors. It is not important to get at objective truth—at exactly who said what and what precisely did he mean, if "he" was a subordinate. If "he" was a superior, that is another matter entirely. The Mediterranean truth was that Tyrrell had not avoided the *male sonans* but had cut a *brutta figura*, and therefore the general and the entire Society of Jesus, who enjoyed a special relationship to the Holy Father, were in imminent danger of being shamed in his eyes. That could not be tolerated.

A MEDITERRANEAN VIEW OF THE JOINT PASTORAL

Another anomaly for the northern European mind is the fact that for Luis Martín the issue raised by Tyrrell's "A Perverted Devotion" was, by his own admission, "much more serious" than the Mivart and Dreyfus affairs. In northern Europe the latter affairs generated far more public notice and outcry than the Tyrrell affair did then or later. But Martín's judgment here is understandable when one realizes that he was not directly responsible for overseeing church order in England, whereas he was directly responsible for overseeing Jesuit order. The situation was quite different, however, for Archbishop Rafael Merry del Val. Because of his English roots and lifelong associations, he was always regarded both officially and unofficially as the pope's sentry over England. Thus, whereas Martín was more concerned about liberalism in the Jesuit order, Merry del Val was more concerned about liberalism in England. These two concerns would coalesce in the generation of the English bishops' joint pastoral condemning liberalism.

As special guardian over England, Merry del Val stood to lose far more face over the Mivart and Dreyfus affairs than Martín did. Thus it was Merry del Val who took the initiative for the impending condemnation of liberalism away from Cardinal Vaughan, secured Leo XIII's approval for a "full doctrinal pronouncement . . . without any regard to persons," and engaged the help of Luis Martín in its composition. Once the task of composition was laid to Martín, the latter took it up with a zeal that seemed to surpass even Merry del Val's—after all, once again, his own and the Society's reputation was on the line. He wanted a scheme that could not fail. He appointed two Jesuits resident in Rome, an Italian and an English-born American, secretly to draft the pastoral, and he himself edited it. He then advised Merry del Val to secure the pope's approval prior to publication so that all the English bishops would be pressured to sign it, and then to have Vaughan release it before his *ad limina* visit to Rome to avoid raising suspicions about the real authorship. Knowledge of this duplicity would have enraged the English bishops and the English church, and Martín and Merry del Val knew it. Nevertheless, they were able to carry out this plan with apparently untroubled conscience because to their Mediterranean minds values were at stake that simply precluded consideration of other moral values.

Baldly stated: to them, the enemy had no rights. This principle is by no means exclusive to the Mediterranean world. What is exclusive to the Mediterranean world is the principle's application: who is perceived as enemy and why, and what measures does this perception justify?[78]

The Other Dimension of Martín's Mind

Few persons arrive at such personal freedom during their lifetimes that they rise above their culture. Jesus was certainly one, as were many of the world's recognized enlightened ones or saints. Ignatius of Loyola perhaps was one of these latter; Luis Martín certainly was not. Indeed, I would argue not only that Martín failed to escape the characterizing influences of Mediterranean culture but that circumstances in his life were such that he became almost a caricature of that culture and had to struggle heroically to gain some measure of aesthetic distance.[79]

We have already seen how external factors such as circumstances of birth, formation, and socio- and ecclesiastico-political factors conspired to mold him into a pro-monarchist and anti-liberal. We have also seen how assuming the office of superior general of the Society of Jesus, which is divided into culturally diverse provinces worldwide, introduced into his life the pressure to strive for indifference toward his own culture and understanding of other cultures. And we have seen from his own testimony what a torture that struggle was, particularly because of the Spanish-American War.

What remains to be seen are the internal, private factors that added a certain edge to all the others and made Luis Martín more than merely another example of the Mediterranean mind, but rather something approaching an exemplar. That he never did become a full exemplar, that he was able to exercise restraint, must be laid to the pressures placed on him as superior general to accept cultural diversity and so to confront his own cultural biases.

The one internal, private factor that most affected Luis Martín throughout his life from adolescence on, in virtually all his dealings, was the struggle with his sexuality. We have already seen how, in the Mediterranean male, sexual and personal identity is particularly troublesome due to the gender-defined divisions of social space, time, and interaction, whereby the male child's only effective adult role models until adolescence are the women of his family, particularly his mother. The process of "dis-identification" from the mother and counter-identification with the father is always troublesome, but in Luis Martín's case it became especially problematic for two main reasons: (1) at the age of twelve he left home to study at a seminary in Burgos and so did not live with his father very much at all after reaching adolescence; (2) while boarding with a family in Burgos, he was assigned a room with an older servant boy with whom for about a year he had to share a bed and who, he confessed, "attempted many evil conversations and reprehensible actions" with him.[80] Although Martín vowed that he tried with all his strength to resist the temptations, the trauma and shame of that experience remained fixed in his memory: "I must say that all the year long this familiarity was a steady occasion of many other faults that I have regretted very much all my life through."[81] In fact, judging from Martín's recurrent references to and interpretations of this shaming, one would have to conclude that the sexual curiosity awakened in him by this experience at puberty became a lifelong and morbid preoccupation. "Morbid" is not my subjective characterization. Martín himself, in returning to this issue with surprising candor throughout his *Memorias*, himself regularly connected it with the chronic ill health that led ultimately to his death.[82]

As a result of his experience with the older servant boy, Martín said that he began to live quite privately, not stopping to chat with the servants or workmen, and usually taking his meals alone. To establish his own psychological space in the house, he "dealt with the servants of the house rather roughly as though I had got angry with them."[83] If it is true that, even in circumstances of normal upbringing, the Mediterranean male's sexual identity is ambiguous and troublesome, one can only imagine—based, however, on Martín's own testimony—how much more troublesome it was for him in such psychically devastating circumstances. We continue with some of that testimony.

Martín made no reference to his troubled sexuality during his novitiate years, but the ambiguity and turmoil surfaced shortly thereafter, in his juniorate years, two or three years after pronouncing his religious vows. He confessed that he struggled terribly against a sexual attraction that he felt first toward another junior, then toward a novice who joined the juniorate. To counter these temptations, he redoubled his spiritual exercises and mortifications, and these "broke down the passions and subdued the reluctant body" at least for a time.[84] But if he successfully "subdued the reluctant body," it was not without a price. He had been appointed "beadle" of the juniors, an office of peer leadership given to one regarded as exceptionally exemplary. The discrepancy between his shameful sexual attractions and the charge laid upon him resulted in a tension that he could scarcely endure. A year later, during the next stage of seminary training (philosophy), Martín came down with a pulmonary ailment, which he saw as the beginning of chronic ill health stemming directly from his struggle with sexuality.

After his course in philosophy Martín went on to regency, a period of training when Jesuit scholastics are usually assigned to teach. Martín was assigned to teach rhetoric to younger Jesuits. He recalled how during this time he began a practice, which soon became compulsive, of reading sexually suggestive materials. He said that he would search out "nearly all of the indelicate passages of Virgil, Horace, Catullus, Tibulo [sic], Ovide [sic], Juvenal, Martial, Plautus, Aristophanes, Theocritus, Anecreonte [sic] and some other writers of the Roman and Greek decay." This adventurism led to the reading of other Italian, Spanish, and Latin works "dealing with scientific subjects." Here, writing in English, Martín concluded that

such a curiosity was unsound and hurtful to me yet my passion was so strong that I did not succeed neither that year nor the following ones to get rid of it. . . . I fell again and again without finding out the way to get rid of it. . . . It was a shame for me to find myself so poor and unable to control my fierce passion and I should not have drawn up any idea of the human weakness if I had not felt such an impotence to overcome a little difficulty like that. I think it was something providential and healthy for me to have been so weak that I should know, first, how powerful is the passion, excited by the occasion, to drag worldly men to the abyss of sin, and keep them there years and years.[85]

When Martín went on to study theology (1873–1877) his compulsive curiosity in reading sexually suggestive materials continued. Nor was it helped, he confessed, by the required study of moral theology. He used to sneak books from the professors' library—books stored in a hallway to make room in the stacks for new books—and he would read them, especially Aristophanes, at times when he should have been at common recreation or doing other things. The trouble increased into his third year of theology, when, without giving further details, he said that "a catastrophe" occurred "with so pitiful and sorrowful circumstances."[86]

After theology and ordination, Martín went on to his final year of training called "tertianship." He did not make this year with his classmates, but was instead assigned to act as assistant to the master of novices. Consequently, he missed the exercises of humility normally assigned to tertians, such as caring for the sick, serving in the kitchen, and cleaning floors. He had also missed these exercises during his novitiate. As a result, he admitted, "I did not tame at all my passions and they went on so unbridled as they had been up to then and perhaps much more." Moreover, he believed that because of his sexual struggles his work with the novices was hypocritical, and he harshly judged that all "I did that year was to interfere with the work of the Master of novices in training them."[87]

In 1878 Martín was assigned to teach theology to Jesuit scholastics at the theologate at Poyanne, the house of studies for exiled Spanish Jesuits. One of the students was the novice, now a theologian, to whom Martín was sexually attracted during his juniorate years. The attraction remained; indeed, Martín confessed, "the former passionate love was forever fixed in my heart."[88]

Two years later, in 1880, Martín was appointed superior of the Jesuit community and professor in the diocesan seminary at Salamanca. In March 1881 the bishop appointed him rector of the seminary. This appointment only aggravated Martín's struggle, for in the circumstances of his position his sexual obsession grew and therefore so did his interior turmoil, especially due to the tension caused by his position as role model and rector. By the beginning of his fourth year at the seminary, the toll to his spirit and physical health became so intolerable that he petitioned the Jesuit superior general Peter Beckx to remove him from office, arguing that his many grave faults—which he neglected to specify—made him unfit to rule. Martín did not quote his letter verbatim in his *Memorias*, but if it resembled his memory of it, it was sufficiently ambiguous as to allow Beckx to give it a virtuous interpretation—which indeed he did. And so, Martín said, Beckx's reply—that from all reports he was doing excellent work and should therefore remain in office—indicated that the general "certainly did not comprehend the gravity of my situation."[89]

Thus Martín's problem at the seminary continued unabated and in fact worsened, as indicated by a practice he now adopted, of using binoculars to spy on the boys at night, sneaking barefoot or in his stocking feet along the gallery of the cortile. At one point, remorse over this behavior drove him to pitch the binoculars down a well, but he soon repented of this act and acquired an even better set. He carried on this way for nearly two more years, when deteriorating health forced him to resign his office. He left the seminary in autumn 1885 to become director of the *Messenger of the Sacred Heart* in Bilbao. Martín's assessment of his years at the seminary was that all his preoccupations, combined with the poor food and climate, "was the seed of the illness that later on tried me for many years."[90]

In his new assignment, Martín's sexual preoccupations diminished due to the altered environment, but they did not disappear. He recalled a particularly disturbing experience of September 1886, when, as elected representative of his province to a congregation of Jesuits at their curia in Fiesole, he took the opportunity to do some sightseeing along the way. At Nice and Monaco, he found his senses and imagination assaulted by the sumptuousness of the cities and the nudity of the bathers. Then, following the meeting at Fiesole, he toured the churches and monuments of Florence. Again he found his imagination overloaded with disturbing images of the unclad subjects of painting and sculpture. Years later he recalled this experience with sadness.[91]

Lest the reader suspect that I am making more of Martín's obsessive curiosity than the evidence warrants, let me cite just one instance of how profoundly Martín's fear of and ambiguity toward his sexuality affected his perceptions of reality and consequently, as he himself testified, his health. I referred above to Martín's chapter on the Spanish-American War. Given his testimony that Spain's defeat caused him greater suffering than he had ever experienced up to that point, it is astonishing to see how he begins this chapter. After his opening sentence, which stated that the war was for him a source of great suffering but also of conversion to God, he launched into a lengthy introspective of the state of his soul. It was the year 1895, Martín had been superior general for some three years now, and he had recently moved the curia from Fiesole to Rome:

It was the first year that I spent in Rome, and my behavior was not very edifying. On the contrary it was quite reprehensible due to the fact that I did not dedicate myself with interest to my duties. Indeed I lost a lot of time looking with curiosity from the upper balconies of the house I had taken possession of just a few days after my arrival in Rome . . . particularly at the hotel (and the guests that were there) that looked toward the Via Santa Susanna. This curiosity, which robbed me of many hours every day, but particularly the first hours of the morning, did me much harm. . . . I used to go [to the upper balconies] at any hour, but particularly in the morning, and some-times after ten at night, running the risk of doing harm not only to my soul but also to my body due to the cold of the night and the malaria of Rome. Furthermore, in those walks I was not as modest as I should have been, and so, during that entire year I was very dry and cold,[92] and when I went to confession I was ashamed to see my in-credible miseries, that were so contrary to the position I held.

Toward the end of that year, the news about the war was increas-ingly alarming, and this was in part to liberate me from the shame of my poor spiritual state and in part to expiate my faults and obtain mercy from God for Spain and Cuba, but it would also be the first step of my conversion that would liberate me from the instrument of my curiosity, some binoculars that I had bought in Rome in 1893, on the occasion of the beatification of the martyrs of Salsette.[93]

Thus, in Martín's view, the increasing intensity of the war and the reports of Spain's failure captured his imagination and feelings more than did his binoculars and thus served to liber-ate him from a shameful habit. Instead of indulging his curios-ity he applied himself to his duties and increased his acts of prayer and mortification to win God's favor for Spain. "But God seemed to be so irritated with me and in general with Spain that as soon as I committed a fault of modesty (as in my trip to Anagni) or in my spiritual exercises, I received bad notices of both wars that profoundly afflicted my heart."[94]

Five more times in the course of this chapter Martín reiter-ated his theme that God, angered by Martín's sins, sent the misfortunes of war as punishment and needed to be placated.[95] So Martín redoubled his acts of penance, but was unable to convince God to give Spain victory. At most, he concluded, his mortification succeeded only in deflecting some of God's wrath from Spain.[96] As to himself, while his suffering may have liberated him from an unhealthy psychological and spiritual habit, it contributed directly to the deterioration of his physical health.[97]

I cite all this data on Martín's sexual history only to establish my argument that (a) Luis Martín did not reach the state of holiness and therefore of liberation from his culture that, say, Ignatius of Loyola had reached; but that (b), on the contrary, the peculiarities of his upbringing and especially his unfortunate and traumatic experience of being sexually abused in adolescence exaggerated the already ambiguous and defensive characteristics of the Mediterranean male personality. While Martín was exceptionally gifted intellectually and possessed admirable qualities of leadership, the exaggerated characteristics of his Mediterranean personality proved to be hindrances in his dealing with people in general and with non-Mediterraneans in particular. He himself confessed that he never had any taste or skill for dealing with people of various types.[98] That he succeeded at all—which is attested by his not-unbiased biographer Peter Chandlery—was due to an heroic effort to deny his inclinations, which in the long run contributed significantly to his ill health.

Given the peculiar pathology of Mediterranean culture and Martín's peculiar character defect within that culture, the man found himself, not entirely against his own will, in a simply tragic situation. At one moment in his life, he nearly transcended the boundaries of honor and shame by revealing his darkest secrets to his superior general. But he failed to come clean and his revelation came off as an act of humility, and so he was thrust into the role of religious superior. He could have escaped the burden of office with its responsibility to become in his own person the paragon of vowed poverty, chastity, and obedience. But he chose not to, and so accepted a life of increasing tension and pressure as he mounted the ladder of authority to its highest rung. His effort to counter the inclinations thrust on him by culture and personal circumstance was heroic, but his achievement fell short. Failing to transcend cultural and personal boundaries, Martín condemned himself to a nearly lifelong secret burden of shame and guilt that only increased with time. It was as if he was doomed to survive the deaths of his entire family—who can know the pain of this in a culture where family meant everything?—only to witness the fall of his nation. He was unable finally to bear up under the strain. His psyche had to find an honorable out.

I make no judgment on the state of Luis Martín's soul before God—that is, on the question of personal sin. I judge only the state of inner turmoil and conflict on the basis of his own testimony. To his religious subjects and associates in Rome, Martín was a religious hero: he had given everything in the battle against the heinous enemies of Holy Mother Church and died a confessor of the faith. But to the readers of his memoirs, another interpretation is possible: namely, that the circumstances of Martín's life set him up for tragedy. His heroic strength only heightened the degree of tragedy. It did not help him convert the tragedy to a romance, at least not in this life, not from the perspective of history; perhaps from the perspective of Gospel faith which believes that God regards intentions and in the end straightens crooked lines.

NOTES

1. In arguing so contrastingly here, I do not wish to overlook scholasticism's effort to harmonize the claims of faith and reason. However, I regard that effort as thoroughly biased on the side of reason. Neo-Scholasticism was no less rationalistic than its predecessor, against which humanists in general and Luther in particular rightly rebelled. Scholasticism, in its effort to harmonize faith and reason, virtually reduced faith to reason and simply dismissed or condemned non-scholastic epistemologies that gave greater place to non-rational ways of human apprehension. See McCool, *Nineteenth-Century Scholasticism*. Moreover, I would caution against reading my remark "primacy is not incompatible with parity" as exaggerating their incompatibility. The ultramontane majority at Vatican I (and subsequently) hailed the defined propositions of that council as the triumph of de Maistre's absolutist views of the papacy, and the upshot was an increasingly centralized and absolutist papacy culminating in Pius XII. But one of the major goals of Vatican II was to redress the balance and define the principle of episcopal collegiality, which included the place of the pope considered as a bishop among bishops. The main point

of that effort was to define the bishops as being equal in authority to the pope (as bishop) in their own local churches. Bishops are not vicars of the pope. Their episcopal authority comes directly from God, and when they meet in council, they meet as equals, although the pope enjoys a primacy of service and exercises certain canonically defined powers in relationship to bishops and council. I do not dispute the primacy of the pope. I dispute how that primacy, defined by Vatican I, has been interpreted by ultramontanes. The latter would come down on the incompatibility of primacy and parity, but Vatican II argued that they are not, and must not be conceived as, incompatible. See *Lumen gentium*, nos. 18–29; Patrick Granfield, *The Limits of the Papacy* (New York: Crossroad, 1987); J. M. R. Tillard, O.P., *The Bishop of Rome*, trans. John de Satgé (Wilmington, DE: Glazier, 1982).

2. See Ignatius of Loyola, *Constitutions of the Society of Jesus*, pp. 68, 79–80, and nn. 17–18.

3. Chandlery, "Biographical Sketch," LN 29 (January 1908) 303, records that in 1895 on the day of the beatification of the Jesuit Bernardino Realino, Leo XIII, "in his address to the assembled Cardinals and Prelates, took occasion to speak in most affectionate terms of the Society, letting it be publicly known how much he cherished it. Never before in public had he expressed such praise and such warm esteem of the Society." He was in fact lavish in his signs of affection and approbation. Chandlery, "Biographical Sketch," LN 30 (January 1909) 24–25, also recorded the following testimony on the occasion of Leo's death: "He loved the Society dearly, and gave proof of his affection by many remarkable favours: (1) the Canonization of three of our Saints, and the Beatification of several of the Society's heroic children: (2) the Confirmation of all our Privileges by his Brief *Dolemus inter*, dated July, 1886: (3) his extraordinary praise of the Society and its work in his address to the Fathers Procurator, 1896, 1899: (4) the granting of a special feast of Our Lady della Strada: (5) also of a special feast of all our Saints: (6) the confiding to the Society of his cherished foundation, the Pontifical Seminary at Anagni: (7) the urging his brother, Cardinal Joseph Pecci, to re-enter the Order, &c."

4. "Biographical Sketch," LN 30 (April 1908) 366.

5. Funeral oration for Leo XIII by Archbishop Kelly of Sydney, reported in Chandlery, "Biographical Sketch," LN 30 (January 1909) 25.

6. Chandlery, ibid., p. 29, recalls that when Pius X was cardinal primate of Venice, "he came frequently to our house in the *Fondamenta nuove*, and was as much at home as if he had been one of the Community. One of his first acts after his elevation to St. Peter's Chair,

was to write an *autograph* letter to the Provincial, Father [Egidio] Rossi, thanking him and the Fathers of Venice for all the favours and acts of kindness he had received from them, and recommending himself to their prayers, at the same time sending his *affectionate* Apostolic Benediction—*Con speciale affetto."*

7. "Quod si incidimus profecto in mala tempora, et asperum, quod fere ubique Ecclesiae eiusque sanctis Institutis infertur bellum, aeternam christifidelium salutem in discrimen adducit, dum iniquam hanc rerum ac temporum conditionem vehementer dolemus, maximas Deo agimus gratias, qui vos Nobis exhibet veluti lectissimam militum aciem, belli peritam, ad pugnandum instructam et ad ducis imperium ac nutum paratam vel inter confertissimos hostes convolare vitamque perfundere." Pius X, "Summi Pontificis Alloquutio ad Patres congregatos," 16 October 1906, ARSJ, S. Sedes 1004–I/16a, p. 2; another copy in ARSJ, Cong. XXV, De Rebus, Pars Secunda, p. 410 overleaf.

8. "Nella Congregatione, fate decreti in favore della 'Scholastica' vi lo raccommando." Meyer commented: "Pare che parlasse del metodo o la forma Scolastica; perche diede questa ragione: 'I nemici della Chiesa temono la "Scholastica"; quando si mettono principi e si tirano conclusioni *in forma*; non hanno che respondere etc. etc.'—Finalmente disse: 'Se fosse necessario, metteremmo il chiodo [drive home a point], come Leone XIII.' Rispose il P. Vicario, che la Compagnia vuole essere obbediente in tutte le cose alla Santa Sede. Ed il S. Padre: 'Non l'ho dubitato mai, non l'ho dubito e non l'ho dubiterò mai. Stimo tutti gli ordini religiosi, ma ho relazione speciali coi Padri Gesùiti. La Compagnia è la mano destra del Papa etc." Meyer, ARSJ, Cong. XXV, De Rebus, P.1: Acta R. P. Vicarii, I.1, p. 6.

9. I have formulated a composite or brief without attribution to any specific author. But I list here the works I found most pertinent to my study: Mariko Asano-Tamanoi, "Shame, Family, and State in Catalonia and Japan," in *Honor and Shame and the Unity of the Mediterranean*, ed. David D. Gilmore, Special Publication 22 (Washington, DC: American Anthropological Association, 1987), pp. 104–20; Jeremy Boissevain, "Toward an Anthropology of the Mediterranean," *Current Anthropology* 20 (1979) 81–93; Stanley H. Brandes, *Metaphors of Masculinity* (Philadelphia: University of Pennsylvania Press, 1980); "Like Wounded Stags: Male Sexual Ideology in an Andalusian Town," in *Sexual Meanings: The Cultural Construction of Gender and Sexuality*, ed. Sherry B. Ortner and Harriet Whitehead (New York: Cambridge University Press, 1981); "Reflections on Honor and Shame in the Mediterranean," in *Honor and Shame*, ed. Gilmore, pp. 121–34; John H. R.

Davis, *People of the Mediterranean: An Essay in Comparative Social Anthropology* (London: Routledge & Kegan Paul, 1977); "Family and State in the Mediterranean," in *Honor and Shame*, ed. Gilmore, pp. 22–34; Carol Delaney, "Seeds of Honor, Fields of Shame," in *Honor and Shame*, pp. 35–48; David D. Gilmore, "Anthropology of the Mediterranean Area," *Annual Reviews in Anthropology* 11 (1982) 175–205; "The Shame of Dishonor," introduction to *Honor and Shame*, ed. Gilmore, pp. 2–21; "Honor, Honesty, Shame: Male Status in Contemporary Andalusia," ibid., pp. 90–103; Gilmore and Gilmore, " 'Machismo' "; Michael Herzfeld, " 'As in Your Own House': Hospitality, Ethnography, and the Stereotype of Mediterranean Society," in *Honor and Shame*, pp. 75–89; Jean G. Peristiany, ed., *Honour and Shame: The Values of Mediterranean Society* (Chicago: The University of Chicago Press, 1966; repr. 1974); *Mediterranean Family Structures* (New York: Cambridge University Press, 1976); Julian A. Pitt-Rivers, *The People of the Sierra* (Chicago: The University of Chicago Press, 1961); Julian A. Pitt-Rivers, ed., *Mediterranean Countrymen: Essays in the Sociology of the Mediterranean* (Paris: Mouton, 1963); "Honour and Social Status," in *Honour and Shame: Values*, ed. J. G. Peristiany, pp. 19–78; "Ritual Kinship in the Mediterranean: Spain and the Balkans," in *Mediterranean Family Structures*, pp. 317–34; Saunders, "Men and Women in Southern Europe"; Jane Schneider, "Of Vigilance and Virgins," *Ethnology* 9 (1971) 1–24; George D. Spindler, ed., *The Making of Psychological Anthropology* (Berkeley: University of California Press, 1978).

10. Jean Masamba Ma Mpolo, "African Symbols and Stories in Pastoral Care," *Journal of Pastoral Care* 39 (1985) 314–26, quoted in David W. Augsburger, *Pastoral Counseling Across Cultures* (Philadelphia: Westminster, 1986), p. 79, points out the ontological significance of belonging for traditional cultures like those in the circum-Mediterranean: " 'Traditional culture defines the individual's identity in the following ontological formula: *Cognatus ergo sum: I belong* [am related], *therefore I am*. To belong is to participate in and contribute to the life and welfare of the family. This is in opposition to the individualistic dictum of Descartes: *Cogito ergo sum: I think, therefore I am*. It is not the individual's capacity to think which is the prime source of his or her identity formation, but rather the reality and the ability of belonging, participating, and sharing. The sharing of one's life with another's leads to wholeness and guarantees health.' "

11. As we shall see below, this is why Martín characterizes as effeminate those by whom the breach comes, why these have to be so carefully watched, and why he insists so firmly on reparation once he feels the Society of Jesus has been shamed.

12. Here, as we shall see, lies the root of Martín's inability to trust the English Jesuits.

13. This, as we shall see, accounts for Martín's aggressive language and style on the outside and his turmoil on the inside.

14. Gilmore, "Shame of Dishonor," p. 4. Julian A. Pitt-Rivers, *People of the Sierra*, p. 116, offered the following perceptive explanation of the symbol of the cuckold: "The word *cabrón* (a he-goat), the symbol of male sexuality in many contexts, refers not to him whose manifestation of that quality is the cause of the trouble but to him whose implied lack of manliness has allowed the other to replace him. To make a man a cuckold is, in the current Spanish idiom, 'to put horns on him.' I suggest that the horns are figuratively placed upon the head of the wronged husband in signification of his failure to defend a value vital to the social order. He has fallen under domination of its enemy and must wear his symbol. He is ritually defiled." But Stanley Brandes, "Like Wounded Stags," p. 229, offers the following correction: "It is not the male rival who puts on the horns, as Pitt-Rivers implies; it is the wife! Thus, one man will say of another, *'Pobrecillo, que no sabe que su mujer le está metiendo los cuernos'* ('Poor guy, for he doesn't know that his wife is placing the horns on him'). Men also wonder aloud of their wives, *'No sé si me habría meti'o los cuernos'* ('I don't know if she ever put horns on me'). In these as in countless other expressions, it is clear that it is the cuckold's wife, not his rival, who bears primary responsibility for the horns on his head."

15. Gilmore, "Shame of Dishonor," p. 5. Although many of these patterns are breaking down in the cosmopolitanism of the modern world, they remain very much in evidence.

16. This could account for Martín's insistence on the so-called masculine virtues, as well as for his simultaneous defensiveness.

17. George R. Saunders, "Men and Women in Southern Europe," p. 441, points out, however, that a man's aggressive sexuality is evaluated only in reference to his status within the family and the community. It may not be used to weaken family bonds. Therefore his manly courage and strength imply continence and may be sexually demonstrated only by keeping his wife pregnant and his other female charges in line. The importance of effective rituals for healthy male development is the subject of Robert Bly's insightful work *Iron John: A Book About Men* (Reading, MA: Addison-Wesley, 1990). Walter J. Ong, in his *Fighting for Life: Contest, Sexuality, and Consciousness* (Ithaca and London: Cornell University Press, 1981), on the basis of intellectual, literary, and cultural history, concludes that males in general are developmentally far more beleaguered and at risk in their sexual iden-

tity than females. His argument, however, does not vitiate that of Mediterranean anthropologists specifically about Mediterranean males. Mediterraneanists would merely point out that their data suggest that, if all the world's males were lined up on a spectrum of beleaguered identity, the Mediterranean male would fall at the extreme end.

18. The argumentation presented here is taken from Gilmore, "Anthropology of the Mediterranean Area" and "Shame of Dishonor."

19. Robert Redfield, *The Little Community/Peasant Society and Culture* (Chicago: The University of Chicago Press, 1967), p. 182.

20. See, for example, Peristiany, *Honour and Shame: Values* and Pitt-Rivers, *Mediterranean Countrymen.*

21. Gilmore, "Anthropology of the Mediterranean Area," pp. 178–79.

22. Ibid., p. 181.

23. See, e.g., Jane Schneider, "Of Vigilance and Virgins," and Jane Schneider and Peter Schneider, *Culture and Political Economy in Western Sicily* (New York: Academic, 1976).

24. Gilmore, "Anthropology of the Mediterranean Area," p. 184.

25. In *Honor and Shame*, ed. Gilmore, pp. 35–48.

26. Ibid., pp. 35–36.

27. Ibid., p. 45.

28. Ibid., p. 44.

29. Ibid., pp. 46–47, nn. 5, 16.

30. Ibid., p. 46. One other causal factor for the dominance of patriarchy which Delaney did not consider is the influence of the male's generally superior physical size, strength, and speed. These traits are not negligible when one considers that the "people of the Book" became a people precisely by fighting for their lives and property. Indeed, to this day, they seem to need enemies over against which to define themselves. Apropos of this last point, see the works of René Girard, beginning with *Violence and the Sacred*, trans. Patrick Gregory (Baltimore: Johns Hopkins University Press, 1977); Raymund Schwager, s.j., *Must There Be Scapegoats? Violence and Redemption in the Bible*, trans. Maria L. Assad (San Francisco: Harper & Row, 1987); and Ong, *Fighting for Life.*

31. Members of the Social Sciences and New Testament Interpretation section of the Society of Biblical Literature have recently engaged this issue. Important monographs emerging from this group are: Bruce J. Malina, *The New Testament World: Insights from Cultural Anthropology* (Atlanta: John Knox Press, 1981), esp. pp. 94–121; *Christian Origins and Cultural Anthropology: Practical Models for Biblical Interpretation*

(Atlanta: John Knox Press, 1986); Bruce J. Malina and Jerome H. Neyrey, *Calling Jesus Names: The Social Value of Labels in Matthew* (Sonoma, CA: Polebridge, 1988); Douglas E. Oakman, *Jesus and the Economic Questions of His Day* (Lewiston, NY: Mellen, 1986); and John J. Pilch, *Hear the Word*, Vol. 1, *Introduction to the Cultural Context of the Old Testament*, and Vol. 2, *Introduction to the Cultural Context of the New Testament* (Mahwah, NJ: Paulist, 1991).

32. Ong's *Fighting for Life*, and many references cited therein, confirm my judgments here and correlate to Delaney's findings. Ong argues: "The Church is sexually defined. To the psyche, the Church is always feminine, Holy Mother Church. Psychoanalytically as well as theologically there is no way to have a 'Father Church.' The femininity of the Church is connected with the nature of the Incarnation itself and of redemption. The Incarnation has a fundamentally feminine human base, particularly as related to the Church's teaching regarding the virgin birth" (p. 172). Ong merely asserts that "the Church is always feminine," that its femininity is "connected with the nature of the Incarnation," and that "the Incarnation has a fundamentally feminine base," but he does not ask why these assertions should be so. Delaney's findings answer this question: The church is feminine because it is for Christians what the land is for Jews. For Jews and all Mediterraneans land is feminine—it receives the male seed.

33. For an illuminating presentation of these points see Jean Lipman-Blumen, *Gender Roles and Power* (Englewood Cliffs, NJ: Prentice-Hall, 1984) and Bryan S. Turner, *The Body and Society: Explorations in Social Theory* (Oxford: Blackwell, 1984).

34. See Walter E. Conn, *Conscience: Development and Self-Transcendence* (Birmingham, AL: Religious Education Press, 1981).

35. McCool, *Nineteenth-Century Scholasticism*, p. 17, cites the argument of Edgar Hocedez (*Histoire de la théologie au XIXe siècle*, vol. 1, *Décadence et réveil de la théologie, 1800–1831* [Brussels: Universelle, 1949], pp. 8–9) that " 'rationalism, in its empirical or idealistic forms, was the only adversary outside the Church which Catholic theologians took seriously'." In assigning cues, it would be remiss not to ask, from whom did the popes take their cues? Protocol might require the answer, from no one but God. However, they depended on their appointed philosophers and theologians of the pontifical universities, and especially on the Jesuits of the Gregorian University, to craft their anti-rationalist/liberalist/Protestant polemics.

36. See Yzermans, *All Things in Christ*, p. xiii.

37. Pius X, *E supremi apostolatus*, par. 2.

38. Ibid., par. 4, 12.

39. Typically the Mediterranean mind leaps from what is judged as not good (evil) to a denial of its existence: I hate you, you don't exist! Banishing someone or something to the status of non-existence, then, justifies any sort of malicious behavior against that person or thing. The philosophical formulation of this behavior is certainly found in non-Mediterranean philosophies, but in the Mediterranean culture the embodiment of this formulation is such that it has become a characteristic and characterizing pattern. It is evident in a spectrum of behaviors from easy assassinations ordered by Mafia or Camorra bosses to kicking a stray dog because it does not belong.

40. This architectural style is typical not only of the large homes of the wealthy, but also of the extended family enclaves of the less wealthy and of older apartment buildings. But in contemporary urbanized society, where family enclaves are less and less common, apartment blocks do not have a cortile, and family existence is more and more reduced to the nuclear family typical of northern Europe and America. Sometimes apartment blocks are constructed around a commons, but the cortile mentality lives on and is expressed in the apartment dwellers' utter disregard for the commons. It is considered a place to discard rubbish, whereas the interior of the apartment is kept meticulously clean and ordered.

41. *Pascendi*, par. 40, quoting *Singulari nos* (25 June 1834) which condemned Lamennais.

42. When Maria Christina (1806–1878), fourth wife of Ferdinand VII (1784–1833), convinced her husband to set aside the Salic law to enable their only child Isabella to succeed to the throne, that excluded the legal pretender, Ferdinand's brother Don Carlos, and precipitated widespread and often violent disputes. The Salic law forbidding females to succeed to titles or offices in a family was prominently enforced by the houses of Valois and Bourbon in France. It was introduced into Spain in the time of Philip V (1683–1746). However, an ancient law of Castile provided that women could rule in their own right. That law was abrogated in 1713. Charles IV restored it in 1789, but because its enactment was never published, its validity was now hotly disputed. Hence the birth of Carlism.

43. See Bangert, *History of the Society of Jesus*, pp. 449–52.

44. *Memorias*, fl. 202r.

45. Ibid., fl. 224v.

46. Adrien Dansette, *Religious History of Modern France*, trans. John Dingle, 2 vols. (Freiburg: Herder; New York: Herder & Herder, 1961) 1:323, observes about this atrocity: "When it comes to fixing the blame, we must remember, if we are to be fair, that none of these

executions took place before the beginning of the terrible week during which the [provisional government's] army from Versailles put to the sword without trial at least 15,000 *communards*."

47. See Graham, *Donoso Cortés*. Gary Lease, an historian of ideas, connects Donoso's political theory to Thomas Hobbes: "As to Hobbes' notion of power/authority, . . . it was the Spanish canon lawyers who picked up *their* notions from Hobbes! Cf. Carl Schmitt: *Politische Theologie: Vier Kapitel zur Lehre von der Souveränität* (Munich/Leipzig: Duncker & Humblot, 1934²). Here he points to Hobbes's great line in Leviathan (chap. 26): *auctoritas non veritas facit legem*, and calls this the basis for his theory of 'decisionism' (pg. 44). Later, in chapter 4, Schmitt refers to Donoso Cortes, whom he typifies as a 'Catholic' *Staatsphilosoph*, as one who exemplified the best kind of development from Hobbes's point of departure. In other words, one whose thought was directed inevitably to a dictatorship, and whose critique was especially hard on all modern forms of 'liberal,' or democratic forms of government. Cortes was, of course, one of the leading Spanish theological and canonical minds of the 19th century, even though he remained a layman. . . . He fought for an official Catholic state (in Spain) and of course supported all efforts on the Vatican's part to free itself from such 'anti-Christian' elements as democratic tendencies." Lease, private correspondence.

Causes are notoriously difficult to substantiate historically, but one could plausibly advance the thesis that there is a causative connection between the ecclesiology of Donoso and the prevailing ecclesiastical reaction to political liberalism in the latter half of the nineteenth century and beyond, and by extension to other forms of liberalism and modernism. One cannot read Pius IX's *Quanta cura* (Syllabus of Errors) without being struck by the similarity of thought and language to Donoso's one and only book, *Ensayo sobre el catolicismo, el liberalismo y el socialismo* (1851).

48. That would have been Donoso's fiery speech of 4 January 1849 to the Spanish parliament, in which he cogently argued for dictatorship under certain conditions. An English translation of the speech is included in Béla Menczer, *Catholic Political Thought, 1789–1848* (Westminster, MD: Newman, 1952), pp. 160–76. Graham, *Donoso Cortés*, pp. 6–7, n. 9, argues that Carl Schmitt, the apologist for dictatorship in Weimar Germany, "truly misrepresented Donoso on dictatorship, either intentionally or because he did not understand him." Graham further argues (p. 149): "To make clear that he [Donoso] justified dictatorship only under crisis conditions as a temporary safeguard of social order, he avowed that were there any choice between liberty

and dictatorship, he would never 'bend the knee' before a dictator. He felt that he had no choice, since liberty did not in fact exist in Europe."

49. *Memorias*, fl. 255v.

50. Chandlery, "Biographical Sketch," LN (1907) 2–5.

51. LN (1907) 4–5.

52. The Liberals passed the Law of Associations, which required all religious congregations to register their members and, when not specifically recognized under the concordat of 1851, to apply for authorization. A new proposal to enforce the law greatly incensed church officials. The papal nuncio announced that Rome would consent to discuss the question only on condition that all requests for authorization would be granted. Margaret Cochrane Storrie, "Spain," *Encyclopedia Britananica* (1970).

53. The Jesuit curia moved from Rome to Fiesole in 1873 to escape the systematic persecution that began in 1870 when the Piedmontese occupied Rome. The Jesuits immediately lost all their colleges, museums, libraries, and observatories. Finally, in 1873, the general and his staff were driven from their residence.

54. Chandlery, "Biographical Sketch," LN 170 (January 1908) 302.

55. Pitt-Rivers points out in "Honour and Social Status," pp. 21–22, that tirades against the mores of the day are common in moralistic literature in which the moralist or the claimant to honor "retains the right to arbitrate claims to honour" and "must get himself accepted at his own evaluation, must be granted reputation, or else the claim becomes mere vanity, an object of ridicule or contempt."

56. *Select Letters*, par. 10.

57. Ibid., par. 25.

58. Ibid., pars. 28, 30–31.

59. Ibid., pars. 35–36.

60. Peristiany, *Honour and Shame: Values*, pp. 14, 11.

61. *Memorias*, published text, vol. 2, fl. 2451r.

62. Thomas E. Sherman (1856–1933) was the son of the great Union general of the American Civil War, William Tecumseh Sherman. Secretary of State John Sherman (1823–1900) was William's brother. A search of the John Ireland Papers, Archives of the Archdiocese of St. Paul and Minneapolis, for the spring of 1898 and of the archdiocesan newspaper, *The Northwest Chronicle*, which published virtually everything Ireland said, produced no reference to a sermon on this occasion. Possibly Martín's memory was of another celebrated sermon preached by Ireland in Washington, D.C., at a memorial for General Calixto García y Iñigues (1839–1898), a leading Cuban insurgent. Mar-

vin O'Connell, in his superb study, *John Ireland and the American Catholic Church* (St. Paul, MN: Minnesota Historical Society Press, 1988), pp. 460–61, includes the following anecdote that suggests the kind of information that Martín was receiving from Vatican sources: "As the Americanist struggle approached its climax, John Ireland too was the victim of small-minded complaints and vexations, his every word and gesture scrutinized, his basic loyalties subjected to examination. On December 13 [1898], for instance, he preached a memorial service in Washington for one of the leading Cuban insurgents, General Garcia, and was alleged to have spoken disparagingly of Spain and to have contrasted 'the Catholicity of the Spanish friars with the free and virile Catholicity of the United States.' Rampolla, still rankled over the humiliating defeat of Spain in the recent war, instructed Martinelli to find out the truth of this charge 'con certezza.' The 'certainty' to emerge from the delegate's investigation was that at the funeral the Protestant hymn 'Nearer My God to Thee' had been sung and that Ireland had said no more than Ireland always said on such occasions: 'This is the pride of America, that nothing keeps a man down but himself. . . . Beneath the American flag is absolute religious liberty, and the very fact that that flag has once touched Cuba is a guaranty given the island she is free in her religion.' The sensible Martinelli found 'nothing incriminating in the form or substance of the sermon.' " Papal Secretary of State Cardinal Mariano Rampolla del Tindaro to U. S. Apostolic Delegate Cardinal Sebastiano Martinelli, the Vatican, 2 January 1899; and Martinelli to Rampolla, Washington, 17 January 1899. Secret Vatican Archives, papers of the Apostolic Delegation to the United States, fasc. 22. Ireland's description of the "virile" American Catholicism in contrast to the—one must suppose "effeminate"—Catholicism of Spain would have stung Martín to fury. I am indebted to Fr. Marvin O'Connell and Dr. Robert L. Gambone, archivist of the Archdiocese of St. Paul and Minneapolis, for this information.

63. *Memorias*, published text, fl. 2451r, 2453r.

64. Ibid., fl. 2451r–2452r.

65. Ibid., fl. 2453r–v.

66. Ibid., fl. 2453v–2454v.

67. Ibid., fl. 2454v–2455r.

68. Ibid., fl. 2455r.

69. Ibid., fl. 2455v, 2457v. The same sentiments are expressed in his letter of 2 July 1898 to the same provincials (fl. 2459v).

70. *Memorias*, published text, fl. 2455v.

71. Ibid., fl. 2458v–2459r.

72. Ibid., fl. 2471r, 2471v.

73. *Memorias*, unpublished manuscript, fl. 2280r–2282r.

74. Ibid., fl. 2282r–v.

75. Institutionalization may have made Merry de Val a paragon of the Mediterranean mind's salient characteristics, but I would argue that institutionalization took so firmly with him because he was culturally predisposed to it. Being born and raised in England did no more to erase his Mediterranean cultural characteristics than being born and raised in America erases those characteristics in first- and second-generation Italians or Puerto Ricans. See above, pp. 12–14, n. 15.

76. As I argued in *George Tyrrell*, p. 424, n. 200.

77. Martin to Charnley, 5 February 1900, Reg. Epp. Angl., vol. 5, pp. 83–84. On that occasion, Tyrrell sent von Hügel apparently his own version of the general's words: "Quidquid sentiat Reverentia Vestra [Charnley] et consultores, hic Romae longe aliter sentitur" ("Whatever Your Reverence and consultors might think, here in Rome the view is very different"). Letter of 14 February 1900, PP, BL, Add. MSS 44927.99. Probably Charnley had told Tyrrell the general's reply without letting him actually see it. In any case, the two versions carry the same meaning.

78. I do not wish to leave the impression that I believe that everything about the modernist crisis would have turned out fine if Rome had taken no action. But I would argue that a *different* course of action would have yielded far better results, because the action Rome took alienated from the church numerous faithful and loyal theologians and hindered all theologians from engaging in serious theological research and teaching. Had an uncontentious, pastoral approach been taken, Rome could have drawn many of the so-called modernists — including Loisy and Tyrrell — into a sympathetic dialogue and not lost them to the church. But, given all that I said about the cultural characteristics of the anti-modernists, and barring a moral miracle (i.e., conversion), Rome's course of action was a foregone conclusion. Even so, I would contend that Rome's actions were moderate compared to what Mediterranean culture might have justified. Rome was driven, at the very least, to demand subjection. Understandably, many of the modernists refused.

79. Peristiany observes that in all societies there is, in addition to honor, the ideal of saintliness, which transcends the ideal of honor. "The definition of saintliness might be that saintliness is above honour and that there is nothing above saintliness." *Honour and Shame: Values*, pp. 17–18. Here I am contending that Martín, unlike Ignatius,

did not rise above his culture's requirements for defending his honor, which, of course, was tied to the honor of the Society of Jesus.

80. *Memorias*, fl. 47r, my translation from the published text.

81. Ibid., Martín's own English words.

82. See, e.g., ibid., fl. 181v, 279r–v, 296r–297r, 306r–v, 347r, 492r–493r, 498v–499r, 519–550 passim.

83. Ibid., fl. 78r&v, Martín's own English words.

84. Ibid., fl. 181v, Martín's own English words.

85. Ibid., fl. 279r–v, Martín's own English words.

86. Ibid., fl. 306r–v, Martín own English words.

87. Ibid., fl. 327r–330v, Martín's own English words.

88. Ibid., fl. 347r, my translation from the published text.

89. Ibid., fl. 495r, my translation from the published text.

90. Ibid., fl. 495r, 499r (Martín's own English words); see also fl. 492r–499r.

91. Ibid., fl. 539r–v.

92. Martín was referring here to his spiritual state.

93. Ibid., fl. 2345r–v, my translation from the published text.

94. Ibid., fl. 2436v, my translation from the published text. Martín had gone to Anagni to visit the Pontifical Seminary which Leo XIII had entrusted to the Jesuits.

95. See ibid., fl. 2450v, 2455v, 2457r–v, and 2459v.

96. See ibid., fl. 2455v.

97. See ibid., fl. 2458r.

98. Ibid., fl. 83v–84v.

CONCLUDING POSTSCRIPT:

HISTORIOGRAPHICAL CONSIDERATIONS

THE ROMAN VIEW *vs.* THE "MODERNIST" VIEW

HARDLY ANYONE WILL DENY that human perception is affected by culture, and those who accept a doctrine of original sin will even grant that human perception is skewed by culture. Such an admission does not gainsay the possibility of knowing and expressing truth, but it ought to temper the claim to know truth perfectly, let alone absolutely, as if anyone, including the pope, could stand outside of history and be immune to his or her cultural context. Still more it ought to temper the claim to express truth in its fullness and purity for all time. But for those like the anti-modernists, whose world view does not embrace historicality, the claim to perceive and express truth without qualification is, apart from the influence of sin, quite simply accepted as a given. And when you add to this ahistoricality the papal prerogative of infallibility as interpreted by ultramontanism, such claims are even perceived as protected from the darkening influence of sin. Thus, for the ultramontanes, there was a one-for-one correspondence between divine revelation and sacred scripture on the one hand, and sacred scripture and its embodiment in doctrine on the other. Nothing more was required for knowing God's mind and will than a simple reading of scripture and the church's tradition—although authorities did not encourage private reading by the laity, as that smacked of Protestantism. The suggestion that revelation might not be merely extrinsically attached to human language but substantially embedded in culture and therefore not neatly extractable was regarded as a suggestion of Satan, part of that "compendium of all heresies" whose father was Luther.

Modernists, for their part, embraced historicality and therefore saw revelation as embedded in a cultural matrix. To receive revelation, they held, one had to read scripture from within its matrix. Therefore one needed hermeneutics and the science of historical criticism; not in the sense of a new dogma—no salvation outside of hermeneutics—at least not for moderates like Tyrrell and von Hügel who affirmed the salutary effect of even an uneducated reading of scripture; but at least in the sense that historical criticism was needed as one check to rank devotionalism. In other words, scripture could not simply mean whatever the reader wanted it to mean. What then did it mean, and who could say what it meant? Modernists did not deny that grace could work through the most naïve reading of scripture. But because they saw revelation as substantially embedded in a particular cultural matrix, they held that its literal (intended) meaning was not simply available to anyone who could read scripture even in its original language, let alone in translation. The uneducated reader could gain much by private reading, but really needed to depend on trained historical critics.

Here is where the battle between the modernists and church authorities was joined. It was a battle over authority, power, control, and it turned on the issue of history and historical criticism. If authorities conceded the modernist viewpoint regarding the need for historical criticism for a truer reading of sacred scripture and reception of revelation, they would be conceding the existence of a secondary kind of magisterium, to which even they were in some sense beholden—unless, of course, they made themselves or at least some of their members historical critics, an option virtually foreclosed by their own cultural determination. They would be alleging that God did not speak plainly to Peter, does not now continue to do so primarily to his successor, and therefore needs an interpreter. They would be acknowledging that in matters magisterial the pope himself required the science of interpretation and so might need to share power with non-infallible inferiors, an option again virtually foreclosed by cultural determination.

Thus it was a battle, one could argue, between opposing cultural determinations, determinations that substantially affected perceptions of reality. Arising out of and allied with the opposing cultural determinations were opposing philosophical schools with their opposing epistemologies: the naïve realism of scholastic Aristotelianism *vs.* the idealism of Kant, the former arising out of Mediterranean culture, the latter out of northern European culture.

Walter Ong's description of the relationship between agonistic behavior and structures (such as those prevalent in Mediterranean cultures) and the noetic world illuminates the point of opposition. He observes that

shifts in agonistic structures within the world of knowledge relate to other major shifts within the noetic world itself: to the shift, for example, from closed-system paradigms [Mediterranean cultures] to open-system paradigms [northern European cultures] in Western thinking generally, and to what analytic psychology has described as the breakthrough of the dark side of the psyche in the West, the conscious recognition of the unconscious and the internalizing in the individual psyche of the evil present in the human lifeworld.[1]

This reflection helps explain why Catholic authorities and their theologians during the nineteenth century assiduously singled out Kant as the epistemological and philosophical arch-enemy: he blurred the boundaries between the interior world of perception and the world perceived out there. After Kant the "enemy" is no longer clearly defined or definable because there is no clearly distinct subject and object set over against each other. There is no longer clearly an "I–it" or "I–you" relationship, because the knowing subject is related to known objects not as they are in themselves but only as they are known through perceptions which the subject at least partially creates. This creative involvement of the subject in every act of knowing means, then, that the object *as known* does not exist as purely and simply other. Human knowledge is never objectively pure or purely objective. Kantian epistemology, therefore, does not allow a distinct opposition between subject and object.

Admission of such an epistemology into church dogmatics would undercut the claim of a clear, transcendently divine transmission of revelation into the distortion-free repository of sacred scripture and church tradition. The blurred focus created by Kantian epistemology infuriates the agonistic Mediterranean mind, which must have a clear adversary to demolish in order to feel powerful. As Huizinga points out, " 'all knowledge—and this includes philosophy—is polemical by nature.' "[2] This is especially true in Mediterranean cultures, where the world of intellectual discourse is dominated by males with insecure egos, who seem to imbibe polemics with their mothers' milk.

Aims and Conclusions of This Study

Much work has already been done on the exposition of the modernist viewpoint(s) by both sides of the dispute. The literature on modernism is filled with friendly exposition by modernist sympathizers and with acrimonious refutation by their opponents. But one looks in vain for any kind of sympathetic exposition of the anti-modernist viewpoint by modernist sympathizers.[3] The present study seeks to leap into that gap, on the conviction that historical truth-telling requires sympathetic understanding.

My aim in this study has been not only to bring into the light, however dimmed by my own subjectivity, the perceptions of the principal anti-modernist figures regarding "modernist errors," but also to offer on the basis of anthropological findings at least a hypothetical rationale for those perceptions. In other words, I tried not only to tell what I could find of the story behind anti-modernist perceptions of the impending crisis (Parts I and II) but also to say what the story means (Part III). In Part I, where I sought to convey the papal perception, I argued that the views of Leo XIII and Pius X virtually coincided, and this by Pius' own intention, driven by the cultural requirement to uphold tradition. I based my exposition almost entirely on official papal documents and published sources. But in Part II I was able to use almost entirely archival sources, private correspondence, and unpublished memoirs. Thus the story became much more intimate, as it was told as far as possible from within the minds of the protagonists.

As to papal perceptions, we saw that Leo XIII and Pius X were of one mind in believing that only the restoration of Catholic monarchies morally and spiritually subordinate to the Holy See could restore the tranquillity of order intended by God for the whole world. Luther and the revolt he instigated, they believed, was the originating cause of the unraveling of the medieval marriage of throne and altar. Luther and Lutheranism were therefore perceived as the enemy behind every anti-Catholic (read, anti-Roman, anti-papal) aggression on the world scene, from the establishment of Protestant states to the sociopolitical revolutions that split church and state; from the establishment of Protestant churches to the intellectual and religious revolutions that split faith and reason. The science of cultural anthropology suggests that it was no accident of history that the unified medieval empire was Roman and that there was a Roman religion to serve as the state's backbone. Unity is the cardinal dogma of Mediterranean order. Chaos is held at bay as long as everyone adheres to the divinely ordained plan that placed the pope as supreme overseer of the universe with cardinals, bishops, priests, and religious orders at his command. In Pius X's view, bishops and their subjects were to be "co-operators" with Christ's vicar against "that sacrilegious war which is now almost universally being stirred up and fomented against God" by dint of "a certain new and fallacious science [historical criticism], which . . . strives to open the door to the errors of rationalism."[4]

I argued that, given the cultural characteristics of the Mediterranean mind, the response of the popes and their subordinate authorities to the liberal/modernist threat was proportional to the danger perceived. The question is, why was the danger so perceived? Why did the popes use wartime rhetoric, equating their struggle with war and calling the action of Catholic liberals/modernists sacrilege, the most egregious abomination a human being could perpetrate? Again, the answer lies in the peculiar quality of the Mediterranean mind which sees world order as ordained by God with earthly authorities hierarchically arranged to maintain it; so that any affront to authority is automatically taken as an affront against God. Thus in the Mediterranean logic of *Pascendi*, the chain of "isms" initiated by Luther had to end in atheism.

We saw that with Leo XIII the Roman Question was the single

most preoccupying concern of his papacy. It was of equal concern to Pius X, but other more immediately urgent matters such as church–state issues in France and Portugal and the modernist crisis claimed his attention.

Why was the Roman Question so central to the papacy? Mediterranean anthropology suggests several interrelated reasons. The single most important injunction for a Mediterranean male is to guard his patrimony. In the tradition of the Roman Catholic Church, the ecclesial patrimony could not be conceptually separated from territory—the Holy Roman Empire was holy because its absolute sovereign was, at least in the papal mind, not the king who ruled, but the pope of Rome, the vicar of Christ who crowned the king. In time, violent insurrections, beginning with the Protestant Revolt, dissolved the medieval marriage of throne and altar along with the empire and reduced the symbolic power of sacred imperium to the Papal States. These too finally fell, inducing an ecclesiastical trauma that required the most wrenching readjustment in thinking on the part of church authorities about the identity of the church and its leadership. Short of a complete liberation from the determinations of Mediterranean culture, the pope who inherited "the keys of the Kingdom" (Matt. 16:19) without a condign temporal sovereignty was equivalently emasculated and reduced to the status of a slave—a man without power, without honor, indeed to the Mediterranean mind no man at all, but a woman. Second, for the pope to have lost the patrimony (the "land") was to have failed in his supreme charge of vigilance over the church (his "woman"). Third, these two failures meant that the church itself had failed in its role as the foundation of divinely ordained social order.

The popes were probably not so naïve as to take the Petrine commission to hold "the keys of the Kingdom of Heaven" in its most materialistic sense as mandating sentry duty at the entrance of an earthly kingdom, at least not consciously so. But subconsciously, if there was a distinction, there was surely no separation between guarding the heavenly and guarding the earthly patrimony. And even consciously, given the historical incarnation of the church into Christendom, one can see that the popes could not, without the most wrenching conceptual conversion, think of shepherding the flock without land. Leo XIII, I would argue, began to restructure the church's consciousness of the papacy with respect to holding territory. He began to think of the ecclesial territory more explicitly in terms of people's souls and consciences, at least until adequate territory could be returned to the papacy.

Meanwhile, to regain the honor attached to his rightful position as holder of "the keys," he attempted to find a way to transcend the precariousness of a control that depended on possession of territory, "where thieves break in and steal" (Matt. 6:19). So he sought a way to secure "the conscience of the peoples," rather than restore "medieval institutions" and to make the church the "moral center of the world" rather than the geographic center.[5] The pope's Christ-appointed position as holder of "the keys" would always be in jeopardy as long as it was tied to possession of land. Of course the gospel mandate went deeper than that. Land was only a symbol of the Kingdom of Heaven, but the symbol could not work if land was not held. But perhaps the land-symbol might become dispensable if spiritual and moral power over "the conscience of the peoples" were strengthened in proportion to the loss of temporal power.

Here entered a renewed concern for the church's teaching authority. The way to strengthen and secure this moral power was to control the church's teachers. The bishops were not a significant problem for the pope, at least not since Vatican Council I, which solidified the power of the papacy vis-à-vis bishops and teaching authority. Philosophers and theologians were another matter. To shore up the ramparts on this front, Leo mandated with *Aeterni Patris* that Thomism and only Thomism be taught as the church's system of philosophy and theology. Thus I would argue (*a*) that *Aeterni Patris* became the principal supporting column of Leo's papacy, and (*b*) that when it came under attack by the "modernists," Pius X felt compelled to rush to its defense with every weapon in his arsenal.

Thomism was born from and appealed to the Mediterranean mind. It was like "Jerusalem, built as a city with compact unity" (Ps. 122:3). One could feel secure within its walls. Its compact unity meant that it was accessible to a single mind, that one person could actually master its complexities and so use it effectively to fight the rising tide of disparate opinions and false teachings. It could be readily incorporated into a teaching manual and inculcated into the minds of disciples. It was the one last bastion against a modern world that authorized anarchy against the church, the one authority that unified religion and provided a principle of order for civil society. Pius X took up Leo's intent and tried to secure the "final solution" by silencing or expelling from the church all proponents of liberal/modernist thinking. Thus theological liberalism was directly linked in papal thinking to political liberalism. Pius saw "nothing new" in modernism—it had been condemned by Pius IX and now it stood condemned anew. Pius X made his own the view of Pius IX and Vatican I, which saw "the doctrine of the faith which God has revealed" as a "divine deposit"—a kind of patrimony or entitled property—"entrusted to the Spouse of Christ to be faithfully guarded and infallibly interpreted."[6]

On the issue of newness, we saw that the Mediterranean mind has an instinctive aversion to novelty, not only because it bears the pejorative implication of strangeness and frivolity, but also because its acceptance implies a sharing of authority. That is, newness in this context is by definition a reality that enters into the galaxy of patriarchal authority and control from beyond and demands recognition on its own merits. For church authority to credit novelty is to grant validity to "outside" reality, to admit that good *can* come from Nazareth, that there might be salvation outside the church, that therefore God can and does work in a saving way apart from the hierarchical structures of the Roman Catholic Church. Such an admission relativizes church authority, and that scares the Mediterranean mind, which, in its dyadic agonism, prefers its realities sharply defined: to admit one reality is to deny its apparent opposite, to acknowledge outside authority is to deny inside authority. Thus the counter-Reformation popes argued that to allow validity to individual sentiment and internal guidance of the Holy Spirit is to deny the necessity of external authority, and so the upshot must be atheism and anarchy.

Fear of just this outcome is what fueled the Vatican reaction to Americanism, at least as it was found in Hecker's thought and parlayed by the likes of Ireland and O'Connell. Hecker wanted to emphasize the "active" virtues and credit the individual with the ability to discern the Spirit and make responsible choices. But to the Mediterranean mind, perhaps what was most inflammatory about Heckerism was the suggestion that the Holy Spirit was working providentially in America (where to Rome's dismay Catholics were consorting with Protestants not only in government but in religious congresses) for the salvation not only of America but of Europe as well. Such a suggestion shocked the Mediterranean mind and provoked aggressive counter-measures. The logic of the Mediterranean mind is seen pointedly from the Anglo-Saxon perspective in Klein's complaint against it: "If we should say that God acts in each soul by His inspirations but that, in order to know whether or not an inspiration comes from Him, we need the aid of the Church, they [read, Mediterranean minds] would seize upon the first part of the sentence and suppress the conclusion; then they would charge us with teaching that today the Holy Spirit suffices for the direction of souls and there is no need for external authority."[7]

Many Europeans were fascinated by America and espoused Americanism, but America and Americanism simply frightened wielders of monarchic power, who in the late nineteenth century were mainly clustered in the circum-Mediterranean. Leo XIII, as we saw, believed that monarchy was virtually the only form of government ordained by God. Thus the Spanish-American War was not simply a war between two sovereign nations but a war between two ideologies, two cultures, one divinely ordained and one ordained by God's enemies. Not only did Spain's defeat mean the end to a way of life, a way of thinking and governing, but it had to mean, in Mediterranean logic, either that God was defeated or that God was using the enemy to punish Spain for some sin. As we saw, this was precisely the thinking of the Jesuit general Luis Martín. The defeat dealt a mortal blow not only to the honor of every red-blooded Spaniard, including Martín, but also to the papacy which supported not just any monarchism but Catholic monarchism.

The cosmic interconnectedness in the Mediterranean mind of

all events and issues allows us to leap, without logical misstep, to any issue, however seemingly disconnected. Thus, I may logically take up here Loisy's contention that Leo XIII, with *Providentissimus Deus*, intended to condemn all biblical criticism without exception. When one brings the contours of the Mediterranean mind to bear upon Loisy's contention, its force becomes more compelling. Loisy argued on the basis of Leo's later letter to the French clergy, *Depuis le jour*, that Leo really wanted to condemn historical criticism outright as applied to the Bible because it would (*a*) remove exegesis from the framework of scholasticism where its sole function was to support dogmatic theses and refute heresies, and (*b*) establish it on its own footing with its own internal authority—that is, the authority that comes from scientific investigation and peer review of published findings rather than an authority delegated from above. So that if the new critics had their way, they would become partners in dialogue with dogmatic theologians and authorities rather than simply servants to externally imposed agenda. In other words, they and biblical criticism would serve by exercising their own internal authority. This would mean power-sharing, a concept distinctly Protestant and wholly repugnant to patriarchal thinking. Thus the Vatican had to ban Catholics from participating in so-called "scientific" congresses where such ideas were common currency.

As we moved into Part II and took up the perceptions of the Jesuit general, we met in Martín's *Memorias* and letters the most evident and personal expressions of the Mediterranean mind. Our reflections began with an encounter in which James Hayes was representing the concerns of the English Jesuits to Martín. It is now clear why Martín seemed so uneasy in that confrontation. The fact that Hayes was complaining about the inability of superiors in Rome to understand the English might have been enough to account for Martín's discomfort. But we have also seen how completely Martín was identified with Spain—in which case England's support of the liberal party against the Spanish monarchists during the nineteenth century and her alignment with the United States during the Spanish-American War were reason enough for Martín to feel more than a little uncomfortable. Recall that after the war he could not stand to look at Rudolf Meyer, his hand-picked English-speaking assistant, or be in the same room with him, because he was American. Nor was Martín able to trust and credit the ability of England's highest religious authorities, the cardinal archbishop of Westminster and the Jesuit provincial superior. Even in the best of situations, it is difficult for Mediterraneans to be trustful of "outsiders." But these were hostile times. It would have taken a miracle of grace for Martín to prevent his antipathy toward England as a nation from seeping into his dealings with the English Jesuits regarding religious discipline and their liberal tendencies.

Indeed Martín did not rise above his cultural influences but comported himself toward England from within the moral framework of the Mediterranean mind. Tyrrell and his provincials and numerous other English Jesuits sensed this attitude, were confounded by it, and tried to cry foul, but their cries, far from gaining them a hearing, only provoked more severe reprisals: Gerard was removed from office, Tyrrell was banished from London to Richmond, and Lucas, the Rickabys, and Thurston among others were roundly reprimanded and subjected to more stringent censorship.

Why were the English confounded? Because their tradition of hearing complaints involved a far different procedure from Rome's. Theirs was based on the Anglo-Saxon understanding of natural law, which promotes equality based on the conviction that every individual possesses certain inalienable rights, among which are the right to a fair hearing before a court of law, the right of legal counsel, and the right to be faced with one's accusers. Church law is also based on natural law, but as assumed into Roman law. Thus its focus and practice is very different, influenced as it is by Mediterranean culture where the primary unit of identification is not the individual but the group. Thus, the good of the church rather than of the individual is the primary concern. Individuals do not have an identity as such. They are always considered as individuals embedded within a network of relationships. Thus rights, duties, and privileges do not accrue to individuals as such, but only insofar as they belong to the group. In a conflict between the group and the individual, presumption of right is on the side of the group, not the individual. To the Anglo-Saxon mind, therefore, the treatment of Tyrrell by Roman officials violated the English sense of "fair play," but to the Mediterranean mind his treatment seemed more than fair. Also, in the matter of securing the patrimony, the rights of the in-group take precedence over the rights of the out-group. Indeed, it might even seem that the out-group has no rights at all compared to the in-group. Thus it would seem perfectly fair and moral for Martín secretly to conspire with Merry del Val to write the English bishops' pastoral condemning liberalism and then pressure all the bishops to sign it by securing the pope's explicit approbation prior to its publication. It would not seem fair or moral to the English. Merry del Val and Martín knew this, which is why they had to keep the letter's authorship strictly secret.

But Mediterranean morality is dominated by what Lawrence Kohlberg calls "conventional morality" and Michael Barnes calls "acceptance morality," in which there is no essential moral distance between the individual and his or her group.[8] Barnes links Kohlberg's stages of morality in the development of the individual with Robert Bellah's four stages of cultural and religious development,[9] and assigns "conventional" or "acceptance morality" to the second stage of cultural and religious development called "archaic," which follows the "primitive" but has not yet reached the "historic," let alone the "modern" stage. The archaic stage incorporates the primitive stage, characterized by tribalism ("small groups living in a one-possibility local world, with magic and spirits at hand all around" and tribal meanings carried largely by folk tale-myths); whereas the archaic stage has seen the aggregation of tribes into "towns with class structure in a larger world, with great and distant gods demanding worship" and collective meanings carried by grand myths.[10] Barnes's description of "acceptance morality" in archaic cultures harmonizes remarkably well with the anthropological description of even contemporary Mediterranean cultures: "Among archaic people as among adolescents, the virtues that are considered praiseworthy are the group virtues of loyalty to one's own people, dedication to the causes of the group, and trustworthiness and honesty in dealing with others in the same group. To be found disloyal or a traitor brings shame and dishonor."[11] Presumably, then, there is no call for trustworthiness and honesty in dealing with outsiders, so that if one becomes defined as an outsider for whatever reason, one should not be surprised to be treated shabbily.[12] Barnes continues:

A stress on honor is a major manifestation of acceptance morality in the late archaic style of culture. Honor even becomes a sacred thing, to be guarded and protected against anything that might profane it. . . .
Archaic cultures . . . will look to a leader. Primitive culture has no formal leader. Tribespeople sit and talk and come to a consensus [often arranged by the strong leader(s)]. . . . Historic cultures . . . suppose that there is a body of law that is superior to individual leaders. But the archaic style of culture knows no good way to make society cohere than to find a strong leader to whom people may give their loyalty and who will reward them with special attention when it is earned by devotion. This style of thought thinks that it is legitimate to break the law in service to one's leader. Laws appear to them only as taboos, of less moral value than loyalty and honor. It often does not occur to them that laws may deserve more reverence than a leader.[13]

If one compares Barnes's correlation of Kohlberg and Bellah with anthropological descriptions of Mediterranean cultures, one must conclude that these cultures are primarily archaic and dominated by acceptance morality. However, according to Kohlberg, one stage of moral development subsumes the previous stage, so that cultures dominated by acceptance morality would also frequently function out of taboo morality. This realization throws light on the difference in attitude toward law between Anglo-Saxons and Mediterraneans. Anyone who has encountered automobile traffic in Italy knows that Italians regard traffic laws as mere suggestions—and presumably other laws too.

All this is to say that the anti-liberal/modernist figures met in this study—Leo XIII, Pius X, Merry del Val, and Martín—were very much caught up in the framework of Mediterranean (archaic) culture and acceptance morality. The Catholic liberals and modernists were mostly denizens of non-Mediterranean cultures that were largely, in Bellah's terms, "historic" or "modern" with a morality dominated by what Barnes calls "universal laws morality" and/or "basic values morality."[14] The two groups, separated by a great wall of cultural differences, thought and behaved in ways quite mysterious to each other. Perhaps their greatest misjudgment of each other came in thinking that if they spoke the same language, they meant the same thing by the same words. They did not. To the Mediterranean ecclesiastical mind requirements of group loyalty militate against individuality and freedom of thought and expression. But to the Anglo-Saxon mind loyalty to one's own individuality takes precedence, militates against knee-jerk conformity, and promotes freedom of thought and expression.

The modernist crisis was about two ecclesial-cultural worlds colliding with each other. The anti-modernists of the Mediterranean world held the reins of power and forced the "modernists" of the Anglo-Saxon and northern European world to pull in their horns, at least for the time being. There have been and will continue to be other collisions. They seem to be endemic to the kind of adversative-processional beings we are, particularly to the males of the species and most especially to Mediterranean males whose behavior has set the pattern for social interaction in the church from the beginning.[15]

On the surface, the modernist crisis was about doctrine, the expression of theological reflection on revelation as incarnated in lived experience. But at the foundational level, the crisis was about the cultures that gave rise to doctrinal thought and expression. The challenge will be for theologians and ecclesiastical authorities to try not to write off immediately forms of thought and expression simply because they are different, but to enter sympathetically into the various cultures that gave rise to those forms. Only on such a cross-cultural basis can pluriform thoughts and expressions be compared and evaluated to see whether or not they are fulfilling Paul's injunction to "have the same thoughts among yourselves as you have in your communion with Christ Jesus" (Phil 2:5). Communion is the rock-bottom issue. But whether or not different parties are actually in communion can be discerned only through linguistic communication. Such communication, however, will never adequately happen until cultural prejudices, fueled by fear, are overcome.

Historians perhaps have an obligation here to their own science, if not to the world before whose feet they lay their findings. They cannot adequately do history, cannot adequately respond to von Ranke's challenge to tell it "as it really was," so long as their perceptions are skewed by cultural bias. Granted that it will never be possible for anyone to stand outside of culture and view reality through lenses grown in outer space; still the effort can be made in that direction if the historian is motivated by that "perfect love [which] casts out fear" (1 John 4:18) to enter sympathetically into foreign cultures. For historians to practice an adequate historiography and be true to it, they must love not their method but the other on whom their method is trained. Perfect love does not require the other to conform to the historian's cultural bias but allows the other to be wholly other. Only on such a foundation can true communion occur and thus true stories be told.

NOTES

1. Ong, *Fighting for Life*, p. 29. See also Ong, *Interfaces of the Word: Studies in the Evolution of Consciousness and Culture* (Ithaca and London: Cornell University Press, 1977).

2. Johan Huizinga, *Homo Ludens: A Study of the Play Element in Culture* (Boston: Beacon Press, 1955), quoted in Ong, *Fighting for Life*, p. 45.

3. I use *viewpoint* in the singular here, because by cultural determination the anti-modernists had, or at least tried to have, a single point of view.

4. See above, pp. 17–18.

5. See above, pp. 21–27. For important insight into this issue and the Roman question, see the study by Halvor Moxnes referred to above, p. 35 n. 7.

6. *Pascendi*, par. 28; Vatican I, Constitution *Dei filius*, chap. 4.

7. See above p. 40.

8. Lawrence Kohlberg, *The Philosophy of Moral Development: Moral Stages and the Idea of Justice*, Vol. 1 of *Essay on Moral Development* (San Francisco: Harper & Row, 1981). Michael Horace Barnes, *In the Pres-*

ence of Mystery: An Introduction to the Story of Human Religiousness, rev. ed. (Mystic, CT: Twenty-Third Publications, 1990). See also Ronald Michael Green's important study *Religion and Moral Reason: A New Method for Comparative Study* (New York: Oxford University Press, 1988), esp. pp. 77–129, for important moral differences between "people of the Book" and those, especially non-Mediterraneans, who are influenced more strongly by other factors.

9. Robert Bellah, "Religious Evolution," *American Sociological Review* 39 (June 1964) 348–74.

10. Barnes, *In the Presence of Mystery*, pp. 5, 9.

11. Ibid., p. 169.

12. My own experience of living in the Mediterranean world confirms this description, but my experience pales next to that of the late Ukrainian Cardinal Josyf Slipyj (1892–1984). In a deal struck by Russia, the United States, and the Vatican, Slipyj was released after eighteen years in Russian gulags and—as one of the conditions of his release—exiled to Rome. After fifteen years in Rome, he complained in writing to Pope John Paul II about the "negative attitude" he consistently encountered from Vatican congregations and confided to a friend (hyperbolically?) "that he had never experienced such mistreatment from the atheists in the Soviet Union as he was experiencing now from fellow Catholics and fellow clergy in Rome." Jaroslav Pelikan, *Confessor Between East and West: A Portrait of Ukrainian Cardinal Josyf Slipyj* (Grand Rapids: Eerdmans, 1990), p. 173. If there was justification for Skipyj's treatment, it does not come out in Pelikan's account.

13. Barnes, *In the Presence of Mystery*, p. 169.

14. Ibid., pp. 173–86.

15. On the adversative nature of human beings, particularly males, see Ong, *Fighting for Life*.

BIBLIOGRAPHY

Archives and Manuscript Collections

Azpeitia, Loyola Castle, Spain. Archivo Histórico de Loyola. FONDO P. MARTIN. *Memorias* of Luis Martín Garcia (1846–1906), superior general of the Society of Jesus; 2712 quarto-size folios, front and back, in Martín's hand, written from 1895, the third year of his generalate, to 1902 when illness prevented his writing.

London. Archives of the Archdiocese of Westminster. HERBERT ALFRED VAUGHAN PAPERS.

London. Archives of the English Province of the Society of Jesus. Papers relating to Luis Martín and George Tyrrell.

London. The British Library, Additional Manuscripts. MAUDE DOMINICA PETRE PAPERS.

London. Franciscan Provincial Archives. DAVID FLEMING PAPERS.

Rome. Archives of the Congregation de Propaganda Fide. ACTA, NEW SERIES, 1892–1906.

Rome. Secret Vatican Archives. PAPERS OF THE APOSTOLIC DELEGATION TO THE UNITED STATES.

Rome. Roman Archives of the Society of Jesus. Papers relating to Luis Martín, the English Province, and George Tyrrell.

St. Andrews (Scotland), University Library. WILFRID WARD PAPERS.

St. Paul, Minnesota. Archives of the Archdiocese of St. Paul and Minneapolis. JOHN IRELAND PAPERS.

Monographs

Appleby, R. Scott. *"Church and Age Unite!" The Modernist Impulse in American Catholicism.* Notre Dame and London: University of Notre Dame Press, 1992.

Arnstein, Walter L. *Protestant versus Catholic in Mid-Victorian England: Mr. Newdegate and the Nuns.* Columbia: University of Missouri Press, 1982.

Aubert, Roger. *The Church in a Secularised Society.* Trans. Janet Sondheimer. Vol. 5 of *The Christian Centuries*. New York and Ramsey, NJ: Paulist, 1978.

Bangert, William V., S.J. *A History of the Society of Jesus*. St. Louis: Institute of Jesuit Sources, 1972.

Barnes, Michael Horace. *In the Presence of Mystery: An Introduction to the Story of Human Religiousness*. Rev. ed. Mystic, CT: Twenty-Third Publications, 1990.

Barmann, Lawrence F. *Baron Friedrich von Hügel and the Modernist Crisis in England*. Cambridge: Cambridge University Press, 1972.

Barraclough, Geoffrey. *Main Trends in History*. New York: Holmes & Meier, 1978.

Beales, Derek, and Best, Geoffrey, eds. *History, Society and the Churches: Essays in Honor of Owen Chadwick*. Cambridge: Cambridge University Press, 1985.

Billot, Louis, S.J. *Tractatus de ecclesia Christi sive continuatio theologiae de verbo incarnato*. Vol. 1, *De credibilitate Ecclesiae, et de intima eius constitutione*. 5th ed. Rome: Gregorian University, 1927. Vols. 2 and 3 in one. Vol. 2 *De potestate ecclesiastica*. Rome: Ex Typographia Polyglotta S. C. de Propaganda Fide, 1899. Vol. 3, *De subiecto potestatis*. Rome: Ex Typographia Polyglotta S. C. de Propaganda Fide, 1900.

Blakiston, Noel, ed. *The Roman Question: Extracts from the Despatches of Odo Russell from Rome, 1858–1870*. London: Chapman & Hall, 1962.

Bly, Robert. *Iron John: A Book About Men*. Reading, MA: Addison-Wesley, 1990.

Brandes, Stanley H. *Metaphors of Masculinity*. Philadelphia: University of Pennsylvania Press, 1980.

Brucker, Joseph. *"Les Études" contre le modernisme de 1888 à 1907*. Paris: Bureaux des Études, 1914.

Buehrle, Marie Cecilia. *Rafael Cardinal Merry del Val*. Milwaukee: Bruce, 1957.

Callahan, William James. *Church, Politics, and Society in Spain, 1750–1874*. Cambridge: Harvard University Press, 1984.

Campbell, Thomas Joseph, S.J. *The Jesuits, 1534–1921: A History of the Society of Jesus from Its Foundation to the Present Time*. Vol. 2. New York: The Encyclopedia Press, 1921.

Caperan, Louis. *L'Anticléricalisme et l'Affaire Dreyfus*. Toulouse: Imprimerie Regionale, 1948.

Carroll, Michael P. *The Cult of the Virgin Mary: Psychological Orgins*. Princeton: Princeton University Press, 1986.

Catholic Church. Pontificia Commissio Biblica. *Enchiridion Biblicum: Documenta ecclesiastica sacram scripturam spectantia*. 2d ed. rev. and enl. Naples: D'Auria, 1954.

Cenci, Pio. *Il Cardinale Raffaele Merry del Val.* Rome and Turin: Berruti, 1933.

Chadwick, Owen. *The Victorian Church.* 2 vols. London: Black, 1966, 1970.

——. *The Secularization of the European Mind in the Nineteenth Century.* The Gifford Lectures, University of Edinburgh, 1973–1974. Cambridge: Cambridge University Press, 1975.

——. *The Popes and European Revolution.* Oxford: Clarendon, 1981.

Chapman, Guy. *The Dreyfus Case: A Reassessment.* London: Hart-Davis, 1963.

Coates, Willson Havelock, White, Hayden V., and Schapiro, J. Salwyn. *The Emergence of Liberal Humanism: An Intellectual History of Western Europe.* Vol. 1, *From the Italian Renaissance to the French Revolution.* Vol. 2, *Since the French Revolution.* New York: McGraw-Hill, 1966, 1970.

Conn, Walter E. *Conscience: Development and Self-Transcendence.* Birmingham, AL: Religious Education Press, 1981.

Cornwallis, Frederick [Fred Conybeare]. *The Dreyfus Case.* London: Allen, 1898.

Corrigan, Raymond. *The Church and the Nineteenth Century.* Milwaukee: Bruce, 1938.

Crehan, Joseph, s.j. *Father Thurston.* London and New York: Sheed & Ward, 1950.

Cresson, William Penn. *The Holy Alliance: The European Background of the Monroe Doctrine.* New York: Oxford University Press, 1922.

Dal-Gal, Jerome. *The Spiritual Life of Cardinal Merry del Val.* Trans. Joseph A. McMullin. New York: Benziger, 1959.

Daly, Gabriel, o.s.a. *Transcendence and Immanence: A Study in Catholic Modernism and Integralism.* Oxford: Clarendon, 1980.

Daniel-Rops, Henri. *The Church in an Age of Revolution (1789–1870).* Trans. John Warrington. Vol. 8 of *History of the Church of Christ.* New York: Dutton, 1965.

Dansette, Adrien. *Religious History of Modern France.* Trans. John Dingle. 2 vols. Freiburg: Herder; New York: Herder & Herder, 1961.

Davis, John H. R. *People of the Mediterranean: An Essay in Comparative Social Anthropology.* London: Routledge & Kegan Paul, 1977.

Demolins, Edmond. *À quoi tient la supériorité des Anglo-Saxons?* Paris: Firmin-Didot, 1897. Translation: *Anglo-Saxon Superiority: To What It Is Due.* New York: Fenno, 1898.

Devas, Charles Stanton. *The Key to the World's Progress, Being Some Account of the Historical Significance of the Catholic Church.* London: Longmans, Green, 1906.

Donoso Cortés, Juan. *Oeuvres de Donoso Cortés*. Trans. Louis Veuillot. 3 vols. Paris: Vaton, 1858.

———. *Essay on Catholicism, Liberalism, and Socialism*. Trans. Madeleine Vinton Goddard. Philadelphia: Lippincott, 1862.

Dooley, Patrick., S.J. *Woodstock and Its Makers*. Vol. 56 of *Woodstock Letters*. Woodstock, MD: College Press, 1927.

Dumont, Louis. *Essays on Individualism: Modern Ideology in Anthropological Perspective*. Chicago: The University of Chicago Press, 1986.

Farina, John, ed. *Hecker Studies: Essays on the Thought of Isaac Hecker*. New York and Ramsey, NJ: Paulist, 1983.

Fogarty, Gerald P., S.J. *The Vatican and the Americanist Crisis: Denis J. O'Connell, American Agent in Rome, 1885–1903*. Rome: Gregorian University Press, 1974.

———. *The Vatican and the American Hierarchy from 1870 to 1965*. Wilmington, DE: Glazier, 1985.

Fülöp-Miller, René. *The Power and Secret of the Jesuits*. Trans. F. S. Flint and D. F. Tait. New York: Viking, 1930.

———. *Leo XIII and Our Times: Might of the Church-Power in the World*. Trans. Conrad M. R. Bonacina. London: Longmans, Green, 1937.

Gargan, Edward T. *Leo XIII and the Modern World*. New York: Sheed & Ward, 1961.

Gibson, Ralph. *A Social History of French Catholicism, 1789–1914*. London and Boston: Routledge & Kegan Paul, 1989.

Gilmore, David D., ed. *Honor and Shame and the Unity of the Mediterranean*. Special Publication 22. Washington DC: American Anthropological Association, 1987.

Girard, René. *Violence and the Sacred*. Trans. Patrick Gregory. Baltimore: Johns Hopkins University Press, 1977.

Gisler, Anton. *Der Modernismus dargestellt und gewürdigt*. 2nd ed. Einsiedeln, Waldshut, Cologne: Benziger, 1912.

Graham, John Thomas. *Donoso Cortés, Utopian Romanticist and Political Realist*. Columbia: University of Missouri Press, 1974.

Granfield, Patrick. *The Limits of the Papacy*. New York: Crossroad, 1987.

Green, Ronald Michael. *Religion and Moral Reason: A New Method for Comparative Study*. New York: Oxford University Press, 1988.

Hales, E. E. Y. [Edward Elton Young]. *Pio Nono: A Study in European Politics and Religion in the Nineteenth Century*. New York: Kenedy, 1954.

———. *The Catholic Church in the Modern World: A Survey from the French Revolution to the Present*. Garden City, NY: Doubleday Image, 1960.

Hartley, Thomas J. A. *Thomistic Revival and the Modernist Era*. Toronto: St. Michael's College, 1971.

Hasler, August Bernhard. *How the Pope Became Infallible: Pius IX and the Politics of Persuasion.* Trans. Peter Heinegg. Garden City, NY: Doubleday, 1981.

Hayes, Carlton J. H. *A Century of Predominantly Industrial Society Since 1830.* Vol. 2 (shorter rev.) of *A Political and Cultural History of Modern Europe.* New York: Macmillan, 1939.

——. *Christianity and Western Civilization.* The Raymond Fred West Lectures at Stanford University, April 5–7, 1954. Stanford: Stanford University Press, 1954.

Hecker, Isaac Thomas. *Exposition of the Church in View of the Recent Difficulties and Controversies, and the Present Needs of the Age.* London: Montagu, 1875.

——. *Questions of the Soul.* New York: Appleton, 1855.

Heiner, Franz. *Der neue Syllabus Pius' X oder Dekret des Hl. Offiziums "Lamentabili" vom 3. Juli 1907.* Mainz: Kirchheim, 1908.

Hocedez, Edgar, s.j. *Histoire de la théologie au XIXe siècle.* Vol. 1, *Décadence et réveil de la théologie, 1800–1831.* Brussels: Universelle, 1949. Vol. 2, *Épanouissement de la théologie, 1831–1870.* Brussels: Universelle, 1952. Vol. 3, *Le Règne de Léon XIII, 1878–1903.* Brussels: Universelle; Paris: Desclée de Brouwer, 1947.

Hoehn, Matthew, ed. *Catholic Authors: Contemporary Biographical Sketches, 1931–1947.* Newark, NJ: St. Mary's Abbey, 1948.

von Hönsbröch, Count Paul. *Fourteen Years a Jesuit: A Record of Personal Experience and a Criticism.* Trans. Alice Zimmern. 2 vols. London: Cassell, 1911.

Holmes, J. Derek. *More Roman Than Rome: English Catholicism in the Nineteenth Century.* Shepherdstown, WV: Patmos Press, 1978.

——. *The Triumph of the Holy See: A Short History of the Papacy in the Nineteenth Century.* Shepherdstown, WV: Patmos Press, 1978.

Houtin, Albert, and Sartiaux, Félix. *Alfred Loisy: Sa vie, son oeuvre.* Ed. Émile Poulat. Paris: Centre National de la Recherche Scientifique, 1960.

Hughes, John Jay. *Absolutely Null and Utterly Void: The Papal Condemnation of Anglican Orders, 1896.* Washington, DC: Corpus, 1968.

Hughes, Thomas A., s.j. *The History of the Society of Jesus in North America, Colonial and Federal.* 4 vols. Cleveland: Burrows; London and New York: Longmans, Green, 1907.

Huizinga, Johan. *Homo Ludens: A Study of the Play Element in Culture.* Boston: Beacon, 1955.

Ignatius of Loyola. *The Constitutions of the Society of Jesus.* Trans. George E. Ganss, s.j. St. Louis: Institute of Jesuit Sources, 1970.

Kedward, Harry Roderick. *The Dreyfus Affair: Catalyst for Tensions in French Society*. London: Longmans, Green, 1965.

Klein, Félix. *Americanism: A Phantom Heresy*. Atchison, KS: Aquin Book Shop, 1951.

Kohlberg, Lawrence. *The Philosophy of Moral Development: Moral Stages and the Idea of Justice*. Vol. 1 of *Essays on Moral Development*. San Francisco: Harper & Row, 1981.

Kurtz, Lester R. *The Politics of Heresy: The Modernist Crisis in Roman Catholicism*. Berkeley: University of California Press, 1986.

Lagrange, Marie-Joseph. *M. Loisy et le modernisme: À propos des "Mémoires."* Juvisy (Seine-et-Oise): Les Éditions du Cerf, 1932.

——. *Père Lagrange: Personal Reflections and Mémoires*. Trans. Henry Wansbrough. New York and Mahwah, NJ: Paulist, 1985.

Larkin, Maurice. *Church and State After the Dreyfus Affair: The Separation Issue in France*. New York: Harper & Row, 1973.

Latourette, Kenneth Scott. *A History of Christianity*. New York: Harper & Row, 1953.

Lemius, Jean-Baptiste, O.M.I. *A Catechism of Modernism*. New York: Society for the Propagation of the Faith, Archdiocese of New York, 1908. Repr. Rockford, IL: TAN, 1981.

Leo XIII. *The Great Encyclical Letters of Pope Leo XIII*. 3rd ed. New York: Benziger Brothers, 1903.

——. *The Pope and the People: Select Letters and Addresses on Social Questions by Pope Leo XIII*. Rev. ed. London: Catholic Truth Society, 1912.

Lipman-Blumen, Jean. *Gender Roles and Power*. Englewood Cliffs, NJ: Prentice-Hall, 1984.

Loisy, Alfred Firmin. *Choses passées*. Paris: Nourry, 1913.

——. *My Duel with the Vatican: The Autobiography of a Catholic Modernist*. Trans. Richard Wilson Boynton. London: Dutton, 1924. Repr. New York: Greenwood, 1968.

——. *Mémoires pour servir à l'histoire religieuse de notre temps*. 3 vols. Paris: Nourry, 1930–1931.

Loome, Thomas Michael. *Liberal Catholicism, Reform Catholicism, Modernism: A Contribution to a New Orientation in Modernist Research*. Tübinger theologische Studien 14. Mainz: Grünewald, 1979.

McAvoy, Thomas T., C.S.C. *The Great Crisis in American Catholic History, 1895–1900*. Chicago: Regnery, 1957.

McCool, Gerald A., S.J. *Nineteenth-Century Scholasticism: The Search for a Unitary Method*. New York: Fordham University Press, 1989. Repr. of *Catholic Theology in the Nineteenth Century: The Quest for a Unitary Method*. New York: Seabury, 1977.

McCormack, Arthur, M.H.M. *Cardinal Vaughan: The Life of the Third*

Archbishop of Westminster, Founder of St. Joseph's Missionary Society, Mill Hill. London: Burns & Oates, 1966.

Maignen, Charles. *La Souveraineté du peuple est une hérésie.* Paris: Roger & Chernoviz, 1892.

———. *Études sur l'Américanisme: Le Père Hecker est-il un Saint?* Paris: Retaux; Rome: Desclée, Lefébvre, 1898. Translated and adapted under the title, *Studies in Americanism—Father Hecker, Is He a Saint?* London: Burns & Oates, 1898.

———. *Nationalisme, Catholicisme, Revolution.* Paris: Retaux, 1901.

Malina, Bruce J. *The New Testament World: Insights from Cultural Anthropology.* Atlanta: John Knox Press, 1981.

———. *Christian Origins and Cultural Anthropology: Practical Models for Biblical Interpretation.* Atlanta: John Knox Press, 1986.

———, and Neyrey, Jerome H. *Calling Jesus Names: The Social Value of Labels in Matthew.* Sonoma, CA: Polebridge, 1988.

Martín, Luis, S.J. *Memorias del P. Luis Martín, General de la Compañía de Jesús.* Vol. 1 (1846–1891), vol. 2 (1892–1906). Ed. José Ramón Eguillor, S.J., Manuel Revuelta González, S.J., and Rafael Maria Sanz de Diego, S.J. Rome: Historical Institute of the Society of Jesus; Madrid: Pontifical University of Comillas; Bilbao: University of Deusto and Ediciones Mensajero, 1988.

Martina, Giacomo, S.J. *Pio IX (1846–1850).* Vol 1. Miscellanea Historiae Pontificiae 38. Rome: Gregorian University Press, 1974.

Menczer, Béla. *Catholic Political Thought, 1789–1848.* Westminster, MD: Newman, 1952.

Merk, Frederick. *The Monroe Doctrine and American Expansionism.* New York: Knopf, 1966.

Merton, Robert K. *Sociological Ambivalence and Other Essays.* New York: Free Press, 1976.

Misner, Paul. *Social Catholicism in Europe: From the Onset of Industrialization to the First World War.* New York: Crossroad, 1991.

Moody, Joseph N., ed. *Church and Society: Catholic Social and Political Thought and Movements, 1789–1950.* New York: Arts, 1953.

Moynihan, James H. *The Life of Archibishop John Ireland.* New York: Harper & Brothers, 1953.

Newman, John Henry Cardinal. *Apologia pro vita sua.* London: Oxford University Press, 1913.

Norman, Edward R. *The English Catholic Church in the Nineteenth Century.* Oxford: Oxford University Press, 1984.

———. *Roman Catholicism in England: From the Elizabethan Settlement to the Second Vatican Council.* Oxford: Oxford University Press, 1985.

Oakman, Douglas E. *Jesus and the Economic Questions of His Day.* Lewiston, NY: Mellen, 1986.

O'Connell, Marvin R. *John Ireland and the American Catholic Church.* St. Paul, MN: Minnesota Historical Society Press, 1988.

O'Toole, George J. A. *The Spanish War: An American Epic—1898.* New York and London: Norton, 1984.

Ong, Walter, J., S.J. *Interfaces of the Word: Studies in the Evolution of Consciousness and Culture.* Ithaca and London: Cornell University Press, 1977.

——. *Fighting for Life: Contest, Sexuality, and Consciousness.* Ithaca and London: Cornell University Press, 1981.

——. *Orality and Literacy: The Technologizing of the Word.* London and New York: Methuen, 1982.

Payne, Stanley G. *Spanish Catholicism: An Historical Overview.* Madison: University of Wisconsin Press, 1984.

Pelikan, Jaroslav. *Confessor Between East and West: A Portrait of Ukrainian Cardinal Josyf Slipyj.* Grand Rapids, MI: Eerdmans, 1990.

Peristiany, Jean G., ed. *Honour and Shame: The Values of Mediterranean Society.* Chicago: The University of Chicago Press, 1966. Repr. 1974.

——. *Mediterranean Family Structures.* New York: Cambridge University Press, 1976.

Petre, Maude Dominica. *Autobiography and Life of George Tyrrell.* 2 vols. London: Arnold, 1912.

Petrie, Charles. *King Alfonso XIII and His Age.* London: Chapman & Hall, 1963.

Phillips, Charles Stanley. *The Church in France, 1848–1907.* 1936. Repr. New York: Russell & Russell, 1967.

Pilch, John J. *Hear the Word.* Vol. 1, *Introduction to the Cultural Context of the Old Testament.* Vol. 2, *Introduction to the Cultural Context of the New Testament.* Mahwah, NJ: Paulist, 1991.

Pitt-Rivers, Julian A. *The People of the Sierra.* Chicago: The University of Chicago Press, 1961.

——, ed. *Mediterranean Countrymen: Essays in the Sociology of the Mediterranean.* Paris: Mouton, 1963.

Piux X. *All Things in Christ: Encyclicals and Selected Documents of Saint Pius X.* Ed. Vincent A. Yzermans. Westminster, MD: Newman, 1954.

Poulat, Émile. *Histoire, dogme, et critique dans la crise moderniste.* Paris: Casterman, 1962.

——. *Modernistica: Horizons, physionomies, débats.* Paris: Nouvelle Éditions Latines, 1982.

Purcell, Edmund Sheridan. *The Life of Cardinal Manning, Archbishop of Westminster.* 2 vols. London: Macmillan, 1895.

Quinn, M. Bernetta, O.S.F. *Give Me Souls: A Life of Raphael Cardinal Merry del Val.* Westminster, MD: Newman, 1958.

Redfield, Robert. *The Little Community/Peasant Society and Culture.* Chicago: The University of Chicago Press, 1967.

Reher, Margaret M. "The Church and the Kingdom of God in America: The Ecclesiology of the Americanists." Ph.D. dissertation. Fordham University, 1972.

Renovation Reading. Rev. and enl. ed. Woodstock MD: Woodstock College, 1931.

Rivière, Jean. *Le Modernisme dans l'Église: Étude d'histoire religieuse contemporaine.* Paris: Letouzey, 1929.

Satolli, Francesco. *Loyalty to Church and State.* Ed. John R. Slattery. Baltimore: Murphy, 1895.

Schneider, Jane, and Schneider, Peter. *Culture and Political Economy in Western Sicily.* New York: Academic, 1976.

Schultenover, David G., S.J. *George Tyrrell: In Search of Catholicism.* Shepherdstown, WV: Patmos Press, 1981.

Schwager, Raymund, S.J. *Must There Be Scapegoats? Violence and Redemption in the Bible.* Trans. Maria L. Assad. San Francisco: Harper & Row, 1987.

Select Letters of Our Very Reverend Fathers General to the Fathers and Brothers of the Society of Jesus. Woodstock, MD: Woodstock College, 1900.

Soderini, Eduardo. *Il Pontificato di Leone XIII.* Vol. 1, *Il Conclave: L'Opera di ricostruzione sociale.* Vol. 2, *Politica con l'Italia e con la Francia.* Vol. 3, *Politica con la Germania.* Milan: Mondadori, 1932. Translation: Vol. 1, *The Pontificate of Leo XIII.* Vol. 2, *Leo XIII: Italy and France.* Trans. Barbara Barclay Carter. London: Burns, Oates & Washbourne, 1934, 1935.

Spindler, George D., ed. *The Making of Psychological Anthropology.* Berkeley: University of California Press, 1978.

Storer, Maria Longworth. *In Memoriam Bellamy Storer: With Personal Remembrances of President McKinley, President Roosevelt and John Ireland, Archbishop of St. Paul.* Privately published, 1923.

Sturzo, Don Luigi. *Church and State.* New York: Longmans, Green, 1939.

Sutcliffe, Edmund F., S.J. *Bibliography of the English Province of the Society of Jesus, 1773–1953.* Roehampton (London): Manresa, 1957.

Sutton, Michael. *Nationalism, Positivism, and Catholicism: The Politics of Charles Maurras and French Catholics, 1890–1914.* Cambridge: Cambridge University Press, 1982.

Tillard, J. M. R., O.P. *The Bishop of Rome*. Trans. John De Satgé. Wilmington, DE: Glazier, 1982.

Todd, Emmanuel. *The Explanation of Ideology: Family Structures and Social Systems*. Trans. David Garrioch. New York: Blackwell, 1985.

T'Serclaes, Charles de. *The Life and Labors of Pope Leo XIII, With a Summary of His Important Letters, Addresses, and Encyclicals*. Ed. Maurice Francis Egan. Chicago: Rand, McNally, 1903.

Turner, Bryan S. *The Body and Society: Explorations in Social Theory*. Oxford: Blackwell, 1984.

Turvasi, Francesco. *The Condemnation of Alfred Loisy and the Historical Method*. Rome: Edizioni di Storia e Letteratura, 1979.

Tyrrell, George. *Notes on the Catholic Doctrine of Purity*. Roehampton (London): Manresa, 1897.

———. *Nova et vetera: Informal Meditations for Times of Spiritual Dryness*. London: Longmans, Green, 1897.

———. *Essays on Faith and Immortality*. Ed. Maude D. Petre. London: Arnold, 1914.

Vance, Norman. *The Sinews of the Spirit: The Ideal of Christian Manliness in Literature and Religious Thought*. New York: Cambridge University Press, 1985.

Vidler, Alec R. *Prophecy and Papacy: A Study of Lamennais, the Church, and the Revolution*. London: SCM, 1954.

———. *A Variety of Catholic Modernists*. Cambridge: Cambridge University Press, 1970.

———. *Scenes from a Clerical Life*. London: Collins, 1977.

Von Arx, Jeffrey Paul. *Progress and Pessimism: Religion, Politics, and History in Late Nineteenth-Century Britain*. Cambridge: Harvard University Press, 1985.

Ward, Maisie. *The Wilfrid Wards and the Transition*. Vol. 2, *Insurrection versus Resurrection*. London: Sheed & Ward, 1937.

Wilson, J. A. *The Life of Bishop Hedley*. London: Kenedy, 1930.

Yzermans, Vincent A., ed. *All Things in Christ: Encyclicals and Selected Documents of Saint Pius X*. Westminster, MD: Newman, 1954.

Essays and Periodicals

Asano-Tamanoi, Mariko. "Shame, Family, and State in Catalonia and Japan." In *Honor and Shame and the Unity of the Mediterranean*. Ed. David D. Gilmore. Special Publication 22. Washington, DC: American Anthropological Association, 1987. Pp. 104–20.

Barry, William Francis. "An American Religious Crusade." *National Review* 193 (March 1899) 115–28.

Bellah, Robert. "Religious Evolution." *American Sociological Review* 39 (June 1964) 348–74.

Bendiscioli, Mario. "Italian Catholics Between the Vatican and the Quirinal: The *Non expedit* at the Time of Leo XIII." In *The Church in the Industrial Age*. Vol. 9 of *History of the Church*. Ed. Hubert Jedin and John Dolan. New York: Crossroad, 1981. Pp. 84–96.

Blanning, T. C. W. "The Role of Religion in European Counter-Revolution, 1789–1815." In *History, Society, and the Churches: Essays in Honor of Owen Chadwick*. Ed. Derek Beales and Geoffrey Best. Cambridge: Cambridge University Press, 1985. Pp. 195–214.

Boissevain, Jeremy. "Toward an Anthropology of the Mediterranean." *Current Anthropology* 20 (1979) 81–93.

Brandes, Stanley H. "Like Wounded Stags: Male Sexual Ideology in an Andalusian Town." In *Sexual Meanings: The Cultural Construction of Gender and Sexuality*. Ed. Sherry B. Ortner and Harriet Whitehead. New York: Cambridge University Press, 1981.

———. "Reflections on Honor and Shame in the Mediterranean." In *Honor and Shame and the Unity of the Mediterranean*. Ed. David D. Gilmore. Special Publication 22. Washington, DC: American Anthropological Association, 1987. Pp. 121–34.

Breton, Stanislas. "Dogme de la Résurrection et concept de la matière." In *Le Modernisme*. Institut Catholique de Paris Philosophy Series 5. Paris: Beauchesne, 1980. Pp. 101–27.

Brucker, Joseph. "Un congrès et un centenaire à Fribourg en Suisse." *Études* 72 (1898) 788–93.

Chandlery, Peter J., s.j. "The Very Rev. Father General Luis Martín, s.j.: A Biographical Sketch." 28 (July, October 1906) 433–50, 510–17; 29 (January, April, July, October 1907; January, April, July, October 1908) 1–13, 73–84, 145–57, 217–30, 296–307, 361–75, 442–57, 535–47; 30 (January, April, July, October 1909; January 1910) 21–36, 119–30, 191–98, 256–63, 291–97.

———. "Father General's Illness." LN 28 (April 1905) 73–82.

———. "Father General's Recent Illness." LN 28 (July 1905) 169–70.

———. "Father General's Convalescence." LN 28 (October 1905) 217–19.

———. "Fatal Termination to Very Rev. Father General's Long Illness." LN 28 (April 1906) 361–69.

Colin, Pierre. "Le Kantisme dans la crise moderniste." In *Le Modernisme*. Institut Catholique de Paris Philosophy Series 5. Paris: Beauchesne, 1980. Pp. 9–81.

"Cronaca contemporanea." *La Civiltà Cattolica* 5, ser. 16 (28 December 1895) 118–24.

Davis, John H. R. "Family and State in the Mediterranean." In *Honor and Shame and the Unity of the Mediterranean*. Ed. David D. Gilmore. Special Publication 22. Washington, DC: American Anthropological Association, 1987. Pp. 22–34.

Delaney, Carol. "Seeds of Honor, Fields of Shame." In *Honor and Shame and the Unity of the Mediterranean*. Ed. David D. Gilmore. Special Publication 22. Washington, DC: American Anthropological Association, 1987. Pp. 35–48.

Dell, Robert Edward. "A Liberal Catholic View of the Case of Dr. Mivart." *Nineteenth Century* 47 (April 1900) 669–84.

Despland, Michel. "What Is a Religious Liberal in the Nineteenth Century?" Proceedings of the Nineteenth Century Working Group of the American Academy of Religion. 1981. Pp. 72–82.

———. "A Case of Christians Shifting their Moral Allegiance: France 1790–1914." *Journal of the American Academy of Religion* 52.4 (December 1984) 671–90.

"Dr. Mivart's Heresy" [Anonymous]. *Tablet* (London), 6 January 1900, p. 5.

Dubarle, Dominique. "Modernisme et expérience religieuse: Réflexions sur un cas de traitement théologique." In *Le Modernisme*. Institut Catholique de Paris Philosophy Series 5. Paris: Beauchesne, 1980. Pp. 181–244.

Fontana, Sandro, and Traniello, Francesco. "Aspetti Politico-Sociali." In *Romolo Murri nella storia politica e religiosa del suo tempo*. Ed. Sandro Fontana, Maurilio Guasco, and Francesco Traniello. Rome: Cinque Lune, 1977. Pp. 15–68.

Gilmore, David D. "Anthropology of the Mediterranean Area." *Annual Reviews in Anthropology* 11 (1982) 172–205.

———. "The Shame of Dishonor." In *Honor and Shame and the Unity of the Mediterranean*. Ed. David D. Gilmore. Special Publication 22. Washington, DC: American Anthropological Association, 1987. Pp. 2–21.

———. "Honor, Honesty, Shame: Male Status in Contemporary Andalusia." In *Honor and Shame and the Unity of the Mediterranean*. Ed. David D. Gilmore. Special Publication 22. Washington, DC: American Anthropological Association, 1987. Pp. 90–103.

Gilmore, Margaret M., and Gilmore, David D. "'Machismo': A Psychodynamic Approach (Spain)." *Journal of Psychological Anthropology* 2 (1979) 281–300.

Hennesey, James. "Leo XIII's Thomistic Revival: A Political and Philosophical Event." *Journal of Religion* 58 (Supplement 1978) 185–97.

Herzfeld, Michael. "'As in Your Own House': Hospitality, Ethnography, and the Stereotype of Mediterranean Society." In *Honor and Shame and the Unity of the Mediterranean*. Ed. David D. Gilmore. Special Publication 22. Washington, DC: American Anthropological Association, 1987. Pp. 75–89.

Ireland, John [J. St. Clair Etheridge]. "The Genesis of 'Americanism.'" *North American Review* 170 (May 1900) 679–93.

Johnson, Harry M. "Religion in Social Change and Social Evolution." In *Religious Change and Continuity: Sociological Perspectives*. Ed. Harry M. Johnson. San Francisco: Jossey-Bass, 1979. Pp. 313–39.

Killen, David P. "Americanism Revisited: John Spalding and *Testem Benevolentiae*." *Harvard Theological Review* 66 (1973) 413–54.

King, Michael J., s.j. "The German Fathers at Ditton and Portico." LN 28 (July 1905) 190–93.

Knowles, M. David. "The Thirteenth Century." In *The Middle Ages*. Vol. 2 of *The Christian Centuries: A New History of the Catholic Church*. Ed. M. David Knowles and Dimitri Obolensky. New York: McGraw-Hill, 1968, Pp. 289–95.

Köhler, Oskar. "The World Plan of Leo XIII: Goals and Methods." In *The Church in the Industrial Age*. Trans. Margit Resch. Vol. 9 of *History of the Church*. Ed. Hubert Jedin and John Dolan. New York: Crossroad, 1981. Pp. 3–25.

——. "The Relationship to the State and the Parties." In *The Church in the Industrial Age*. Trans. Margit Resch. Vol. 9 of *History of the Church*. Ed. Hubert Jedin and John Dolan. New York: Crossroad, 1981. Pp. 233–45.

——. "The Position of Catholicism in the Culture at the Turn of the Century." In *The Church in the Industrial Age*. Trans. Margit Resch. Vol. 9 of *History of the Church*. Ed. Hubert Jedin and John Dolan. New York: Crossroad, 1981. Pp. 245–56.

Lease, Gary. "Merry del Val and Tyrrell: A Modernist Struggle." *Downside Review* 102 (April 1984) 133–56.

Leclair, P., s.j. (Pseud.). "Leo XIII and le modernisme biblique." *Le Revue Apologétique* (Brussels), 9 (16 January 1908) 631–44.

Leo XIII. *Diuturnum illud* (29 June 1881). *Acta Leonis* 2:269–87.

——. *Au milieu des sollicitudes* (16 February 1892). *Acta Leonis* 12:21–34. In *The Papal Encyclicals*. Vol. 2, *1878–1903*. Ed. Claudia Carlen. Wilmington, NC: McGrath, 1981. Pp. 277–81.

——. *Onorare le ceneri* (1 March 1892). *Acta Leonis* 12:383–85.

——. *Nostra erga Fratres Minores* (25 November 1898). *ASS* 31:264–67.

——. *Depuis le jour* (8 September 1899). *Acta Leonis* 19:157–90; ASS 32:193–213. In *The Papal Encyclicals*. Vol. 2 *1878–1903*. Ed. Claudia Carlen. Wilmington, NC: McGrath, 1981. Pp. 455–64.

——. *Graves de communi* (18 January 1901). *Acta Leonis* 21:8–10. In *The Papal Encyclicals*. Vol. 2, *1878–1903*. Ed. Claudia Carlen. Wilmington, NC: McGrath, 1981. Pp. 481–82.

Loisy, Alfred Firmin. "La Théorie individualiste de la religion." *Revue du clergé français* 17 (1 January 1899) 202–14.

—— [Isidore Desprès]. "Opinions catholiques sur l'origine du Pentateuque." *Revue du clergé français* 17 (15 February 1899) 526–57.

——. "La Lettre de Léon XIII au clergé de France et les études d'Écriture Sainte." *Revue du clergé français* 22 (1 June 1900) 5–17.

Lyng, Stephen G., and Kurtz, Lester R. "Bureaucratic Insurgency: The Vatican and the Crisis of Modernism." *Social Forces* 63 (June 1985) 901–22.

Martín, Luis, S.J. "On Some Dangers of Our Times." In *Select Letters of Our Very Reverend Fathers to the Fathers and Brothers of the Society of Jesus*. Woodstock MD: Woodstock College, 1900. Pp. 501–46.

Masamba Ma Mpolo, Jean. "African Symbols and Stories in Pastoral Care." *Journal of Pastoral Care* 39 (1985) 314–26.

Mivart, St. George Jackson. "Happiness in Hell." *Nineteenth Century* 32 (December 1892) 899–919.

——. "The Happiness in Hell: A Rejoinder." *Nineteenth Century* 33 (February 1893) 320–38.

——. "Last Words on the Happiness in Hell." *Nineteenth Century* 33 (April 1893) 637–51.

——. "The Roman Catholic Church and the Dreyfus Case." *Times* (London), 17 October 1899, pp. 13–14.

——. "The Continuity of Catholicism." *Nineteenth Century* 47 (January 1900) 51–72.

——. "Some Recent Catholic Apologists." *Fortnightly Review* N.S. 67 (1 January 1900) 24–44.

Moran, Valentine G. "The 'Breakings' of George Tyrrell." *Downside Review* 102 (July 1984) 174–85.

Moxnes, Halvor. "Patron–Client Relations and the New Community of Luke-Acts." In *The Social World of Luke-Acts: Models for Interpretation*. Ed. Jerome H. Neyrey. Peabody, MA: Hendrickson, 1991. Pp. 241–68.

Norman, Edward R. "Cardinal Manning and the Temporal Power." In *History, Society, and the Churches*. Cambridge: Cambridge University Press, 1985. Pp. 235–56.

Pitt-Rivers, Julian A. "Honour and Social Status." In *Honour and Shame: The Values of Mediterranean Society*. Ed. Jean G. Peristiany.

Chicago: The University of Chicago Press, 1966. Repr. 1974. Pp. 19–78.

———. "Ritual Kinship in the Mediterranean: Spain and the Balkans." In *Mediterranean Family Structures*. Ed. Jean G. Peristiany. New York: Cambridge University Press, 1976. Pp. 317–34.

Pius X. *E supremi apostolatus*. In *The Papal Encyclicals*. Vol. 3, *1903–1939*. Ed. Claudia Carlen. Wilmington, NC: McGrath, 1981.

Pollen, John Hungerford, S.J. "The Rise of the Anglo-Benedictine Congregation." *Month* 90 (December 1897) 581–600.

Portier, William L. "Isaac Hecker and *Testem Benevolentiae*: A Study in Theological Pluralism." In *Hecker Studies: Essays on the Thought of Isaac Hecker*. Ed. John Farina. New York and Ramsey NJ: Paulist, 1983. Pp. 11–48.

Quigley, Carroll. "The Mexican National Character and Circum-Mediterranean Personality." *American Anthropology* 75 (1973) 319–22.

Reher, Margaret M. "Leo XIII and 'Americanism.'" *Theological Studies* 34 (1973) 679–89.

Rivière, Jean. "Qui rédigea l'encyclique 'Pascendi'?" *Bulletin de littérature ecclésiastique* 47 (1946) 143–61.

Root, John David. "English Catholic Modernism and Science: The Case of George Tyrrell." *Heythrop Journal* 18 (July 1977) 271–88.

———. "George Tyrrell and the Synthetic Society." *Downside Review* 98 (January 1980) 42–59.

———. "The Philosophical and Religious Thought of Arthur James Balfour (1848–1930)." *Journal of British Studies* 19 (Spring 1980) 120–41.

———. "The Final Apostasy of St. George Jackson Mivart." *Catholic Historical Review* 71 (January 1985) 1–25.

Saunders, George R. "Men and Women in South Europe: A Review of Some Aspects of Cultural Complexity." *Journal of Psychoanalytic Anthropology* 4 (Fall 1981) 435–66.

Schmandt, Raymond H. "The Life and Work of Leo XIII." In *Leo XIII and the Modern World*. Ed. Edward T. Gargan. New York: Sheed & Ward, 1961. Pp. 15–48.

Schmitt, Carl. "The Necessity of Politics: An Essay on the Representative Idea in the Church and Modern Europe." In Carl Schmitt, Nicholas Berdyaev, and Michael de la Bedoyère. *Vital Realities*. New York: Macmillan, 1932. Pp. 23–82.

Schneider, Jane. "Of Vigilance and Virgins." *Ethnology* 9 (1971) 1–24.

Schultenover, David G., S.J. "George Tyrrell: Caught in the Roman Archives of the Society of Jesus." In *Three Discussions: Biblical Exegesis, George Tyrrell, Jesuit Archives*. Proceedings of the Working Group on Roman Catholic Modernism of the American Academy of Religion. Ed. Ronald Burke and George Gilmore. Mobile, AL: Spring Hill College, 1981. Pp. 26–33.

———. "Rome and the English Bishops' Joint Pastoral: Implications for the Historiography of the Modernist Period." In *Historiography and Modernism.* Proceedings of the Working Group on Roman Catholic Modernism of the American Academy of Religion. Ed. Ronald Burke, Gary Lease, and George Gilmore. Mobile, AL: Spring Hill College, 1985. Pp. 8–29.

———. "A Critique of Lester R. Kurtz's *The Politics of Heresy: The Modernist Crisis in Roman Catholicism.*" In *Varieties of Modernism.* Proceedings of the Working Group on Roman Catholic Modernism of the American Academy of Religion. Ed. Ronald Burke, Gary Lease, and George Gilmore. Mobile, AL: Spring Hill College, 1986.

———. "Toward a Contextualization of Modernism in the Other Isms of the Day." In *Modernism: Contexts in History.* Proceedings of the Working Group on Roman Catholic Modernism of the American Academy of Religion. Ed. Ronald Burke, Gary Lease, and George Gilmore. Mobile, AL: Spring Hill College, 1987.

Schwertner, Thomas M., o.p. "The Genius of Père Berthier." *Catholic World* 122 (January 1926) 452–58.

Smith, Sydney F. "The Jesuits and the Dreyfus Case." *Month* 93 (February 1899) 113–34.

———. "Mr. Conybeare Again." *Month* 93 (April 1899) 405–12.

Storrie, Margaret Cochrane. "Spain." *Encyclopedia Britannica.* 1970.

Sturzo, Don Luigi. "The Catholic Church and Christian Democracy." *Social Action Magazine* (15 May 1944) 5–43.

de la Taille, Maurice, s.j. "Ami du clergé." *Études* 29 (26 September 1907) 872.

Tilliette, Xavier. "Maurice Blondel et la controverse christologique." In *Le Modernisme.* Institut Catholic de Paris Philosophy Series 5. Paris: Beauchesne, 1980. Pp. 129–60.

Tyrrell, George. "A Perverted Devotion." *Weekly Register* 100 (16 December 1899) 797–800. Repr. in *Essays on Faith and Immortality* by George Tyrrell. Ed. Maude D. Petre. London: Arnold, 1914. Pp. 158–71.

Vaughan, Herbert Cardinal, and the Bishops of the Province of Westminster. "The Church and Liberal Catholicism: A Joint Pastoral Letter" (29 December 1900). *Tablet* (London) 97 (5, 12 January 1901) 8–12, 50–52.

Ward, Wilfrid. "Liberalism and Intransigeance." *Nineteenth Century* 47 (June 1900) 960–73.

Weaver, Mary Jo. "George Tyrrell and the Joint Pastoral Letter." *Downside Review* 99 (January 1981) 18–39.

INDEX